Published by:
Airlife Publishing Ltd
101 Longden Road
Shrewsbury SY3 9EB
England
Telephone: (01743) 235651
Fax: (01743) 232944

Produced by Aerospace Publishing Ltd and
published jointly with Airlife Publishing Ltd

© Aerospace Publishing Ltd 1994

Authors:
David Donald
Günter Endres
Robert Hewson
Jon Lake
Lindsay Peacock

Sub-Editor:
Karen Leverington

Design:
Robert Hewson

First published 1994
Reprinted 1996

ISBN 1-85310-538-4

Printed in Hong Kong.

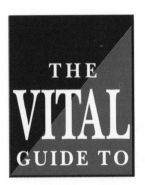

THE VITAL GUIDE TO

COMMERCIAL AIRCRAFT
AND AIRLINERS

INCLUDING A GUIDE TO AIRLINES AND THEIR COLOUR SCHEMES

EDITOR: ROBERT HEWSON

Airlife
England

ATR 42, ATR 72 and ATR 82

Regional aircraft development was the impetus behind the union in October 1981 of Aeritalia (now Alenia) of Italy and Aérospatiale of France, who set out to develop a whole new family of twin-turboprop regional airliners. The **ATR 42** designation was derived from Avion de Transport Régional (the new company name) and the intended number of seats (42). The first prototype flew on 16 August 1984, and type certification was received on 24 September 1985 in France and Italy.

The aircraft features a high-set wing, mounted above the fuselage so that the carry-through structure does not reduce cabin height. The tailplane is mounted near the top of the swept-back fin, while the undercarriage is housed in sponsons on the fuselage side. On the flight deck are two pilot seats, with a folding seat for an observer. Main access is via a door on the rear port side with an integral stairway. The space between the flight deck and passenger cabin is used for baggage stowage, with additional capacity at the rear of the cabin, where the toilet, galley and cabin attendant's seat are located.

Air Littoral received the fourth aircraft, and put the ATR 42 into service on 9 December 1985. Since then it has become a very popular choice on many regional routes around the world. The basic

The ATR 42s of UK airline Cityflyer Express now wear the colours of British Airways after the two airlines entered into a franchise agreement in 1993.

Finland's Kar-Air, long a swing-tailed DC-6 freighter operator, was one of the earliest customers for the stretched ATR 72.

ATR 42-300 version (PW120 engines) is complemented by the **ATR 42-320**, with PW121s for hot-and-high performance. The **ATR 42-500** is a PW127-powered proposal for even better performance. Other variants include the **ATR 42 Cargo**, with a reconfigurable cabin and cargo door, **ATR 42F** military freighter with air-opening side door for paradropping, and the **ATR 42 Calibration** for testing navigation aids.

Always intended to be a family, the ATR design gave rise to the stretched **ATR 72-200**, which first flew on 27 October 1988. Powered by PW124B engines, the stretched fuselage can accommodate 64-74 passengers. Certificated in the autumn of 1989, the first recipient was Kar-Air of Finland, which received its initial aircraft on 27 October 1989. Further variants include the **ATR 72-210** (subject of a 60-aircraft order from American Airlines), with PW127 engines for hot-and-high performance, the **ATR 52C** military freighter with rear loading ramp, and the stretched 80/86-seat Allison AE2100-powered **ATR 82**, which is scheduled to first fly in 1996.

By December 1993, ATR had achieved 422 firm orders, comprising 282 ATR 42s and 140 ATR 72s, with 362 aircraft delivered. This figure represents 53 per cent of the world market in this class.

SPECIFICATION:
ATR 42-300
Powerplant: two 1,800-shp (1342-kW) Pratt & Whitney Canada PW120 turboprops,
Accommodation: two (flight deck), maximum of 50 passengers
Dimensions: span 80 ft 7½ in (24.57 m); height 24 ft 10½ in (7.586 m); length 74 ft 4½ in (22.67 m)
Weights: operating empty 22,674 lb (10285 kg); maximum take-off 36,817 lb (16,700 kg)
Performance: maximum cruising speed at 17,000 ft (5180 m) 305 mph (490 km/h); maximum operating altitude 25,000 ft (7620 m); maximum range with reserves 3,131 miles (5040 km)

Aerospacelines Guppy

O f all the commercial aircraft still active today, the 'Guppy' family is easily the most unusual. The need to transport outsize components for the space programme in the early 1960s prompted Aerospacelines to undertake the conversion of a Boeing Stratocruiser in 1961. The process involved inserting an extra fuselage section (into the second Stratoliner delivered to Pan American) aft of the wing and building up a huge 'bubble' fuselage structure able to take items of up to 9-ft 9-in (6.02- m) diameter. This aircraft made its maiden flight on 19 September 1962 and acquired the nickname **'Pregnant Guppy'**, which lead to the official designation **Model 377PG**.

Following trials, the aircraft operated under contract to NASA and was used to transport Saturn rocket sections. Such was the success of the original piston-engined aircraft that eight more Guppies were built during 1965-83. Three were **Mini Guppies (Model 377MG**, but later **Model 101)**, with the first using Pratt & Whitney R-4360 radial engines, while the later two had Allison 501 turboprops. They were smaller, with loading facilitated by a hinged aft section. These three aircraft were 'produced' between 1967 and 1970.

The most numerous version and also the largest is the **Super Guppy (Model 377SG)**. This flew for the first time at the end of August 1965 and was fitted with Pratt & Whitney YT34 turboprops inherited from the YC-97J on which it was based. Unlike its predecessors, this version was loaded from the

Nothing in the aviation world quite compares with the Super Guppy. Combined with Airbus Skylink's colour scheme, it is truly an impressive sight.

front, with the entire nose swinging through a 90° arc to port for access to the hold, which could accept items of up to 25-ft (7.62-m) diameter.

The original Super Guppy was also used to support the space project, and was the only aircraft able to carry a third-stage section of a Saturn V rocket. Subsequently, four more Super Guppies appeared, all being fitted with Allison 501 engines from the outset. The first two were completed in 1970 and 1973 and used by Airbus Industrie (though operated by Aeromaritime) to move large components between the various European factories involved in the Airbus production programme. The final two were built in 1982-1983 and were actually assembled by the French airline Union de Transports Aériens in 1982-83 from Stratocruiser and C-97 parts furnished by Aerospacelines.

The Super Guppies are still busy with Airbus work, but are to be replaced by a quartet of Airbus A300-600ST Super Transporters in 1995-98. Combining jet speed with modern technology, the A300-600ST will be able to carry a maximum payload double that of the hardworking Super Guppy.

Despite the advent of the A300-600ST, the last of the 1953-vintage Super Guppies will soldier on with Airbus until 1999.

SPECIFICATION:
Aero Spacelines (Boeing) 377SGT Guppy-201
Powerplant: four 4,912-ehp (3659-kW) Allison 501-D22C turboprops
Accommodation: four (flight deck)
Dimensions: span 156 ft 3 in (47.62 m); height 48 ft 6 in (14.78 m); length 143 ft 10 in (43.84 m)
Weights: empty 100,00 lb (45359 kg); maximum payload 54,000 lb (24494 kg); maximum take-off 170,000 lb (77110 kg)
Performance: maximum level speed, below 14,800 ft (4510 m) 242 mph (390 km/h); service ceiling, max certified 25,000 ft (7620 m); range, with max payload 505 miles (813 km)

Airbus A300

Born in the mid-1960s, Airbus Industries and the **A300** grew from an informal requirement expressed by several major European carriers for a new wide-bodied airliner for use on busy, medium-range European routes. The aircraft that became the A300 had its roots in the Anglo-French **HBN100**, a design proposed by Hawker Siddeley, Breguet and Nord. Sud-Aviation and a conglomeration of German manufacturers joined the project, and by 1967 the planned design was renamed A300.

A lengthy period of indecision led finally to a Memorandum of Understanding (MoU) to proceed, providing Sud-Aviation received design leadership and the future powerplants would be built by Rolls-Royce. Another factor of the MoU was the expectation of 75 orders each from the national airlines BEA, Air France and Lufthansa. The A300 continued to grow in size until finally, in 1968, it was fixed as a 252-seat, 275,500-lb (124966-kg) design renamed the **A300B**. In 1969 France and Germany announced they would proceed with this design, in the face of British apathy towards the project, but British Aerospace (then BAC) did become a major manufacturing partner in Airbus Industrie, which was founded in December 1970. Currently, work is divided between Aérospatiale (37.9 per cent), Deutsche Aerospace (37.9 per cent), BAe (20 per

Monarch Airlines is one of an increasing number of UK Airbus operators. Its current fleet includes four CF6-powered A300-605Rs.

cent) and CASA (4.2 per cent), with other contributions being made by Fokker and Belairbus (Belgium).

The first A300 to fly, an **A330B1**, took to the air on 28 October 1972. Air France took delivery of two of these, but the dominant early production version was the slightly stretched **A300B2**. A long-range version, the **A300B4**, followed in 1974.

The current production version is the **A300-600** (initially named the **Advanced A300B2/B4**) and the extended-range **A300-600R**, which features a fin fuel tank and a computerised fuel trimming system. The A300-600 offers a fully 'glass' EFIS cockpit for two-crew operations, increased use of composite materials and much improved aerodynamics. Spurred by interest from Federal Express, Airbus developed the **A300-600F** freighter. The first of these was delivered to FedEx on 27 April 1994, and Airbus is now working on four **A300-600ST**s (Super Transporter) to replace Aerospacelines Super Guppies used to transport Airbus parts to Toulouse for final assembly. The first of these, the widest civil jet ever at 24 ft 2 in (7.4 m) across, was rolled out on 23 June 1994.

By mid-1994, Airbus A300 orders stood at 472 aircraft with 416 delivered, 248 of which are Airbus A300B2/B4s.

Japan Air Systems (formerly TOA Domestic) liked Airbus' house colours so much they adopted them for with their new A300s in 1980.

SPECIFICATION: Airbus A300-600R
Powerplant: two 61,500-lb (273.6-kN) General Electric CF6-80C2A5 or 58,000-lb (258-kN) Pratt & Whitney PW4158 turbofans
Accommodation: two (flight deck), maximum of 375 passengers
Dimensions: span 147 ft 1 in (4.84 m); height 54 ft 3 in (16.53 m); length 174 ft 10½ in (53.30 m)
Weights: (with CF6-80C2A5s) operating, empty 198,003 lb (89813 kg); maximum take-off 378,535 lb (171700 kg)
Performance: max cruising speed at 30,000 ft (9150 m) 557 mph (897 km/h); max operating altitude 40,000 ft (1220 m); max range with reserves 4,800 miles (7725 km)

Airbus A310

European airliner-building experience which began with the Airbus A300 highlighted the need for a smaller, short-range Airbus, initially proposed as the **A300B10**. Interest was expressed by Swissair, Lufthansa and Eastern Airlines, and the design that emerged was launched in 1978 as the **A310**. The main cabin is 11 frames shorter than the A300, while retaining the same cross-section, and features a new 'advanced technology' wing, modified undercarriage, and increased use of composites. A two-crew 'glass' EFIS cockpit is standard and engine choices included the General Electric CF6, Pratt & Whitney JT9D and Rolls-Royce RB.211 turbofans. In the event, no orders were received for the Rolls-Royce-powered version.

The first A310 flew on 3 April 1982, with an order book of 181. Airbus had intended to offer two versions, the 2,300-mile (3704-km) range regional **A310-100** and longer-range **A310-200**, which could cover an additional 1,150 miles (1852 km) with 210 passengers. Swissair placed the first orders, for 10 series -200 aircraft with 10 on option, and all subsequent orders were for A310-200s. No A310-100s were ever built.

In 1982 Airbus announced a third version, the **A310-300**, aimed at even longer routes than the previous models. The programme was announced during the handover of Swissair's first A310, and that same airline again became the launch customer. Outwardly, the A310-300 is almost identical to previous versions, although it does carry small,

Swissair subsidiary Balair (which merged with CTA to form BalairCTA), relies on four A310-324s to serve IT holiday charter destinations worldwide.

but distinctive winglets. Power is provided by either General Electric CF6 or Pratt & Whitney PW4000-series engines. Internally, the aircraft is fitted with a fin fuel tank (which was later applied to the A300-600R). Optional tanks can be carried in the hold and a computerised fuel trimming system ensures maximum performance in the cruise. Many airlines have qualified the A310-300 for EROPS operations, by upgrading its navigational systems and communications fit.

By mid-1994, 258 A310s of all versions had been ordered, with 247 delivered. The current price for a new A310-300 is roughly $66 million. Airbus developed a cargo-convertible version, the **A310-200C**, but only one example was sold, to Dutch airline Martinair. Federal Express is converting 13 leased Lufthansa A310-200s to **A310-200F** freighter configuration with a large cargo door. The first was delivered in July 1994. The Airbus partners are now discussing a military **Multi-Role Tanker Transport (MRTT)** version of the A310 with a side-cargo door and a 66,000-lb (30,000-kg) payload, or underfuselage fuel cells and wing-mounted refuelling pods.

Troubled airline Alyemda was the carrier of the former South Yemen. In 1993 it took delivery of a single A310-304, leased from the manufacturer.

SPECIFICATION: Airbus A310-300
Powerplant: two 59,000-lb (262.4-kN) General Electric CF6-80C2A8 or 56,000-lb (249.1-kN) Pratt & Whitney PW4156A turbofans
Accommodation: two (flight deck), maximum of 280 passengers
Dimensions: span 144 ft (43.89 m); height 51 ft 10 in (15.80 m); length 148 ft 0¾ in (53.30 m)
Weights: (with CF6-80C2A8 engines) operating, empty 177,095 lb (80329 kg); maximum take-off 330,695 lb (150000 kg)
Performance: cruising speed at 31,000 ft (9150 m) Mach 0.80; max operating altitude 40,000 ft (1220 m); max range, with reserves and standard load 4,951 miles (7968 km)

Airbus A320

Realising that American dominance of the airliner market had been shaken by the A300/A310 family, Airbus launched a rival for the Boeing 737 and McDonnell Douglas DC-9/MD-80 families in the form of the **A320**. From the outset, Airbus determined to use as much 'new technology' as possible to dramatically reduce operating costs and worked hard to persuade the staid airline market to accept something new. The design had its roots in a myriad of European small airliner studies dating back to the early 1970s, but when Airbus launched the definitive A320 in 1981 it was built around a then-unique fly-by-wire (FBW) control system and a choice of two new turbofan engines. Three fuselage lengths were initially proposed, but the team at Toulouse settled on just two: the 130/140-seat **A320-100** and the 150-160 seat **A320-200**.

Air France announced a letter of intent for both versions at the Paris air show of 1981, where Boeing was also exhibiting the new 737-300. In the face of continued airline interest, Airbus decided to concentrate on a single fuselage length, seating approximately 150 passengers, while offering two versions still dubbed A320-100 and -200. The difference was in payload/range, as the 'new' A320-100 had wing fuel tanks only, as opposed to the higher MTOW A320-200 with additional fuselage centre-

Since 1985, Hong Kong's Dragonair has filled a gap in regional services beneath the island's dominant airline, Cathay Pacific. Six A320s are now in service.

Air Lanka operates a pair of V2500-A1-powered Airbus A320-231s that replaced Boeing 737-200s on the airline's short-haul routes during 1992-93.

body fuel tanks. The type was finally launched in 1984, with its first orders from British Caledonian Airways. Orders continued to grow until the A320 first flew on 22 February 1984. The first deliveries were made to Air France in March 1988, these being of the lightweight A320-100 version (only 21 of which were built). The first A320-200 was delivered to Ansett Airways in June 1988.

Airbus offers several versions of the CFM International CFM56-5A engine for the A320, along with the newly developed International Aero Engines (IAE) V2500-A1, which claims a much improved fuel burn. Over half the orders so far (67 per cent) have been for CFM-engined aircraft. A more radical innovation is the five-computer, quadruplex Thomson-CSF/Sfena digital FBW control system that provides the pilot with a side-stick controller instead of a more normal control column. The cockpit features colour, multi-function displays, a unique Electronic Centralised Aircraft Monitor system and only 13 main panel instruments.

Perhaps the ultimate compliment came in May 1994 when Boeing tried to acquire a (second-hand) A320 for display in Seattle, to 'motivate its employees'. By mid-1994, 645 A320s (at an approximate price of $36 million each) had been ordered, with 457 delivered.

SPECIFICATION: Airbus A320-200
Powerplant: two 25,000-lb (111.2-kN) IAE V2525-A5 or 26,500-lb (117.9-kN) CFM International CFM56-5B4 turbofans
Accommodation: two (flight deck), maximum of 179 passengers
Dimensions: span 111 ft 3 in (33.91 m); height 38 ft 9½ in (11.80 m); length 123 ft 3 in (37.57 m)
Weights: (with CFM56 engines) operating, empty 91,675 lb (41583 kg); maximum take-off 169,765 lb (77,000 kg)
Performance: cruising speed at 31,000 ft (9150 m) Mach 0.80; max operating altitude 40,000 ft (1220 m); max range, with reserves and standard load 3,222 miles (5190 km)

Airbus A319 and A321

The early years of the A320 saw a variety of models proposed. A longer-fuselage version had been planned, but was put aside in favour of a dedicated higher-capacity design initially referred to as the **'Stretched A320'** or **'A320 Stretch'**. In June 1989 this formally became the **A321**, a minimum-change version of the A320. The aircraft was 6.93 m (273 in) longer than its antecedent, with reinforced centre fuselage and landing gear, and redesigned trailing-edge flaps. The fuselage stretch, accommodating a normal load of 176 passengers, comprised two plugs forward and aft of the wing. This has to the repositioning of the four emergency exits to either side of the wing leading- and trailing-edges.

Airbus is offering one version initially, the **A321-100**, with a choice of CFM56-5B or IAE V2530-A5 turbofans. It was initially assumed that the new type would be assembled alongside the A320 on the Toulouse line but, instead, it has become the first Airbus to be assembled in Germany, at DASA's Otto Lilienthal facility, Hamburg. The first A321 was rolled out on 3 March 1993, and the maiden flight took place on 11 March 1993. Four aircraft underwent an 850-hour flight test programme that led to the type's European JAA certification in December 1993, with CFM56 approval following on 15 February 1994.

Launch customers were Lufthansa, which chose the higher-powered V2530 for its aircraft (20), and Alitalia (40). Lufthansa took delivery of the

Launch A321 customer Lufthansa was also the first operator, introducing the type, in 182-seat configuration, on European routes in January 1994.

first production A321 on 27 January 1994, followed by Alitalia (with CFM56-5B engines) on 22 March. By mid-1994, orders for the $47.5-million airliner stood at 131, with eight in service.

The short-fuselage **A319** was announced in May 1992 as the third member of the A320 'family'. Using the similar systems, avionics and structure to the A320, the A319 will offer the more powerful engine choices of the A321, and be built alongside the latter, in Hamburg. The A319 will have the longest range of the three versions at 3,105 miles (5000 km), will be some 12 ft 3 in (3.73 m) shorter than the A320, and carry a normal load of 130 passengers. Airbus formally launched the project at the 1993 Farnborough air show, after an earlier order for six aircraft from leasing firm ILFC in December 1992. The A319 first flew on 25 August 1995, and service entry is planned for early 1996. In January 1994, Air Inter placed orders for nine aircraft, with options on a further nine (though these may be converted to A320s or A321s). Swissair has also signed for three of the type, followed by Air Canada with an order for 25.

Air Inter has signed up for perhaps as many as 18 A319s and, along with Swissair, will become one of the first airlines to operate the A319, A320 and A321.

SPECIFICATION: Airbus A321
Powerplant: two 30,000-lb (133.4-kN) CFM International CFM56-5B or 31,000 (137.9-kN) IAE V2530-A5 turbofans
Accommodation: two (flight deck), maximum of 220 passengers
Dimensions: span 111 ft 10 in (34.09 m); height 38 ft 9 in (11.81 m); length 146 ft (44.51 m)
Weights: operating, empty 104,746 lb (47512 kg); maximum take-off 182,984 lb (83,000 kg)
Performance: cruising speed at 31,000 ft (9150 m) Mach 0.80; maximum operating altitude 40,000 ft (1220 m); maximum range, with reserves and standard load 2,648 miles (4260 km)

Airbus A330

Having successfully established its credentials as a major aviation manufacturer, in the early 1980s Airbus Industrie announced the latest and largest members of its airliner family, the **A330** and A340. Both aircraft are closely related, sharing structural, wing and cockpit design, and each uses the same Airbus-developed fly-by-wire control system. The twin-engined A330 (which utilises different engines to the A340), is aimed at less 'global' routes then the very-long-range A340, and is perhaps better viewed as a Boeing 767-300ER competitor, despite being larger than the rival design from Seattle.

The A330 is now the largest twin-engined airliner in production (beating the 267-seat A300-600) and, like many Airbus designs, has its roots in the A300. When the outlines of long-range Airbus variants began to be drawn up in the mid-1970s, the aircraft were referred to as the **A300B9** and **A300B11**. The latter grew into a four-engined design and led to the A340. As studies progressed, the A300B9 was renamed the **TA9** (Twin Aisle), and two versions (long-range with 230 passengers, or medium-range with 270 passengers) were foreseen. In January 1986, the TA9 officially became the A330, powered by either General Electric CF6-80C2 or Pratt & Whitney PW4000-series turbofans.

Air Inter was the A330 launch customer, with an order for 15. Some of these aircraft may soon be abandoned in favour of smaller A319s, however.

Along with Malaysian Airlines, which has ordered 10, Thai Airways' eight A330s will be the first deliveries fitted with Pratt & Whitney PW4168 engines.

Airbus continued to juggle a number of fuselage lengths and seating configurations before settling on the definitive first production version, the **A330-300**, which shares the same fuselage as the A340-300. The first orders, for 15, came from Air Inter in 1987, and that same year Roll-Royce engines became an option for the first time on any Airbus. The first A330 flew over a year after the A340, on 2 November 1992, powered by CF6 engines. Three aircraft were involved in a 1,100-hour flight test programme. A PW4168-powered A330 joined the programme on 14 October, and the first Rolls-Royce Trent 700-powered aircraft finally flew on 31 January 1994. Joint FAA and JAA certification was achieved on 21 October 1993, and deliveries began, to Air Inter, in January 1994.

Extended-Range Twin-engined OPerationS (ETOPS) approval was granted in May 1994, and by mid-1994 the type was already in transatlantic service with Aer Lingus. In mid-1994, orders for the $92-million design stood at 118. Unlike the A340, problems have afflicted the A330's early days. Difficulties with the landing gear and PW4000 thrust reversers were overshadowed by the tragic loss of a prototype during single-engined certification trials at Toulouse on 30 June 1994. Hopefully, this will have little effect on the A330's future.

SPECIFICATION: Airbus A330-300
Powerplant: two 63,820-lb (285-kN) to 72,000-lb (320-kN) General Electric CF6-80E1A2, Pratt & Whitney PW4168, or Rolls-Royce Trent 768 turbofans
Accommodation: two (flight deck), maximum of 440 passengers (335 standard)
Dimensions: span 197 ft 8 in (60.3 m); height 54 ft 11 in (16.74 m); length 208 ft 9 in (63.7 m)
Weights: operating, empty 263,448 lb (1119500 kg); maximum take-off 467,372 lb (212000 kg)
Performance: max cruising speed Mach 0.82; max operating altitude 40,000 ft (1220 m); max range, with reserves 5,219 miles (8400 km)

Airbus A340

European aviation's most potent symbol today is probably the **A340**. Airbus Industrie's 'World Ranger', the consortium's largest design to date, is an advanced-technology, two-crew, ultra-long-range transport intended to offer the first real competition to Boeing's 747.

The A340 has common roots with the A330, as they began life as early developments of the A300. In the case of the A340, its initial designation of **A300B11** led to the **TA11** design of 1980. Airbus toyed with the idea of making its new long-range design a three-engined aircraft, but by the 1982 Farnborough air show the TA11 had become a four-engined airliner with a design range of 6,830 nm (12650 km; 7,860 miles). As the TA9 and TA11 design became increasingly similar, Airbus dropped plans for an over-complicated variable-camber wing. The TA11 was renamed, in 1986, the A340 (the same time as the TA9 became the A330).

Airbus had hoped to power the A340 with a 'SuperFan' – an ultra-high bypass development of the CFM56 or V2500. Plans for this powerplant were not successful and Airbus had to rely on improved versions of existing turbofan engines to achieve its promised range. The first commitments, from Lufthansa, had already been received on the understanding that these new engines, or at least an aircraft with their performance, would be available. To solve its problems, Airbus increased the A340's wingspan by adding 9-ft (2.75-m) winglets, and CFM International announced an uprated version of

Air France was the first airline to place the standard (long-fuselage) A340-300 into revenue service in March 1993. It is configured with 287 seats.

its CFM56, the CFM56-5C2. The A340 received its formal go-ahead in July 1987.

Two versions are on offer, the 375-seat (standard) **A340-300** or the short-fuselage, extended- range **A340-200**, normally seating 263 passengers. The first A340 to fly was a -300 on 25 October 1991. The A340-200 followed on 1 April 1992. Both versions are built alongside the A330, at a new production facility at Toulouse. The flight decks of the A340 and A330 are virtually identical, and very similar to the A320. As a result, the FAA has certified crew cross-cockpit qualification for the first time ever. Cold weather trials were undertaken at Yakutsk in February 1993. During the Paris air show that year, Airbus flew an A340 named 'World Ranger' around the globe with only one stop, breaking many previous records set by a Boeing 747SP. Lufthansa and Air France introduced the A340-200 and -300 into service in March 1993, and Lufthansa has stated that it has been the most trouble-free introduction of a new type in the company's history. By mid-1994, orders for the A340 (at $98-103 million each) stood at 127 with 33 delivered.

Lufthansa opted for extended-range, short-fuselage A340-200s as its initial version. The aircraft have 228 seats, arranged in three classes.

SPECIFICATION: Airbus A340-300
Powerplant: four 31,200-lb (138.8-kN) CFM International CFM56-5C2 turbofans
Accommodation: two (flight deck), maximum of 440 passengers (375 standard)
Dimensions: span 197 ft 8 in (60.3 m); height 54 ft 11 in (16.74 m); length 208 ft 9 in (63.7 m)
Weights: operating, empty 278,843 lb (126481 kg); maximum take-off 566,588 lb (257000 kg)
Performance: maximum operating speed Mach 0.86; maximum operating altitude 40,000 ft (1220 m); maximum range, with reserves and standard load 7,560 miles (12300 km)

Antonov An-2 (SAP Y-5)

Poland (China)
Single-engined utility biplane

When the **Antonov An-2 'Colt'** flew for the first time on 31 August 1947, production was initially undertaken in the Soviet Union, where several thousand were built. Subsequently, other assembly lines were established in China and Poland. The various factories completed somewhere in the region of 20,000 examples, making it one of the most numerous aircraft to be built since World War II.

The An-2's rather antiquated appearance perhaps tends to disguise its characteristics and capabilities. The fuselage, for example, is an all-metal, stressed-skin, semi-monocoque structure and is quite robust, while the wing is a mix of ancient and modern, utilising an all-metal, two-spar structure but also incorporating fabric covering material to the rear of the front spar. High-lift devices such as leading-edge slots on the upper wing and trailing-edge flaps on both upper and lower wings result in impressive STOL performance, and also help bestow docile handling qualities.

In addition to being easy to fly, the An-2 has also demonstrated a good degree of versatility, with suitably adapted versions being used for photographic survey, fire-fighting, weather research and casualty evacuation. The basic **An-2P** general-purpose transport can carry up to 4,519 lb (2,000 kg). The provision of a generously-proportioned side door

The An-2 serves in large numbers in its native Poland, in a wide variety of roles. This particular example serves as a sport parachute aircraft.

permits reasonably bulky loads to be carried or, alternatively, it can take up to 19 adults in tip-up seats. The **An-2R** is an agricultural version fitted with fuselage hoppers and underwing spraybars, while the **An-2T** and **An-2TP** are passenger-configured for 12 occupants in standard seats.

Power for the An-2 is usually provided by a PZL Kalisz ASz-62IR nine-cylinder radial piston engine, but Antonov has developed and tested an updated turboprop installation for agricultural tasks. Known by the bureau as the **An-3**, this is fitted with a 1,450-shp (1081-kW) Glushenkov TVD-20 engine and also embodies short 'plugs' inserted fore and aft of the wings to lengthen the fuselage. As far as is known, the An-3 is available only as a modification of the An-2, with the conversion project centred upon a factory in Kiev.

The An-2 remains in production at PZL's Mielec plant, which has completed nearly 12,000 (since 23 October 1960) for service at home and for export to 20 countries, from Afghanistan to Venezuela. Since 1970, over 225 Chinese aircraft have been built by the Shijiazhuang Aircraft Plant (previously Huabei/Nanchang) as the **SAP Y-5N** (Yunshuji 5 – transport aircraft 5) with Chinese-built HS5 engines and differing avionics fit. The **Y-5B** is a dedicated agricultural version and first flew on 2 June 1989.

Among its varied fleet, Cubana flies a single An-2 specially modified with panoramic windows for sight-seeing flights around the island.

SPECIFICATION:
Antonov (PZL-Mielec) An-2
Powerplant: one 1,000-hp (746-kW) PZL Kalisz ASz-621R air-cooled, radial piston engine
Accommodation: two (flight deck), maximum of 19 passengers (seated)
Dimensions: span, upper 59 ft 7¼ in (18.18 m), lower 46 ft 8½ in (14.24 m); height, tail down 13 ft 2 in (4.01 m); length, tail down 40 ft 8¼ in (12.40 m)
Weights: empty 7,605 lb (3450 kg); maximum take-off 12,125 lb (5500 kg)
Performance: max level speed 160 mph (258 km/h); service ceiling 14,425 ft (4400 m); max range, with standard load 560 miles (900 km)

Antonov An-12 (Shaanxi Y-8)

Ukraine (China)
Four-engined rear-loading transport

Seen in the West for the first time at the Paris air show of 1965, the **An-12** made its maiden flight during 1958 and entered service in the following year. Built alongside the commercial **An-10 Ukraina** at first, it was adapted with the military very much in mind. Consequently, it introduced a revised aft fuselage (with hardly any windows) that permitted the transfer of cargo directly from trucks, as well as allowing vehicles to be loaded with the assistance of a separate ramp. A rear gun turret was another sign of its military roots, though later civil versions did delete this feature. Several hundred examples of the basic **An-12BP 'Cub-A'** were obtained for service with the state airline, although Aeroflot's unique status resulted in these often being employed for military duties.

In addition, the Soviet air force also received a substantial number for tactical airlift tasks. However, the introduction of the Ilyushin Il-76 in 1974 has resulted in a decline of the 'Cub' fleet. As well as production for the home market, a reasonably large number of An-12s were exported, with other operators including several air arms that traditionally looked to the Soviet Union as a source of military hardware, such as those of Algeria, Egypt, India, Iraq and Syria. Several of these nations operated aircraft in dual civil/military markings but many of these have now been withdrawn, following replacement by more modern equipment.

With the break-up of Aeroflot in the early 1990s, substantial numbers of An-12s have passed into

A single An-12 remains (nominally) on charge with LOT Polish Airlines. It is based alongside an air force An-26 transport unit at Kracow-Balice.

service with a plethora of often colourful (and ever-changing) new airlines throughout the former Soviet Union. The An-12's availability and relative ease of operation ensures that it will be a regular sight for years to come.

The type's future is secure for it is still in production in the People's Republic of China, as the **Shaanxi** (Shaanxi Aircraft Company) **Y-8**. Chinese 'licence'-production started at the Xian factory in 1969 and the first example flew on 25 December 1974. SAC undertook production the following year and the type now exists in several versions. Commercial models include the **Y-8B**, a civilianised military transport; the fully-pressurised **Y-8C** (only a small forward cabin section of Soviet-built aircraft was pressurised); the **Y-8D**, fitted with Collins avionics for export; and the somewhat specialised **Y-8F** 'goat transporter', with up to 350 livestock pens. Amazingly, the latest of these versions, the **Y-8C**, first flew as recently as 17 December 1990. While by mid-1994 over 50 aircraft were in airline service in China, very small numbers have been exported, and only to military customers.

Many An-12s remain in daily use with a number of new airlines in the former Soviet Union. Most retain their former Aeroflot schemes, with revised markings.

SPECIFICATION:
Antonov An-12
Powerplant: four 3,495-ehp (2942-kW) Ivchenko AI-20K turboprops
Accommodation: five (flight deck)
Dimensions: span 124 ft 8 in (38 m); height 34 ft 6½ in (10.53 m); length 108 ft 7¼ in (33.10 m)
Weights: empty 61,730 lb (28000 kg); maximum payload 44,090 lb (20000 kg); maximum take-off 134,480 lb (61000 kg)
Performance: maximum level speed 482 mph (777 km/h); service ceiling 33,500 ft (10200 m); maximum range, with max payload 2,236 miles (3600 km)

Antonov An-24/-26/-32 (Xian Y-7)

Twin-engined utility transports

Originally conceived in the late 1950s to replace Ilyushin Il-12s, Ilyushin Il-14s and Lisunov Li-2s on short-haul routes, the twin-turboprop **An-24 'Coke'** bore a distinct resemblance to the Fokker F27 and flew for the first time on 20 December 1959. Entry into Aeroflot service came in July 1962.

Approximately 1,100 examples had been built by 1978, with the original 44-seat An-24 being supplanted by the 50-seat **An-24V** which offered improved performance. Other variants that appeared later included the **An-24TV** and **An-24RT** freighters, and the **An-24RV**. The latter sub-type had a Tumanskii RU-19-300 turbojet instead of the original TG-16 gas turbine auxiliary power unit, to bestow better take-off performance.

Elsewhere, after receiving about 40 aircraft from the Soviet Union, China initiated licence-production of the An-24 as the **Xian Y-7**, with deliveries starting in 1984. Further refinement, including the fitment of winglets, resulted in the **Y-7-100** and China has since conceived more versions, including the **Y-7-200A** with Pratt & Whitney Canada PW127 engines; the **Y-7-200B** with Harbin WJ5E powerplants; and the cargo-carrying **Y-7H-500**, which is, in fact, a copy of the all-cargo An-26.

Ongoing development in the USSR led initially to the **An-26 'Curl'** which made its Western debut at

The An-32 is an up-engined hot-and-high freighter that has found some civil sales outside the former Soviet Union, such as this Nicaraguan example.

China took the 1959-vintage Antonov An-24 and, during the 1970s, developed the Y-7, which first appeared in 1982. The current Y7-100 boasts winglets.

the 1969 Paris air show. This dedicated light tactical transport (**An-26A**) was fitted with a rear loading ramp and also had a booster engine as a standard feature. The improved **An-26B** can accommodate three standard freight pallets. Small numbers of An-26s are in civilian service, and Antonov has also developed a water-bomber fire-fighting version.

Other members of the family comprise the **An-30 'Clank'** and the **An-32 'Cline'**. The former is optimised for the aerial survey role and is instantly recognisable by its glazed nose. Equipment varies according to the nature of the survey work being undertaken, but includes cameras and other sensor systems. Production estimates indicate that about 130 have been built.

The An-32 is also primarily a tactical transport derivative and was unveiled at the 1977 Paris air show. It has been modified quite extensively to ensure improved hot-and-high/short-field performance and is fitted with considerably more powerful engines driving larger propellers. The revised clearance requirement necessitated fitting the engines in overwing nacelles, giving the 'Cline' a distinctive 'hunch-back' appearance. The **An-32B** is a dedicated flying hospital, while the **An-32P Firekiller** is a fire-fighting version with water tanks scabbed on to the fuselage side.

SPECIFICATION:
Antonov An-24RV
Powerplant: two 2,550-ehp (1899-kW) Ivchenko AI-24A turboprops, plus one 1,985-lb (8.8-kN) RU19-300 auxiliary turbojet
Accommodation: three (flight deck), maximum of 50 passengers (44 standard)
Dimensions: span 95 ft 9½ in (29.20 m); height 27 ft 3½ in (8.32 m); length 77 ft 2½ in (23.53 m)
Weights: empty 29,320 lb (13300 kg); maximum take-off 46,300 lb (21000 kg)
Performance: cruising speed at 19,700 ft (6,000 m) 280 mph (450 km/h); service ceiling 27,560 ft (8400 m); range, with max payload and reserves 341 miles (550 km)

Antonov An-28 and An-38

Nominally developed from the piston-engined **An-14** and originally given the designation **An-14M**, the Antonov **An-28 'Cash'** made its initial flight in the USSR during September 1969, with testing continuing into 1972. Production may have been undertaken in the Soviet Union for Aeroflot, but responsibility for manufacture of the An-28 was transferred to PZL-Mielec of Poland in 1978. In the event, the first Polish-built example completed a successful maiden flight in July 1984, with Polish certification following in February 1986. Production of the initial An-28 ended in the early 1990s, but PZL has gone on to offer several developments with an eye on Western markets. In 1992 the **An-28B1T** appeared, optimised for parachuting/air drops with a sliding rear door, which retracts under the fuselage. The **An-28PT** boasts new PT6A-65B engines driving five-bladed Hartzell props, with Bendix/King avionics and colour weather radar.

Subsequent developments at Antonov's design centre in Kiev led to the joint Russo-Ukrainian **An-38** project, which culminated in a first flight of the prototype at the Chaklov production plant in Novosibirsk on 22 June 1994. This has a rather longer fuselage and is also significantly heavier, but has cabin accommodation for up to 27 passengers, while also possessing the potential to undertake utility transport tasks. At the time of the maiden flight, officials associated with the programme stated that 136 options had been taken for the An-38 but that no firm orders had yet been placed. Nevertheless,

PZL-Mielec built the standard An-28, chiefly for Aeroflot, until 1984. Small numbers operate on the Polish civil register and with the air force.

it is being keenly marketed as a replacement for types such as the An-2, An-24 and Let L-410 in Russia and its neighbouring states.

The An-38 breaks new ground in so far as it is fitted with a considerable amount of Western equipment. Foremost among these are the engines: two Allied Signal (Garrett) TPE-331-14GR turboprops driving five-bladed Hartzell propellers. Testing is now underway, with a view to achieving Russian certification in 1995. It is intended to push for Western certification at the same time, although company representatives were realistic enough to acknowledge that this may well slip.

Production of the An-38 will be centred in Novosibirsk and is to be launched in 1995 at a rate of 10 per year, with a view to reaching a peak of 20 per year in 1999. That will, of course, be dependent upon sufficient orders being obtained and, with a baseline price tag equivalent to $3.5 million, they may not be. However, those backing the project have drawn up lease and loan arrangements for potential customers and are confident that many options will be converted into sales.

At the 1991 Paris air show, PZL exhibited this PZL-10S-powered An-28 as the 'Safari', in the colours of Sprint Airlines with a Polish registration.

SPECIFICATION:
Antonov (PZL-Mielec) An-28PT
Powerplant: two 1,100-ehp (820-kW) Pratt & Whitney Canada PT6A-65B turboprops
Accommodation: two (flight deck), maximum of 17 passengers
Dimensions: span 72 ft 4¼ in (22.063 m); height 16 ft 1 in (4.90 m); length 41 ft 7½ in (12.68 m)
Weights: empty, equipped 8,598 lb (3900 kg); maximum take-off 14,330 lb (6500 kg)
Performance: maximum cruising speed at 9,850 ft (3,000 m) 217 mph (350 km/h); service ceiling 19,685 ft (6000 m); range, with reserves 848 miles (1365 km)

Antonov An-124 and An-225

When it first flew on 26 December 1982, the An-124 **Ruslan** (a giant of old Russian folk tales) was the world's largest production aircraft, dwarfing even the USAF's Lockheed C-5 Galaxy. Developed to meet a joint Aeroflot and air forces requirement for a heavy strategic freighter, the An-124 (**'Condor'** to NATO) is of similar configuration to the C-5, although it has a conventional low-set tailplane rather than a T-tail. It has a rear loading ramp and an upward-hinging visor-type nose to allow loading from both ends simultaneously. The constant-section main hold has a titanium floor, and can be lightly pressurised. Winches and travelling cranes are provided, the latter with a total capacity of more than 44,000 lb (20,000 kg). The upper cabin (seating 88) behind the wing carry-through is fully pressurised. The aircraft can be made to kneel, giving the hold floor a slope of up to 3.5° to assist in loading or unloading.

A relatively high-tech aeroplane, the An-124 has a fly-by-wire control system, and even the relatively low percentage of composites used for some skin panels and fairings give a weight saving of more than 4,410 lb (2000 kg). Despite its enormous size, the An-124 is designed to operate from semi-prepared strips, including hard-packed snow or even ice-covered swamps.

The sole An-225 Mriya visited the Paris air show in 1989 carrying the Soviet Buran orbiter. It first flew in that configuration in May of that year.

Aeroflot still flies a considerable number of An-124s. Aircraft are increasingly being operated by other former Soviet Union and Western airlines.

Britain's Air Foyle manages commercial An-124 operations in North America, Europe and the Persian Gulf on behalf of Antonov, and operates up to three wet-leased An-124s. Another British company, HeavyLift, has a joint venture with Russian specialist cargo operator Volga-Dnepr, operating three An-124s from its London-Stansted base.

The **An-225 Mriya** (Dream), which first flew on 21 December 1988, was a stretched derivative of the An-124 primarily intended for the carriage of outsized loads for the Soviet space programme. Thus, while the fuselage is stretched by 26 ft 2 in (8 m), giving a corresponding increase in hold length (to 141 ft/43 m) and volume, the rear loading ramp is actually deleted. The most important effect is to increase the length available for the carriage of external 'piggyback' loads, for which two upper fuselage hardpoints have been provided, and for which the tail unit has also been redesigned, with increased span and endplate fins replacing the single centreline tailfin of the An-124. The aircraft has a new centre-section, with two further Lotarev D-18T turbofans, bringing the total to six. Only one An-225 has been built (with another still uncompleted), and after a period in storage has been put into service by Antonov's own charter cargo airline. It can carry payloads of up to 551,146 lb (250000 kg).

SPECIFICATION: Antonov An-124
Powerplant: four 51,590-lb (229.5-kN) ZMKB Progress D-18T turbofans
Accommodation: six (flight deck), passenger cabin for 88 aft of flight deck
Dimensions: span 240 ft 5¾ in (73.30 m); height 68 ft 2¼ in (20.78 m); length 226 ft 8½ in (69.10 m)
Weights: operating, empty 385,800 lb (175000 kg); maximum payload 330,693 lb (150000 kg); maximum take-off 892,872 lb (405000 kg)
Performance: maximum cruising speed at 32,800 ft (10,000 m) 497 mph (800 km/h); maximum range, with maximum payload 2,795 miles (4500 km)

Avro Regional Jet 70, 80 and 100 Four-engined regional airliners

Initially developed by Hawker Siddeley as the **HS 146**, the **British Aerospace 146** uses four low-powered turbofans and a highly efficient wing to achieve very low noise levels and outstanding field performance. Flying on 3 September 1981, the first aircraft was a short-body **Series 100**, able to accommodate 82 to 94 passengers in an 85-ft 11-in (26.19-m) fuselage. On 1 August 1982 came the first **Series 200**, stretched to 93 ft 10 in (28.60 m) to carry up to 112; the even longer (by 7 ft 10 in/2.38 m) **Series 300**, which first flew on 1 May 1987, could carry up to 128 in maximum density.

British Aerospace achieved notable 146 sales, particularly to airlines operating into noise-conscious areas. The launch customer was Dan-Air, which began operations on 27 May 1983. The first Series 200 went into service with Air Wisconsin in June 1983, this airline also being responsible for the first Series 300 service in December 1988. Other US airlines bought the aircraft for commuter services, and the type became the only jet allowed into several downtown airports, including London City Airport and John Wayne, Orange County.

Special variants of the 146 were the **146-QT Quiet Trader** all-cargo aircraft with an upward-hinging cabin-side freight door, which was purchased by TNT for overnight parcel deliveries, the **146-QC** which could be rapidly-reconfigured from passenger to cargo carriage, and the **Statesman**, fitted out for VIP transport. Production of the 146 ended in early 1993, with 209 aircraft built.

Conti-Flug operates a pair of BAe 146-200s (similar in size to the RJ85), in 79-seat configuration, from its base at Cologne to several European destinations.

Using the three 146 variants as a solid basis, BAe launched the **Avro Regional Jetliner (RJ)** series in a (still to be formalised) partnership with the Taiwan Aerospace Corporation. The RJ family currently comprises the **RJ70**, **RJ85** and **RJ100**, based on the 146-100, 146-200 and 146-300 fuselage lengths respectively. The principal difference is the adoption of Textron Lycoming LF507 turbofans in place of the ALF 502s of the 146. These offer full-authority digital engine control (FADEC), in addition to greater economy and slightly more power.

Further variants of the RJ family include the **RJ115**, similar in length to the RJ100 but with greater fuel capacity, mid-cabin exits and uprated cabin systems for the carriage of 116 passengers in standard layout. The QT option is still offered for cargo carriers, while the **RJX** is a proposal for a twin-engined variant.

The first RJ85 (for Crossair) flew on 27 November 1992. By mid-1994, the active fleet of BAe 146s/ Regional jets numbered 237, and in June 1994 Avro announced that Lufthansa would acquire the RJ85, in preference to the Fokker 70/100.

The RJ100 is Avro's largest current version and accommodates up to 128 passengers. For the time being, aircraft are still assembled at Woodford.

SPECIFICATION:
Avro RJ100
Powerplant: four 7,000-lb (31.14-kN) Textron-Lycoming LF 507 turbofans
Accommodation: two (flight deck), maximum of 128 passengers (100 standard)
Dimensions: span 86 ft (26.21 m); height 28 ft 2 in (8.59 m); length 101 ft 8¼ in (30.99 m)
Weights: operating, empty 55,915 lb (25362 kg); maximum take-off 97,500 lb (44225 kg)
Performance: maximum operating speed 351 mph (565 km/h); maximum range, with max payload 1,342 miles (2159 km)

Beechcraft Model 99

During the early 1960s, the growth in commuter traffic prompted Beech to develop a twin-turboprop airliner based on its successful Queen Air executive twin. The resultant Beech **Model 99 Airliner** first flew in July 1965. Retaining the overall low-wing, swept-tail layout of the Queen Air, the Model 99 had a stretched fuselage allowing the aircraft to carry 15 passengers in addition to the two pilots. The Queen Air's three main cabin windows were increased to six. The lengthened nose had a hatch for the carriage of baggage, and there was a moveable internal bulkhead to allow the cabin to be rapidly reconfigured for the carriage of freight, passengers or a mixture. The seats were easily removable, and a cargo door was an option, installed forward of the standard passenger door, which incorporated an airstair. A large ventral baggage pannier was another option later seen on many aircraft. Full airways navigation equipment was standard, but the individual equipment could be varied to meet customer requirements. Anti-icing for the propeller blades was also standard, but pneumatic de-icing boots for the leading edges of the wings and tail unit were optional extras.

On 2 May 1968 the first production Model 99 was delivered to Commuter Airlines Inc. Production ran until the end of 1975, by which time a total of

Many operators opted to add the ventral freight/baggage 'speedpak'. The Beech 99 could also be configured to carry just freight in the cabin.

While the Beech 99 Airliner was a popular choice for many US feeder airlines, it has largely been superseded, with the majors at least, by new types.

164 aircraft had been built for 64 customers. During this run, there were two improved versions, the **A99** and **B99**, which featured numerous improvements. Both variants were powered by the PT6A-27 680-shp (507-kW) engine in place of the original 550-shp (410-kW) PT6A-20.

Some four years after shutting the production line, Beech announced on 7 May 1979 that it would re-enter the feederliner market with an improved **C99 Commuter**, powered by the 715-shp (533-kW) PT6A-36. To speed the certification process, a B99 was bought back from Allegheny Commuter to serve as a prototype and was initially fitted with PT6A-34 engines. The first of the new-production aircraft took to the air on 20 June 1980, and heralded a minor revival of the type's fortunes, which also spurred the development of the larger Beech 1900 series.

Production of the C99 raised the total figure to 239, the final aircraft being manufactured in 1986. By this time, the 1900 was established as the company's main competitor in the commuter market, and many other manufacturers had produced highly popular designs (notably EMBRAER). A small number of Beech 99s remain in service on feeder work, and many regard the type as the true pioneer of the commuter market.

SPECIFICATION:
Beechcraft B99 Airliner
Powerplant: two 680-ehp (506-kW) Pratt & Whitney (Canada) PT6A-27 turboprops
Accommodation: two (flight deck), maximum of 15 passengers
Dimensions: span 45 ft 10½ in (14.00 m); height 14 ft 4¼ in (4.38 m); length 44 ft 6¾ in (13.58 m)
Weights: empty, equipped 5,872 lb (2663 kg); maximum take-off 10,900 lb (4944 kg)
Performance: maximum cruising speed at 12,000 ft (3650 m) 282 mph (454 km/h); service ceiling 26,313 ft (8020 m); maximum range, with reserves 838 miles (1348 km)

Beechcraft 400

The aircraft that is now a well-known product in the US business-jet market began life in Japan. Mitsubishi designed a small biz-jet in the mid-1970s with the aim of offering superb performance, low cabin noise and the roomiest cabin in its class. The aircraft had a standard biz-jet layout with T-tail, low-set wing, pod-mounted JT15D turbofans and a wrap-round windscreen. The resulting **MU-300 Diamond I** first flew in Japan on 29 August 1978, and was joined on flight test duties by the second on 13 December. Following completion of the trials, both aircraft were shipped to MAI, the US-based distributor for Mitsubishi aircraft, who reassembled the aircraft for FAA certification, beginning on 10 August 1979. After four aircraft had been delivered from Japan, they began to arrive as major sub-assemblies from the parent company, for final assembly by the US factory in Dallas.

FAA certification was received on 6 November 1981, and 65 Diamond Is were delivered before the **Diamond IA** was introduced in January 1984. This aircraft featured uprated engines, higher weight and better avionics, and a small number were added to the overall total. The **Diamond II** first flew in June 1984, a similar-looking aircraft but powered by JT15D-5s and with a revised interior.

In December 1985 Beech acquired the rights to the Diamond II, and MAI ceased to market the Diamond on March 1986. Renamed **Beechjet 400**, the design was assembled at Beech's Wichita factory from Mitsubishi-supplied kits. Two options for the

The Beechjet 400A has been the current production model since 1989, and the first deliveries were made in 1990. External changes are negligible.

Diamond II, namely tailcone baggage compartment and extended-range tank, were adopted as standard. The first Beech-assembled aircraft was rolled out on 19 May 1986. In 1989 all production moved to Beech, but the company continued to support earlier Diamond deliveries.

At the 1989 NBAA show, Beech announced an improved aircraft, known as the **Beechjet 400A**. While retaining the overall dimensions, the 400A introduced a larger cabin and a new-look 'glass' cockpit, with an electronic flight instrumentation system (EFIS), and an increase in certificated cruising altitude. The cabin usually accommodates eight, with fold-down tables between each pair of facing seats. This is the current version, of which 29 had been sold by mid-1994 to follow 64 Beechjet 400s. A massive order was received from the US Air Force for the **Beechjet 400T**, or **T-1A Jayhawk**, to fulfil a multi-engined trainer requirement. Up to 180 may be ordered, with 148 firm so far. Bringing the Beechjet's story full circle, three similar aircraft have been sold to the Japanese air force (as **T400s**) to serve as trainers also.

Beechjets are flying in Australia, Brazil, Canada, Czech Republic, France, Germany, India, Italy, Mexico, South Africa, UK, USA and Venezuela.

SPECIFICATION:
Beechcraft Beechjet 400A
Powerplant: two 2,900-lb (12.9-kN) Pratt & Whitney Canada JT15D-5 turbofans
Accommodation: two (flight deck), maximum of eight passengers
Dimensions: span 43 ft 6 in (13.25 m); height 13 ft 11 in (4.24 m); length 48 ft 5 in (14.75 m)
Weights: operating, empty 10,450 lb (4740 kg); maximum take-off 16,100 lb (7303 kg)
Performance: maximum level speed at 27,000 ft (8230 m) 539 mph (867 km/h); maximum operating altitude 45,000 ft (13715 m); maximum range, with reserves 2,187 miles (3521 km)

Beechcraft 1900

Design of the **Beechcraft 1900** commuter airliner was launched in 1979, with Beech beginning the fabrication of a trio of flying prototypes, a static test airframe and a pressure test specimen during the course of 1981. Assembly of the these prototypes was completed in 1982, and the formal roll-out of the initial example was followed by a successful maiden flight on 3 September 1982.

Testing of the newest Beechcraft was carried through swiftly and culminated in FAA certification being achieved during November 1983 (including certification for single-pilot operations), by which time work was well in hand on an initial batch of production machines. The first major version to appear was the **Beech 1900C**, which found favour with a number of commuter operators in the USA. Deliveries began in February 1984 and 255 were completed. Aircraft built with a 'wet wing', incorporating 563-Imp gal (2559-litre) fuel tanks, are designated **Model 1900C-1**s. Beech also marketed a similar version that was specifically aimed at the business community. Known initially as the **King Air Exec-Liner** (later as the **Model 1900C/-1 Exec-Liner**), the first example was handed over to the General Telephone Company of Illinois during the summer of 1985. Eleven are in use in the United States, Saudi Arabia and Zambia.

The original Beech 1900s has an altogether more streamlined shape, although, inside, passengers have to step over the main spar on the cabin floor.

The ungainly-looking Beech 1900D displays all the evidence of some severe aerodynamic revisions. Despite this, it performs and handles well.

Not content with limiting itself to the civilian market, Beech has also supplied a modest quantity of suitably adapted aircraft of this basic type to military customers. These include the Egyptian air force, Republic of China air force and the USAF Air National Guard, where its serves as the **C-12J** mission support aircraft.

Deliveries of the Model 1900C continued until 1991, when Beech switched its production resources to the improved **Model 1900D**. Based on the 1900C, the newest variant entered service with Mesa Airlines (a United Express carrier) of Farmington, New Mexico, during the course of 1991, and is proving just as popular with commercial and business operators as its predecessor did. By mid-1994, 92 of the $4.7-million type had been delivered. Among the obvious improvements introduced in the 1900D are its increased cabin height (with almost 30 per cent more interior volume), winglets, finlets and rear fuselage strakes, bigger windows and a larger passenger door. New Pratt & Whitney Canada PT6A-67D turboprops are installed as standard on the 1900D version, as is a four-screen, monochrome/colour, Collins EFIS cockpit. A **Model 1900D Exec-Liner** is also available, with three in use by mid-1994 and production (of all versions) continuing at four per month.

SPECIFICATION: Beechcraft 1900D
Powerplant: two 2,900-lb (12.9-kN) Pratt & Whitney Canada PT6A-67A turboprops
Accommodation: two (flight deck), maximum of 19 passengers
Dimensions: span, over winglets 57 ft 11⅞ in (17.67 m); height 14 ft 11⅜ in (4.57 m); length 57 ft 10 in (17.63 m)
Weights: operating, empty 10,550 lb (4785 kg); maximum take-off 16,950 lb (7688 kg)
Performance: maximum cruising speed at 25,000 ft (7620 m) 320 mph (515 km/h); service ceiling 33,000 ft (10058 m); maximum range, with 10 passengers and reserves 1,725 miles (2776 km)

Bell Model 212, 214 and 412

With the highly successful Model 205 Huey established as the world's leading assault helicopter, Bell teamed with Pratt & Whitney of Canada in the late 1960s to develop a version powered by the PT6T-3 Twin-Pac powerplant. This engine consisted of two turboshafts driving through a common gearbox and single drive shaft. The whole installation was flat-rated to 1,290 shp (962 kW) for take-off but, if one turbine failed, the other could give 1,025 shp (764 kW) through the common gearbox, more than sufficient for continued safe flight over a short period.

With this powerplant, the **Model 212** was developed for both civil and military markets. In the civil field, the type was of particular interest to gas/oilfield exploration work, where the twin-engined safety was vital. Able to carry 14 passengers, the 212 is also available in a float-equipped version, which is certified for single-pilot IFR operation. The uprated PT6T-3B was introduced in 1980, and in 1988 production was moved to Mirabel in Canada, from where it continues. The type is also built under licence in Italy as the **Agusta-Bell AB 212**.

Using the airframe of the 212, Bell developed the **Model 214**, which was powered by a single Avco Lycoming T5508D turboshaft flat-rated to 2,250 shp (1678 kW) for take-off. This engine made the 214 extremely powerful, and a natural for work where heavy loads needed to be carried. A dedicated civil model was the **214B BigLifter**, which could carry 8,000 lb (3629 kg) on an external cargo hook,

The Bell Model 214ST has obvious Huey parentage, but was a development of a model specifically designed for the Imperial Iranian army.

or specialised fire-fighting equipment. Internal accommodation remained at 14 passengers or a sizeable cargo load.

From the basic 214 was developed the **Model 214ST** 'Supertrans', with a revised and lengthened airframe able to carry 17 passengers. Twin-engined power was restored using 1,625-shp (1212-kW) General Electric CT7-2 turboshafts, driving through a common gearbox. Full IFR instrumentation was standard and, as with other models, weather radar was often fitted in a thimble radome on the nose. The 214ST could carry external loads, and could be fitted with emergency flotation gear.

Bell's current major civil helicopter type is the **Model 412**, which is very similar to the 212 except that it features a four-bladed rotor. A **412SP** version offered better performance and 55 per cent greater fuel capacity than the original design, but this has now been superseded by the **412HP**. The powerplant is the PT6T-3BE offering 1,800 shp (1342 kW) for take-off. Like its predecessors, it is a highly versatile helicopter that can be used for passenger air taxi work, supplying rigs, fire-fighting and cargo lifting.

For the first time on any production Bell helicopter, the Model 412 introduces a four-bladed main rotor. Italian 412s are built as the 'Gryphon'.

SPECIFICATION: Bell 412HP
Powerplant: two 1,800-shp (1342-kW) Pratt & Whitney Canada PT6T-3BE Turbo Twin-Pac turboshafts
Accommodation: single pilot, maximum of 14 passengers
Dimensions: main rotor diameter 46 ft (14.02 m); height, tail rotor turning 15 ft (4.57 m); length, rotors turning 56 ft 2 in (17.12 m)
Weights: empty, equipped 6,759 lb (3066 kg); maximum take-off 11,900 lb (5397 kg)
Performance: max cruising speed, at sea level 140 mph (226 km/h); hovering ceiling, in ground effect 10,200 ft (3110 m); maximum range, with no reserves 463 miles (745 km)

BAC/Aérospatiale Concorde

The world's only successful SST (SuperSonic Transport) began life as a French project in 1957. Sud-Aviation, Dassault and Nord-Aviation, in association with Air France, answered a French government-inspired SST requirement, and their first design was a 70-passenger, delta-winged, Mach 2.2 airliner based on the SE.210 and dubbed **Super Caravelle**. At the same time in the UK, a similar airline/industry programme was underway, headed by the British Aircraft Corporation and Hawker Siddeley. Their design, the **BAC 223**, was a four-engined, 100-seat aircraft, but by the early 1960s both groups were coming closer and closer together. So much so, in fact, that on 29 November 1962 a historic Anglo-French supersonic aircraft agreement was signed, which almost uniquely featured a 'no-break clause' that made the resultant design virtually immune to vacillation or cancellation.

This design emerged as the **Concorde**, with no little effort expended to finding a name acceptable to both nationalities. A needle-nosed and slender fuselage (with only an 8-ft 8-in/2.68-m cabin) sat above a graceful, ogival, delta wing, under which were slung four Rolls-Royce/SNECMA Olympus afterburning turbojets. The aircraft's most distinctive feature is its unique 'droop snoot' nose, which can be lowered by up to 12.5° to improve crew visibility

Air France operates six Concordes, chiefly on services to New York. Like British Airways aircraft, they are in 100-seat, four-abreast configuration.

Seven aircraft are currently active at BA's Heathrow home, operating scheduled services to New York, Washington and Barbados.

for take-off and landing. Pre-production aircraft differed slightly in detail, and all had shorter fuselages.

Concorde was assembled both at Filton and Toulouse, and the premier French **Concorde101** was rolled out on 11 December 1967, flying on 2 March 1969. It was followed by the first British **Concorde 102** on 9 April. Air France had signed for five aircraft in May 1963, and subsequently 18 airlines made commitments for 80 aircraft. Firm orders came from British Airways and Air France for five (later seven) and four (later six), respectively, but all other interest lapsed. On 21 January 1976 both airlines placed the type into transatlantic service.

When British Airways was privatised in 1984, the UK government 'sold' its Concordes (entirely funded by the taxpayer) to the airline, with an eighth 'spares ship', for a mere £9.3 million. Air France now operates six aircraft, using a seventh for spares. Structural problems surfaced in the early 1990s when British Airways' aircraft suffered rudder failures, but the importance of Concorde to the airline saw a major investigation undertaken to iron out any more serious complications. 1994 sees the 25th anniversary of the first flight, and since that time the fleets of Air France and British Airways have clocked up some 175,000 flying hours, of which 120,000 have been at supersonic speeds.

SPECIFICATION:
BAC (BAe)/Aérospatiale Concorde
Powerplant: four 38,050-lb (169.3-kN) Rolls-Royce/SNECMA Olympus 593 Mk 610 turbojets
Accommodation: three (flight deck), maximum of 144 passengers (standard 100)
Dimensions: span 83 ft 10 in (25.56 m); height 37 ft 5 in (11.40 m); length 203 ft 9 in (62.10 m)
Weights: operating, empty 173,500 lb (78700 kg); maximum take-off 408,000 lb (185065 kg)
Performance: maximum cruising speed, at 51,000 ft (15635 m) Mach 2.04 (1,345 mph; 2179 km/h); service ceiling 60,000 ft (18290 m); max range, with reserves 4,090 miles (6580 km)

BAC/ROMBAC One-Eleven Twin-engined short- to medium-range airliner

The **BAC One-Eleven** was a successful design that achieved considerable initial sales only to be left behind by developments of rival aircraft which the One-Eleven had beaten into service. When BAC was formed in 1960 by the conglomeration of Hunting, Vickers and others, it inherited the **Hunting 107** design that later formed the basis of the One-Eleven. British United Airways launched the project, ordering 10 80-seat aircraft in May 1961, and Aer Lingus was the first non-UK operator. While the first One-Eleven made its maiden flight on 20 August 1963, the flight test programme was hit when this aircraft was lost just two months later. It entered an unrecoverable 'deep stall', a phenomenon unique to T-tailed designs and previously unknown.

The first production version, the 93-ft 6-in (28.4-m) **One-Eleven 200**, was finally certified in April 1965 and won substantial orders in the US and Europe. A total of 58 was built. Next came the heavier, Spey Mk 511-engined **One-Eleven 300** that could accommodate 89 seats over a reduced operating range. Nine were built before this version was superseded by the **One-Eleven 400**. FAA regulations limiting American Airlines' two-crew operations to aircraft below 80,000 lb (36288 kg) led to the short-range Series 400, which was a Series 300 development with a restricted MTOW. After a first flight on 13 July 1965, 70 were built.

Inspired by a BEA requirement, the next variant was the stretched (by 13 ft 6 in/12.3 m) **One-Eleven**

The One-Eleven has proved to be a popular 'biz-jet', with 38 currently in use around the world. This One-Eleven/414EG is operated by a US resort hotel.

500, which first flew on 30 June 1967. The delay in building this version meant that the DC-9-30 was already firmly established, and no Series 500s were sold in the US. Some aircraft, with the suffix 'DW' (Developed Wet), can use water boosting for extra power on take-off. Eighty-six were completed before this version, and the entire One-Eleven line, was transferred to Romania in the early 1980s. The last UK-built version, the **One-Eleven 475**, combined the more powerful engines of the Series 500 with the short fuselage of the Series 200. Twelve were built, including two side-loading freighters.

Romaero SA, based at Bucharest-Baneasa airport, obtained all BAe's (formerly BAC) One-Eleven tooling with the intention of building a further 22 **ROMBAC One-Eleven 500**s. Production proceeded slowly, with only nine completed (ending in 1988), albeit to a very high standard.

Dee Howard attempted to offer a Rolls-Royce Tay 650 re-engining programme for the One-Eleven, flying a prototype in 1990. This Stage 3/Chapter 3- compliant version was bogged down in legal wrangles that were finally settled in January 1994.

Ireland's Ryanair was one of the 'foreign' operators of the ROMBAC One-Eleven, flying a sizeable number of British- and Romanian-built aircraft.

SPECIFICATION:
BAC (BAe) One-Eleven Series 500
Powerplant: two 12,500-lb (55.6-kN) Rolls-Royce Spey Mk 512DW turbofans
Accommodation: two (flight deck), maximum of 119 passengers (standard 99)
Dimensions: span 93 ft 6 in (28.50 m); height 24 ft 6 in (7.47 m); length 97 ft 4 in (29.67 m)
Weights: operating, empty 54,582 lb (24,758 kg); maximum take-off 104,500 lb (47400 kg)
Performance: maximum cruising speed, at 21,000 ft (6400 m) 541 mph (871 km/h); maximum cruising altitude 35,000 ft (10670 m); maximum range, with reserves 2,165 miles (3484 km)

Boeing 707 and 720

Four-engined short-/medium- and long-range airliners

The design that established Boeing as 'plane maker to the world' is the **Model 707**. The first US jet transport to enter service, the 707 had its roots in the **Model 387-80** (or simply the **Dash 80**), which first flew on 15 July 1954. This one-off company funded demonstrator also gave rise to the military **Model 717** (**C-135**) family.

Work began on a the civil aircraft, and in October 1955 Pan American Airways announced an order for 15. The first 707 proper flew on 20 December 1957. Initial production model was the marginally-transatlantic **707-100**, chiefly serving the US domestic market. Powered by four Pratt & Whitney JT3C turbojets, it could carry an absolute maximum of 189 passengers, with a more normal load of 137. This version lead to the **707-100B** with more efficient JT-3D turbofans. A long-range, short-fuselage development, the **707-138B**, was produced solely for QANTAS. Only five **707-200**s were built for Braniff, with hot-and-high JT4A turbojets. The final production version was the truely intercontinental stretched **707-300**. Powered by JT4As, this version first flew in January 1959, but soon became the **707-300B** with the substitution of JT3D turbofans. The **707-400** was a 707-300 with its JT4As replaced by Rolls-Royce Conway 508s, for service with BOAC, Air India, El Al, VARIG and Lufthansa.

Several 707s serve as extremely plush 'biz-jets' and even a pair of Saudi-registered Boeing 720-047Bs (below) continue to fly in this role.

The number of passenger-configured Boeing 707s is now very small but, until hit by a UN air transport embargo, Iraqi Airways had three in regular use.

The final and most popular 707 version was the cargo/passenger (Combi) **707-300C**, featuring a large cargo door in the forward fuselage. Certified in 1963, 337 were built until 1979, when the last civil 707 (No. 938) was delivered to TAROM. Including military variants of the design, such as the **E-3 Sentry**, 1,012 (916 civil) Model 707s were built, before the line finally closed in 1992. The ultimate 'civilian' airframe was the unique **707-700**, a CFM56-powered prototype that was refitted with JT3Ds and delivered to the Moroccan air force in 1982.

The **Model 720** was a short- to medium-range version intended for the US market, and first flew on 23 November 1959. Similar to the 707-100, it had a fuselage of only 136 ft 2 in (41.5 m) – 8 ft 2 in (2.5 m) shorter – and seated 130 passengers. Sixty-five were completed, followed by 89 JT3D-powered **Model 720B**s. Eleven 720s were converted also to 720B standard. The last airline operator is MEA, a handful of 720s survive as VIP transports and Pratt & Whitney Canada flies one as an engine testbed. About 200 707s are still in service, chiefly as freighters. Several have been hush-kitted by Comtran (**Q707**) to avoid Stage 2/Chapter 2 noise regulations, although no hush-kit currently meets the impending Stage 3/Chapter 3 requirements.

SPECIFICATION: Boeing 707-320C
Powerplant: four 18,000-lb (80-kN) Pratt & Whitney JT3D-3B turbofans
Accommodation: three (flight deck), maximum of 219 passengers (standard 150)
Dimensions: span 145 ft 9 in (44.42 m); height 42 ft 5 in (12.93 m); length 152 ft 11 in (46.61 m)
Weights: (freighter) operating, empty 141,100 lb (64000 kg); maximum payload 88,900 lb (40324 kg); maximum take-off 333,600 lb (151315 kg)
Performance: maximum level speed 627 mph (1010 km/h); service ceiling 36,000 ft (10972 m); maximum range, with maximum payload and reserves 3625 miles (5835 km)

Boeing 727

For many years, until finally overtaken by the 737, the **Boeing 727** was the world's 'favourite airliner', selling a total of 1,831 until production ended in 1984. Boeing's second jetliner was originally planned with three Allison-built Rolls-Royce Spey engines. When the launch order was received from Eastern Airlines for 40 727s, however, this had changed to a trio of Pratt & Whitney JT8Ds. The 727 was structurally very similar to the 707, but featured a more dramatically swept wing with many high-lift devices and a T-tail, in the style of the rival Hawker Siddeley Trident. The first 727 (which, with the advent of subsequent versions, became the **727-100**) flew from Renton on 9 February 1963, with 131 orders including 12 from Lufthansa, the first overseas customer. Boeing next stretched the design by 20 ft (6.09 m) to produce the **727-200**. Engine power was later increased by the addition of JT8D-11 and -17 turbofans, enabling the 727 to operate at progressively higher gross weights. The final major version was the **727-200 Advanced** of 1970, which featured JT8D-15, then JT8D-17 and -17R engines. The JT8D-17R could provide 16,400 lb (73 kN) of thrust when using automatic power reserve in the event of engine failure.

During the 1970s, Boeing proposed a further 18 ft 4 in (5.6 m) fuselage stretch to produce the **727-300**, but instead opted for a new design, the 757. Before production finally closed, Boeing developed a 727 freighter, the **727-200F**, 15 of which were built for Federal Express. Powered by JT8D-17A

While older models are fast disappearing, the Boeing 727-200 is still in widespread service with the major US carriers, such as Northwest Airlines.

engines, this version has a strengthened cabin floor, a large freight door and, of course, no windows. The last of 1,260 727-200s was delivered to Allegheny Airlines on 30 November 1982.

Since then several companies have improved on Boeing's work. Valsan, in association with Pratt & Whitney and Rohr, has refitted aircraft with JT8D-217C or -219 engines, acoustically treating the centre nacelle (while removing the thrust reverser) to quieten the aircraft. This improves take-off performance, while complying with Stage 3/Chapter 3 noise restrictions that come into force in 1999. A two-man cockpit can be added. Valsan also developed a 727 winglet refit, which first appeared on two Delta aircraft in late 1993, to further improve performance. In a somewhat ironic move, Rolls-Royce, in association with Dee Howard, is now bidding to replace the engines of 150 Delta 727s and 737s with 16,500-lb (70-kN) Tay 655 turbofans. Dee Howard is already fitting Tay 651s and Collins EFIS cockpits to 44 UPS 727-100s (**727QF** – Quiet Freighter). Federal Express Aviation Services has developed its own 727 hush-kit, for use on its own and other customer's aircraft.

Libyan Arab Airlines has nine 727s, chiefly Advanced 727-2L5s delivered in the mid-1970s. In mid-1994, the country was still subject to a UN air embargo.

SPECIFICATION:
Boeing 727-200
Powerplant: three 15,500-lb (68.9-kN) Pratt & Whitney JT8D-15 turbofans
Accommodation: three (flight deck), maximum of 189 passengers (standard 145)
Dimensions: span 108 ft (32.92 m); height 34 ft (10.36 m); length 153 ft 2 in (46.69 m)
Weights: operating, empty 99,600 lb (45178 kg); maximum take-off 190,500 lb (86405 kg)
Performance: maximum operating speed Mach 0.90; service ceiling 42,000 ft (9144 m); maximum range, with reserves 2510 miles (4040 km)

Boeing 737-100 and -200 Twin-engined short- to medium-range airliners

When Boeing launched its 'baby', the **Model 737**, it seemed like the company was again playing 'catch-up', as the BAC One-Eleven and DC-9 were already on offer. Again using the nose and fuselage cross-section of the 707/727, Boeing launched the design in November 1964 and worked hard to gain its first order, which came from Lufthansa. This was the first time Boeing had launched a design with no US orders and, initially, Lufthansa wanted only 10 aircraft. This first version became known as the **737-100** and made its maiden flight on 9 April 1967. Entering service in Germany in February 1968, only 30 were built (by 1969) before Boeing switched to the longer and heavier **737-200**, as required by United Airlines, which had ordered 40 and taken 30 options. The 737-200 first flew on 8 August 1967, entering service in April 1968 with United.

Boeing continued to aerodynamically refine the basic aircraft while adding thrust reversers and revising the flap design. Continued improvements to the wing leading edge, engine mounts, Krueger flaps, braking system and undercarriage led to the the **737-200 Advanced**, introduced from the 280th production example. A range of engine options became available over the 737's life, from the JT8D-9 to the -17, and the operating weight of the 737

Lufthansa and Air New Zealand are two airlines already operating 737-200s fitted with the new Nordam-developed hush-kit and thrust reverser.

TACA International (Transportes Aéreos Centro Americanos) of El Salvador currently operates seven US-registered 737-200s of differing versions.

increased accordingly. The 737-200 Advanced could also accommodate additional fuel tanks in the belly hold. Some aircraft were delivered with add-on rough-field landing gear for gravel strip operations, and 104 freighter versions, the **737-200C** and **QC** (Quick Change), were built between 1965 and 1985. Towards the end of its life, increased use of composites was made in the 'first-generation' 737. The last of 865 -200 Advanced aircraft was delivered to CAAC on 18 December 1987, bringing to a close the production run of 1,144 aircraft.

While Boeing's attention moved to subsequent CFM56-engined versions, other companies began to upgrade the older 737s, over 500 of which are still in use. Nordam, of Tulsa, Oklahoma, has developed an FAA-approved Stage 3/Chapter 3-compliant hush-kit for the 737-200, and now has 160 outstanding orders from operators such as Air New Zealand, Lufthansa and USAir. California-based Avro is developing a rival 737 kit.

Hush-kitting is an attractive option for many airlines, as it enables them to carry on operating aircraft that are 'bought and paid for' at a fraction of the cost of their replacements (the Nordam kit costs $3 million; a new 737-500 costs $26 million). Such figures could even see the return to service of 737s that are currently in storage around the world.

SPECIFICATION:
Boeing 737-200 Advanced
Powerplant: two 15,500-lb (68.9-kN) Pratt & Whitney JT8D-15 turbofans
Accommodation: two (flight deck), maximum of 130 passengers (standard 120)
Dimensions: span 93 ft (28.35 m); height 37 ft (11.28 m); length 96 ft 11 in (29.54 m)
Weights: operating, empty 60,507 lb (27445 kg); maximum take-off 115,500 lb (52390 kg)
Performance: maximum cruising speed 532 mph (856 km/h); service ceiling 33,000 ft (10060 m); maximum range, with reserves 2913 miles (4688 km)

Boeing 737-300 to -700
USA
Twin-engined short- to medium-range airliners

After 17 years of building 737s, Boeing took the family into a new era with the introduction of the stretched, re-engined 128-seat **737-300**. Revealed at the Farnborough show of 1980, Boeing was already working on the 757 and 767, and a 'new-generation' short-haul airliner was an obvious next step. Launch customers were Southwest and USAir. The 737-300 is 109 ft 7 in (33.4 m) long, some 8 ft 8 in (2.68 m) longer than the 737-200. There is still 70 per cent airframe commonality between the two, but the -300 boasts colour weather radar, a digital flight management system and auto-throttle, all in a 'glass' EFIS cockpit. The most obvious difference is the CFM56-3B (or -3C) engines, with their distinctive flat-bottomed nacelles. The first 737-300 was rolled out on 17 January 1984 and made its maiden flight on 24 February. The type received FAA certification on 14 November after 1,300 flight-test hours.

Boeing next examined the market for a 150-seat design, potentially an all-new design, the **7-7**. In 1983 this became the **737-400**, but Boeing stated that it did not expect to build such an aircraft for several years. Finally, after much indecision, the 737-400 was launched, in 1986, with an order for 25 from Piedmont Airlines. The new aircraft is stretched by 10 ft (3.04 m) and has a tailskid to protect the longer fuselage from over-rotation on take-off. The 737-400 also has two overwing exits in place of the 737-300's one. First flight occurred on 19 February 1988, with service entry in October that year.

Southwest Airlines has introduced several startling colour schemes, such as its trio of 'Shamu' killer whale 737s, painted for Sea World.

Boeing still planned a new short-fuselage 737 (the **737 Lite**), which in the face of rising competition from other smaller jets was launched as the **737-500** 1987, making its maiden flight on 30 June 1989. Braathens SAFE, of Norway, was the launch customer. The 737-500 measures 101 ft 9 in (31 m), almost exactly the same size as the 737-200. By mid-1994, deliveries for the 737-300/400 ($27-31 million) stood at 1,227, and at 277 for the 737-500 ($26 million).

In November 1993, Southwest Airlines launched the next chapter in the 737 story with an order for 63 Boeing **737-X**s, with another 63 on option. The 737-X will be offered in three sizes, seating between 108 to 157, and all powered by an uprated CFM56-3X engine. Southwest has ordered the 110-ft 2-in (33.6-m) **737-700** (formerly **737-300X**), but on either side of this model (in terms of size) will be a **737-500X** (now **737-600**) and **737-400X** (now **737-800**). Each aircraft will have a much improved aerodynamic configuration and significantly improved performance. Roll-out for the first 737-X is planned for December 1996.

Boeing's 737 is the world's most common airliner. Strong sales seem set to continue, with the next-generation '737-X' family now firmly underway.

SPECIFICATION:
Boeing 737-400
Powerplant: two 22,000-lb (97.86-kN) CFM International CFM56-3C-1 turbofans
Accommodation: two (flight deck), maximum of 171 passengers (standard 146)
Dimensions: span 94 ft 4 in (28.88 m); height 36 ft 6 in (11.13 m); length 119 ft 7 in (36.45 m)
Weights: operating, empty 73,710 lb (33434 kg); maximum take-off 138,500 lb (62822 kg)
Performance: maximum cruising speed 564 mph (908 km/h); cruising altitude 35,000 ft (10668 m); maximum range, with reserves 3,105 miles (5000 km)

Boeing 747-100, -200 and -300
Four-engined long-range airliner

Combining work done on the USAF's CX-HLS competition of 1962 (eventually won by Lockheed C-5) with preliminary designs for a new high-capacity airliner Boeing, began planning a 'double-bubble'-fuselage aircraft with 10-abreast seating and a gross weight of approximately 530,000 lb (240400 kg). Pan American again set its seal on a piece of aviation history when it signed a letter of intent for 25 in December 1965. The **Model 747-100** was formally launched in 1966, followed by the heavier **747-100B**, an all-cargo **747-100F** and the combi **747-100C**. Pratt & Whitney JT9D turbofans were chosen to power the type. With an upsurge of orders, Boeing built a new 43-acre (17.4-ha) facility at Paine Field, Seattle, where the first aircraft was rolled out on 30 September 1968, making its first flight on 9 February 1969 (three months behind schedule). Pan Am operated the first revenue service between London and New York on 22 January 1970. Two hundred and five 747-100s of all versions were completed, but before production had finished Boeing introduced a heavier (by some 10 per cent) development, the **747B**, or **747-200** with much improved payload/range capability owing to its increased fuel load. Certified in December 1970, the first of these entered service with KLM Royal Dutch Airlines, in February 1971.

Air India is a 747 operator that counts the 747-200 (pictured), 747-300 and 747-400 in its current fleet. All carry this distinctive 'window frame'.

Tower Air is a New York-based airline with an expanding fleet of 16 480-seat 747-100s and -200s, operated largely on charter work.

The next version was the nose-loading **747-200F** freighter, which entered service with Lufthansa in April 1972. The **747-200(SCD)** is a freighter with a side cargo door. Also in 1972, Japan Airlines introduced the **747SR**s (Short Range), identical to the 747-100 but restressed to carry 523 passengers over an increased number of flying cycles. In total, 384 747-200s of all versions were delivered.

Boeing continued to look at ways of increasing the 747's passenger load, and in June 1980 revealed the **747SUD** (Stretched Upper Deck). Essentially a Series 200 with the upper deck extended by 23 ft (7 m), it was renamed the **747-300** by the time of its maiden flight on 5 October 1982. Swissair was the launch customer, and the SUD modification could be and was applied retrospectively. Eighty-one such aircraft were completed.

As the older 747s have begun to approach their design life of 20,000 flights or 60,000 hours, they have undergone the 'Section 41' modification that inspects and repairs potential cracks in the nose-frames around section 41. Former passenger 747s are undergoing freighter conversions with Bedek, in Israel, through the addition of a side cargo door, handling system and total refurbishment. The first deliveries were made to Electra Aviation, in 1992, and later to Lufthansa .

SPECIFICATION: Boeing 747-200B
Powerplant: four 52,500-lb (233.5-kN) General Electric CF6-50E2, or 53,110-lb (236.25-kN) Rolls-Royce RB211-524D4-B, or 54,750-lb (243.5-kN) Pratt & Whitney JT9D-7R4G2 turbofans
Accommodation: three (flight deck), maximum of 480 passengers (standard 365)
Dimensions: span 195 ft 8 in (59.64 m); height 63 ft 5 in (19.33 m); length 231 ft 10 in (70.66 m)
Weights: operating, empty 383,600 lb (173998 kg); maximum take-off 775,000 lb (351534 kg)
Performance: maximum level speed 610 mph (981 km/h); cruising altitude 45,000 ft (13715 m); maximum range, with 366 passengers 7,940 miles (12778 km)

Boeing 747SP

Soon after the launch of the 747 it became clear that many customers needed a similar aircraft capable of covering great distances, without the penalties of the 747's 'excessive' passenger capacity. As a result, in August 1973 Boeing announced that an extended-range, short-bodied development of the 747-100, the **747SP** (Special Performance), was underway. This new version indeed boasted improved performance with rate of climb, cruising altitude and cruising speed all increased in comparison with the 747-100, and a range in excess of 6,904 miles (11112 km). The distinctive 747SP is 47 ft 1 in (14.35 m) shorter than the standard 747-100/-200, and has a fin extended by 5 ft (1.52 m) fitted with a double-hinged rudder. The centre-section was redesigned to retain the aircraft's trademark upper deck, along with the rear fuselage that is radically 'pinched in' to reduce its width. This reduction in length necessitated an an extension of the tailfin by 5 ft (1.5 m)and the tailplanes have been changed and lengthened by 10 ft (3 m). The 747SP can be powered by a range of engines, which originally included the General Electric CF6-45A2, but no GE-powered 747SPs were ever delivered.

The launch order came from Pan American, which ordered 10 in September 1973. The first SP, the 265th production 747, was rolled out on 19 May 1975 and first flew on 4 July. Pan Am accepted its premier aircraft on 5 March 1975 and the type entered service on the Los Angeles-Tokyo route on 25 April of that year. A total of 45 747SPs (39 with

Until the advent of its new Airbus A340s, the Boeing 747SP was the only aircraft that could undertake Air Mauritius' long-range 'thin' routes.

Pratt & Whitney engines and six with Rolls-Royce) were built for customers such as Braniff, CAAC, China Airlines, Iran Air, Korean Air Lines, Pan Am, QANTAS, South African Airways, Syrian Arab Airlines and TWA, with the last delivery coming in 1989. This was, in fact, a specially ordered VIP aircraft, and the last true airline delivery occurred in 1982. Subsequently, 747SPs have appeared in the colours of American Airlines, Australia Asia, Air Mauritius, Luxair and Namib Air. The largest operator today is United Airlines, which obtained Pan Am's 10 aircraft when it took over the latter's Pacific routes during the late 1980s.

The 747SP has also proved to be an unusual yet somewhat popular 'biz jet'. Six are currently flown by government/Royal owners, two each in Oman, the United Arab Emirates (Dubai) and Saudi Arabia, the latter also boasting a private 747-300. At least one each of the Omani and UAE examples have been heavily modified and fitted with a satellite communications dome behind the main 'hump'. More recently, the Kazakhstan government placed a former American Airlines example into service.

United Airlines inherited Pan American's fleet of 747SP-21s and is currently the last United States airline to operate the type, with 10 on charge.

SPECIFICATION: Boeing 747SP

Powerplant: four Pratt & Whitney JT9D-7A, or Rolls-Royce RB211-52B2/-524C2/-524D4 turbofans, rated between 46,250 lb (205.7 kN) and 53,110 lb (236.325 kN)
Accommodation: three (flight deck), maximum of 440 passengers (standard 276)
Dimensions: span 195 ft 8 in (59.64 m); height 65 ft 5 in (19.94 m); length 184 ft 9 in (56.31 m)
Weights: operating, empty 333,900 lb (151454 kg); maximum take-off 700,000 lb (317515 kg)
Performance: max speed 619 mph (996 km/h); service ceiling 45,100 ft (13745 m); max range, with 276 passengers 7,658 miles (12324 km)

Boeing 747-400

At the 1984 Farnborough air show, Boeing announced an **'Advanced 747-300'**, so great was the interest in its stretched upper deck design. With a further increased wingspan and higher operating weight, the new 747 would be lighter than previous models, with much use of composite materials in its construction. Four General Electric, Pratt & Whitney or Rolls-Royce turbofans would increase its range to over 8,400 miles (13520 km), while its EFIS cockpit could be managed by just two crew. The cockpit design is a major advance over previous 747s with two colour multi-function displays available to each pilot for their Honeywell/Sperry FMS (Flight Management System). The Collins autopilot is certified to autoland in Category 3B conditions (visibility of 310 ft/5 m). To increase range, 6-ft (1.8-m) winglets and an additional tailfin fuel tank were added. Northwest Airlines became the launch customer with an order for 10 on 22 October 1985.

The first 747-400 was rolled out on 26 January 1988, and took to the air on 29 April. Certification with PW4056 engines came on 10 January 1989, followed by CF6-80C2Bs on 8 May and RB211-524Gs on 8 June 1989. Finally, the RB211-524H was added on 11 May 1990. That same month the 747-400 became the only 747 on offer to customers, but Boeing was not long in adding to its new family.

Thai Airways International is one of a large number of important Asian and Pacific Rim airlines to have added 747-400s to its existing 747 fleet.

Founded in 1988, Korea's Asiana Airlines flies an all-Boeing fleet of 26 737-400 and -500s, 15 767-300s and 11 747-400s, either in service or on order.

In February 1990 a freighter version, the **747-400F**, was formally launched. While this has all the improvements (including the winglets) of the -400, it possesses the short upper deck of the 747-200. The 747-400F can carry 244,000 lb (110676 kg) of cargo 4,950 miles (7970 km). Air France became the launch customer in September 1989. The first example flew on 7 May 1993 and, by mid-1994, 16 had been ordered by six customers.

In October 1990 Boeing began development of the **747-400D** (Domestic) in association with Japan Air Lines and All Nippon Airways. In a similar fashion to the 747-200SR, the 747-400D is a high-capacity transport intended for the Japanese domestic market. It has no winglets, five additional windows in the upper deck and a total of 566 seats, with underfloor cargo. Certified in October 1991, 19 had been delivered by mid-1994.

A **747-400 PIP** (Performance Improvement Package) was announced in April 1993, which makes aerodynamic and structural changes to increase range to 8,000 nm (14816 km; 9,206 miles). Beyond future 747-400 PIPs, Boeing is working on the stretched, rewinged **747-X**, powered by a new generation of 75,000-lb (333-kN) turbofan engines as a short-term answer to airline needs for even larger commercial transports.

SPECIFICATION: Boeing 747-400

Powerplant: four General Electric CF6-80C2B1F/C2B1F1/C2B7F, or Pratt & Whitney PW4056/60/62, or Rolls-Royce RB211-524G/H turbofans, rated between 56,750 lb (252.4 kN) and 62,000 lb (275.8 kN)

Accommodation: two (flight deck), maximum of 568 passengers (standard 390)

Dimensions: span 211 ft 5 in (64.44 m); height 63 ft 8 in (19.41 m); length 231 ft 10 in (70.66 m)

Weights: operating, empty 402,900 lb (182754 kg); maximum take-off 870,000 lb (394625 kg)

Performance: max level speed 612 mph (984 km/h); service ceiling 45,000 ft (13716 m); max range, with 420 passengers 8,314 miles (13398 km)

Boeing 757

By the mid-1970s the end of sales of the Model 727, Boeing's best seller, was in sight. Certainly the company's designers were working on several 'new-generation' airliners and a 727 replacement was a priority. A stretched, rewinged and re-engined 727 was considered before Boeing, after much dialogue with a variety of airlines, settled on the 190/200-seat **7N7** ('N' for narrow). Bearing a marked resemblance to the 727, this aircraft received the go-ahead, after firm orders for 40 from British Airways and Eastern Airlines, in 1979.

Later that year, however, the appearance of the new type, now named the **Model 757**, was completely revised, emerging far more similar to the 767 that was in parallel development. Finding themselves with two new airliners at once, Boeing set out to make the two designs as compatible to design, manufacture and operate as possible, transforming the 757 into its current shape. A prototype was rolled out on 13 January 1982 and made its maiden flight on 19 February. For the first time, Rolls-Royce engines had been chosen as the launch powerplant, and the airframe and RB211 engine combination was certified in the US and UK by January 1983. Eastern placed their aircraft into service first, on 1 January 1983, followed by British Airways on 9 February.

In 1984 PW2037 engines were flown on the 757, as Delta Airlines had specified the more efficient engines for its aircraft. Rolls-Royce developed correspondingly improved versions of the RB211.

Since 1992, Chile's LADECO Airlines has flown a pair of 159-seat 757s from its Santiago home, alongside BAC One-Elevens, 737-200s, 727-200s and a single 707.

In 1985 the **757-200(ER)** (Extended Range) was certified for EROPS with Rolls-Royce engines, followed by Pratt & Whitney-powered 757s in 1990.

In 1985 an order from UPS for 20 aircraft launched the **757-200PF** (Package Freighter). This version has no windows or passenger doors, a new crew entry door, a large cargo door in the port forward fuselage and a 9g cargo restraint system. The 757-200PF first flew on 11 August 1987, and the first delivery took place on 16 September. A second cargo version, the combi **757-200C**, was launched with an order from Royal Nepal Airways in 1986. Featuring the same cargo door as the Package Freighter, the 757-200C retains standard seats and cabin fittings and can carry 164 passengers plus freight pallets in the forward fuselage. To date only one 757-200C has been delivered, to Nepal on 15 September 1988.

The 757 got off to a slow start, receiving only 273 orders between 1979 and 1987. This situation has improved considerably, and by mid-1994 nearly 640 aircraft of all versions (beginning at $42 million each) had been delivered, with 268 still on order.

Four 757s serve currently as executive transports. Two are in military hands, while the civil examples fly from the USA and Switzerland, as seen here.

SPECIFICATION: Boeing 757-200
Powerplant: two 37,400-lb (166.4-kN) Rolls-Royce 535C, or 38,200-lb (170-kN) Pratt & Whitney PW2037, or 40,100-lb (178.4-kN) Rolls-Royce 535E4, or 41,700-lb (185.5-kN) Pratt & Whitney PW2040 turbofans
Accommodation: two (flight deck), maximum of 239 passengers (standard 178)
Dimensions: span 124 ft 10 in (38.05 m); height 44 ft 6 in (13.56 m); length 155 ft 3 in (47.32 m)
Weights: operating, empty 126,060 lb (57180 kg); maximum take-off 250,000 lb (113395 kg)
Performance: max operating speed Mach 0.80; service ceiling 40,000 ft (12192 m); max range, with 186 passengers 4,603 miles (7408 km)

Boeing 767

Both the 757 and the **Model 767** can trace their roots back to Boeing's 7X7 designs of the mid-1970s. At one stage, Boeing considered a tri-jet long-range **7X7LR**, which it planned to develop with Italian and Japanese partners. The design matured until finally allocated its 767 title in early 1978. Three versions were planned, the first and smallest as a direct competitor to the Airbus A310. This initial 180/190-seat **767-100** was never actually built. Instead, the mid-range, 200/210-seat, 159-ft 2-in (48.51-m) **767-200** was launched in 1978, with orders for 30 from United Airlines.

The first 767 was rolled out on 4 August 1981 and flew on 26 September; the type was certified in July 1982, with PW JT9Ds. United put its 767-200s into service on the Denver-Chicago route on 19 August 1982. The first development was the higher MTOW **767-200ER** (Extended Range). Only Air Canada and El Al acquired this early version, which offered little improvement over the basic 767-200. A new series 767-200ER, this time with increased fuel capacity, flew on 30 May 1984, with initial deliveries being made to Ethiopian Airlines. The 767-200ER later gained higher-rated CF6-80C2 and PW4052 engines.

Orders from Japan Air Lines launched the stretched 269-seat **767-300**, which first flew on 30

Taiwan's EVA Air (founded in 1989) took delivery of five 767-300ERs between 1991 and 1992, and four 767-200s in 1994.

Britannia Airways is the UK's oldest charter airline and the first English carrier to acquire the 767, in 1984. It now operates 10 767-200s and -300s.

January 1986. The 767-300 is structurally similar to the 767-200, but lengthened by 21 ft 1 in (6.43 m). Boeing again offered a **767-300ER**, from 1987 onwards, with a higher MTOW and extra fuel. American Airlines was the first to order this version, with an initial purchase of 15. Several variations of this long-range model followed, almost customer-by-customer, as different engines and increased gross weights became available. Several 767/engine combinations have been qualified for EROPS (twin-engined operations over transoceanic distances), although these aircraft are not necessarily all 767-200ER/-300ERs.

UPS launched the **767-300F**, a freighter version similar in configuration to the company's 757-200PF, with an order for 30 (with 30 options) in January 1993. First flight for this version, with a projected payload/range of 112,000 lb (50802 kg) over 3,000 nm (5550 km; 3,450 miles), is planned for 1995. Boeing is also considering potential developments of the type, designated **767ERX** (with additional fin tank fuel) and **767ERY** (with a larger 'wingletted' wing and additional fuel). By mid-1994, deliveries of current models of 767 stood at 219 767-200s (priced from $62 million) and 331 767-300s (priced from $66 to $80 million for the 767-300F), with 157 of all versions still on order.

SPECIFICATION:
Boeing 767-300ER
Powerplant: two 56,750-lb (252.4-kN) Pratt & Whitney PW4056, or 60,000-lb (266.9-kN) General Electric CF6-80C2B4, or Pratt & Whitney PW4060 turbofans
Accommodation: two (flight deck), maximum of 290 passengers (standard 250)
Dimensions: span 156 ft 1 in (47.57 m); height 52 ft (15.85 m); length 180 ft 3 in (54.94 m)
Weights: operating, empty 179,400 lb (81374 kg); maximum take-off 400,000 lb (181437 kg)
Performance: cruising speed Mach 0.80; service ceiling 40,000 ft (12192 m); maximum range with reserves 6,978 miles (11230 km)

Boeing 777

At various stages throughout its history, Boeing has been faced with make-or-break decisions to develop a new type that will dictate the future of the company. The Model 707 and 747 are two such examples, and it is fair to say that they have now been joined by the **Model 777** as a milestone in the Boeing story.

Boeing's first fully fly-by-wire airliner began life as the **7J7** in the early 1980s. It later became the **767-X** as airlines asked the manufacturer to come up with a design that fitted in between the 767-300 and 747-400. The 777's final configuration was revealed in 1989 and formally launched, as the **777-200**, in October 1990 with an order for 34 (and 34 options), from United Airlines. While the 777 retains the outward appearance of an enlarged 767, it is a fundamentally new aircraft with many unique design features, materials and manufacturing techniques involved. Fuselage width is second in the world only to the 747-400, and up to 440 passengers can be accommodated, with standard three-class seating set at around 320.

Two versions are currently available, the so-called **'A-Market'** and **'B-Market'** models. The first of these is a (US) domestic transport with a range of 3,450-5,750 miles (5556-9260 km), while the latter will be capable of reaching destinations over 8,490 miles (13670 km) away. While both 777s will be the same size, the **777-200B** will have an increased MTOW with extra fuel and more powerful engines. The 'B-Market' 777 was launched with an order

On its maiden flight, the 777 was piloted by Captain John Cashman, the project chief pilot. The flight lasted 3 hours and 48 minutes.

from Euralair, of France, in June 1991. An entirely new family of engines, the Pratt & Whitney 4073/4084, General Electric GE90 and Rolls-Royce Trent 800, is under final development for the 777.

Boeing has developed an entirely new FBW system and its award-winning cockpit layout boasts newly developed 'cool' CDUs (Control Display Units), visible in all lighting conditions and from all angles. Under the cabin floor is space for 32 standard LD-3 freight containers, plus additional space for irregular bulk cargo. Boeing has many partners in the project including Mitsubishi, Kawasaki and Fuji, who together are responsible for building 20 per cent of the airframe. On 9 April 1994 the first 777, a **777-200A**, was rolled out at the Everett plant and made its maiden flight on 12 June 1994, powered by a pair of Pratt & Whitney PW4084 turbofans. The second 777 flew on 15 July, in full United Airlines markings. By October, five were in the air.

The first 777 service was inaugurated by United Airlines on 17 May 1995, followed by British Airways, in November. By early-1996, announced 777 orders and options stood at 230.

The 777 was first certified with Pratt & Whitney PW4000 engines, followed by General Electric GE90s and then Rolls-Royce Trents.

SPECIFICATION:
Boeing 777-200 'A-Market'
Powerplant: two 71,200-lb (317-kN) Rolls-Royce Trent 870/1, or 73,500-lb (327-kN) Pratt & Whitney PW4073/A, or 74,500-lb (331-kN) General Electric GE90-B2/3 turbofans
Accommodation: two (flight deck), maximum of 440 passengers (standard 375)
Dimensions: span 199 ft 11 in (60.93 m); height 60 ft 6 in (18.44 m); length 205 ft 11½ in (62.78 m)
Weights: operating, empty 299,550 lb (135875 kg); maximum take-off 535,000 lb (242670 kg)
Performance: max cruising speed Mach 0.87; service ceiling 43,100 ft (13136 m); maximum range, with reserves 4,660 miles (7505 km)

Britten-Norman Islander/Trislander Multi-engined transports

Originally launched as a private venture enterprise, design of John Britten and Desmond Norman's **Islander** got under way during April 1964, with construction of the prototype beginning a few months later, in September. The two partners held a 25 per cent stake in Cameroon Air Transport and the Islander was produced to fulfil its requirements, and those of other airlines operating in 'austere' environments. The maiden flight was made on 13 June 1965, with subsequent testing resulting in a switch of powerplant from the 210-hp (157-kW) Rolls-Royce Continental to Avco Lycoming's O-540. Featuring the revised engine installation and a slight increase in wingspan, a production prototype made its debut in August 1966. UK certification occurred almost exactly a year later, on 10 August 1967, and paved the way for initial deliveries of the **BN-2A** that month. In addition to production at Bembridge, licence agreements were reached with Romania (ROMAERO, first flight on 4 August 1969, 450 built and still in production) and the Philippines (PADC, 47 built).

Subsequent developments led to the **BN-2B** model which made its debut in the late 1970s, at about the same time as Pilatus of Switzerland acquired Britten-Norman. The BN-2B benefited from increased landing weight, and incorporated

The BN-2 family has proved immensely popular all around the globe. Rugged countries such as Bolivia are prime operating environments.

Aurigny Air Services operates nine BN-2A Mk III Trislanders on services to the Channel Islands and mainland Britain. All the aircraft are now yellow.

changes in cabin design as well as being offered with a choice of powerplant. Two extra seats were added in the long-nosed **BN-2S**, but the next major development came with the addition of turboprops. On 6 April 1977 the first such example flew with two Lycoming LTP 101 powerplants, but these were changed to 400-shp (298-kW) Allison 250-B17Cs for the production **BN-2T Turbine Islander**, which first flew on 2 August 1980. Total deliveries of all Islanders exceeded 1,200 by mid-1994.

Perhaps the most distinctive variation on the successful Islander theme was the **BN-2A Mk III Trislander**. Flown for the first time on 11 September 1970, this had a lengthened fuselage with capacity for up to 17 passengers and also featured a third engine mounted in a much modified tail unit assembly. Production was launched not long after, and 12 were subsequently built in the USA by the International Aviation Corp. as the **Tri-Commutair**. Other versions were the increased MTOW **BN-2A Mk III-1**, long-nosed **Mk III-2** and auto-feather-equipped **Mk III-3**. The last of 73 UK-built aircraft was delivered in September 1984. In a surprise development, in 1994 Pilatus Britten-Norman has been discussing reinstating the Trislander as a production type, in China, as part of a deal with the Shenzhen General Aircraft Company.

SPECIFICATION:
Pilatus Britten Norman BN-2A Islander
Powerplant: two 260-hp (194-kW) Textron Lycoming O-540-E4C5 flat-six piston engines
Accommodation: single pilot (flight deck), maximum of 10 passengers
Dimensions: span 49 ft (14.94 m); height 13 ft 0¾ in (4.18 m); length 35 ft 7¾ in (10.86 m)
Weights: empty, equipped 4,114 lb (1866 kg); maximum take-off 6,600 lb (2993 kg)
Performance: maximum cruising speed 160 mph (257 km/h); service ceiling 11,300 ft (1445 m); maximum range, with standard fuel 870 miles (1400 km)

CASA 212 and 235 Twin-engined regional airliners and utility transports

Developed in response to a Spanish air force requirement, the **CASA C.212 Aviocar** first flew on 26 March 1971. Following the successful test programme, the original **C.212-100** derivative began to enter service in the late spring of 1974, but was supplanted by the **C.212-200** in 1979. This new version introduced more powerful Garrett (now AlliedSignal) TPE331-10 turboprops and an increased MTOW. Further redesign in the 1980s led to the **C.212-300**, which was certified in December 1987. With a longer, pointed nose and distinctive winglets, the -300 is available as the 23/26-seat **C.212-300 Airliner** and **C.212-300 Utility**. Since 1976 the C.212 has also been built by IPTN in Indonesia as the **NC.212**. Strangely, Series 300s built by IPTN are known as **NC.212-200**s. Over 400 C.212s of all versions (with a C.212-300 selling for approximately $1 million) had been delivered by mid-1994.

Experience with the C.212 and the relationship that existed between CASA and IPTN resulted in the formation of the Airtech company to develop a larger 45-seat twin-turboprop, the **Airtech CN.235**. Design work was launched in January 1980 on a 50-50 basis, and each production centre (at Seville and Bandung) completed one prototype. CASA's flew first, on 11 November 1983, with IPTN's following six weeks later, on 30 December 1983. CASA is responsible for the wing centre-section, centre and forward fuselages, while IPTN builds the rear fuselage, tail section and outer wing.

The CASA C.212 Aviocar has had a long life, its latest incarnation being the 'wingletted' C.212-300. Several civilian and military versions are available.

Delivery of the first production examples got under way in late 1986, Merpati Nusantara being the first customer to accept an Indonesian-built machine, while CASA's initial example went to the Royal Saudi air force in February 1987. Each manufacturer built 15 **CN.235-10**s with CT7-7A engines, before moving on to the CT7-9C-powered **CN.235-100**, with composite engine nacelles. In March 1992 the current production version, the **CN.235-200**, was introduced, featuring a higher operating weight, refined rudder and tail, reduced field-length requirements and improved (almost doubled) range. A quick-change cargo/passenger version, the **CN.235-200QC**, was certified in 1992 also. Apart from several Spanish and Indonesian regional airlines, the CN.235 serves with only one other operator, Japan's Asahi Airlines. By mid-1994, 34 had been delivered, and military sales of the $9.3-million type have outstripped civil sales by approximately 6:1. The CN.235 has provided valuable experience for IPTN's proposed **N-250** advanced regional turboprop and CASA's projected **CASA 3000** airliner.

The CASA (more correctly Airtech) CN.235 has achieved nearly six times as many military as civil sales. Spain's Binter Canarias flies four CN.235-10s.

SPECIFICATION:
CASA C.212 Series 300 Airliner
Powerplant: two 900-hp (671-kW) Garrett TPE331-10R-513C turboprops
Accommodation: two (flight deck), maximum of 26 passengers
Dimensions: span 66 ft 6½ in (20.28 in); height 21 ft 7¾ in (6.60 m); length 52 ft 11¼ in (16.15 m)
Weights: empty 8,333 lb (3780 kg); maximum take-off 16,975 lb (7700 kg)
Performance: maximum cruising speed 220 mph (354 km/h); service ceiling 26,000 ft (7925 m); maximum range, with 25 passengers and reserves 273 miles (440km)

Canadair CL-215 and CL-415 Twin-engined fire-fighting amphibian

The need to protect Canada's substantial forests from fire prompted the development of a purpose-built fire-fighting aircraft in the mid-1960s. After a symposium on the subject was held in Ottawa, in 1963, Canadair began to develop an amphibian that could scoop up water without lengthy periods spent reloading on the ground. The provincial government of Quebec, and France's Securité Civile organisation, approached Canadair and placed the launch orders for the **CL-215**.

While the Canadian company had no previous experience in building such an aircraft, it developed a simple yet rugged design, proofed against salt water corrosion and of considerable bulk. Its single-step hull hides a fully retractable nosewheel, while the main gear folds into fuselage recesses beneath the high wing. For its main fire-fighting role, the CL-215 can carry 1,200 Imp gal (5455 litres) of water, or retardant, in two tanks. Lake or sea water can be scooped up through two retractable inlets under the hull while the aircraft skims across the surface, before taking off once more. It takes just under one second to release the entire load and, as Canada is privileged to have so much inland water, the CL-215 can make a drop on a given target approximately every 10 minutes. Most, though not all, customers operate the CL-215 in this way.

The CL-215's impressive fire-bombing capability will be improved even further by the CL-415, which can collect its load and transit to a fire much faster.

The CL-415 is a new-build turboprop-powered fire-fighter, renamed to make it distinct from re-engined versions of the piston-powered CL-215.

With a first flight on 23 October 1967, 125 CL-215s were built before production ended in 1990. Current operators include the governments of eight Canadian provinces along with France, Greece, Italy, Spain, Thailand (SAR version for navy), Venezuela and the former Yugoslavia. On 8 June 1989 a Quebec aircraft, fitted with Pratt & Whitney Canada PW123AF turboprops in place of the original Pratt & Whitney R-2800 radial piston engines, made its maiden flight. This version, the **CL-215T**, is now available to any existing CL-215 customer, and Spain ordered 15 conversion kits, delivered by the end of 1993.

On the production line, Canadair introduced the **CL-415** in 1991. Intended as a turboprop design from the outset, the CL-415 has prominent winglets and finlets for added control at high power settings. It also possess a much refined structure and a Honeywell EFIS cockpit. The first example flew on 6 December 1993 and Quebec is again the launch customer. The CL-415 will be capable of skimming 1,350 Imp gal (6137 litres) of water in 12 seconds while flying over a lake, even with waves of 2½ ft (0.76 m). The first of Quebec's 12 aircraft was to be delivered, after a delay of three months from the planned date, in October 1994, and these will be joined by four aircraft for Italy.

SPECIFICATION:
Canadair CL-415
Powerplant: two 2,380-hp (1775-kW) Pratt & Whitney Canada PW123AF turboprops
Accommodation: two (flight deck)
Dimensions: span 93 ft 11 in (28.63 m); height 29 ft 5½ in (8.98 m); length 65 ft ½ in (19.82 m)
Weights: operating, empty 27,190 lb (12333 kg); disposable payload 13,500 lb (6123 kg); maximum take-off, water 37,850 lb (17168 kg)
Performance: maximum cruising speed 234 mph (376 km/h); take-off distance, water 2,670 ft (814 m); scooping distance, at sea level 4,240 ft (1293 m)

Canadair Challenger and Global Express

The aircraft that evolved into the **Challenger** began as Bill Gates' (of Learjet fame) proposed **LearStar 600**. A deal was struck in April 1976 under which Canadair secured exclusive rights covering the design, manufacture and marketing process. Further development soon resulted in important changes being made and the aircraft was renamed **Canadair Challenger** in March 1977.

Three pre-production examples were produced for development work and the first of these made its maiden flight on 8 November 1978, with the initial production specimen following suit on 21 September 1979. Canadian certification of the Avco Lycoming-ALF502L-2-powered **Challenger 600** (**CL600**) was accomplished in August 1980, while the General Electric CF34-powered and winglet-equipped **Challenger 601** (**CL601**) passed this milestone in February 1983, having made its maiden flight on 17 September 1982. Eighty-three CL600s were built and 76 have been refitted with winglets, to be referred to as the **CL600S**. The initial CF34-powered aircraft, 66 of which were delivered, were re-designated **CL601-1A** when the improved **CL601-3A** was introduced. The CL601-3A boasts CF34-3A engines and an EFIS cockpit, while the **CL601-3A/ER** is an extended-range aircraft with a lengthened rear fuselage housing additional fuel. By mid-1994, 140 CL601-3As of all versions had been delivered. Canadair became part of the Bombardier Group in 1992 and is currently developing the **Challenger 604**. To be powered by CF34-3B engines, the **CL604** will

The Challenger CL601-3A is powered (somewhat unsurprisingly) by a pair of General Electric CF34-3A turbofans, and is the current baseline model.

have an increased range of 4,600 miles (7400 km), Collins ProLine 4 avionics and a fin fuel tank. Certification and first deliveries are scheduled for December 1995.

Development of the **Global Express** (which slightly resembles the Canadair Regional Jet) long-range executive jet was formally launched in December 1993. The ultra-long-range, eight/30-seat Global Express is to be powered by a pair of 14,680-lb (65.3-kN) BMW Rolls-Royce BR710-48-C2 turbofans and the first of four test examples is due to make its maiden flight in September 1996, with production deliveries commencing the following year. Japan's Mitsubishi Heavy Industries is a key partner in the collaborative project, developing and manufacturing the supercritical wing and fuselage centre-section. Other major contributions will come from Shorts, which is to supply the all-composite tailplane, forward fuselage and other components. Orders now stand at 40 aircraft and the break-even point is estimated at about 100 aircraft, but Bombardier is optimistic that sales will eventually reach 250 after 12 years.

Many early Challenger operators elected to have their CL600s upgraded to CL600S standard, by retrofitting winglets in the style of the CL601.

SPECIFICATION:
Canadair Challenger 601-3A(ER)
Powerplant: two 9,140-lb (40.66-kN) General Electric CF34-3A turbofans
Accommodation: two (flight deck), up to 19 passengers
Dimensions: span 64 ft 4 in (19.61 m), over winglets; height 20 ft 8 in (6.30 m); length 68 ft 5 in (20.85 m)
Weights: operating, empty 24,935 lb (11310 kg); maximum take-off 44,600 lb (20230 kg)
Performance: max cruising speed 548 mph (882 km/h); max operating altitude 41,000 ft (12500 m); max range, with 5 passengers and reserves 4203 miles (6764 km)

Canadair Regional Jet

Canadair first proposed a stretched Challenger in the early 1980s, the **CL610 Challenger E**, before returning to the original design and developing the CL601-3A in 1986. From the outset, the wide-bodied Challenger had been designed with an airline market in mind, and research showed a market for a 50-seat regional airliner version. The purchase of Canadair by the Bombardier Group provided the impetus and funding to develop such a version, soon named the **Regional Jet**. By adding two 'plugs' to the CL601 fuselage, the new design could accommodate 48 seats, and had a maximum range of 1,380 miles (2222 km). Other manufacturers began to announce similar designs (such as the EMBRAER EMB-145 and Shorts RJX) and competition for orders hotted up. Bombardier went on to acquire Shorts in June 1989, leading to the cancellation of the RJX but assuring substantial work as a sub-contracter for the Northern Irish firm (which builds Regional Jet fuselage centre-sections and other major components).

By the late 1980s the Regional Jet (in its definitive form) became a 50-seat aircraft and a launch order for six was signed in March 1989 by German airline DLT. Canadair finished that year with 126 orders and options, and by early 1989 production of the prototype aircraft was well under way.

Canadair Regional Jets are now flying in Europe in the hands of Lufthansa Cityline, Austria's Lauda Air and Air Littoral, the latter in Air France markings.

Cincinnati-based Comair is a Delta Connection operator and Canadair RJ launch customer. By mid-1994, 19 were in service with more on order/option.

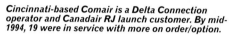

The first 'RJ' flew on 2 August 1991 and three prototypes undertook the flight test programme, leading to Canadian certification in July 1992. One of these aircraft was tragically lost in a spinning accident in July 1993. Deliveries began to Lufthansa Cityline (formerly DLT) on 29 October 1992, and final European JAA and US FAA certification was granted by 21 January 1993. The standard 50-seat, 1,128-mile (1816-km) range aircraft is designated the **Regional Jet 100**. It has since been joined by the **Regional Jet 100ER** (first customer Lauda Air), with additional fuel boosting its range to 1,865 miles (3002 km). Canadair refers to the type as the **CL600RJ**, and RJ 100ERs have been registered as the **CL600-2B19**. An executive version is also available, the first of these 30-seat aircraft being delivered to the Xerox Corp in 1993. By mid-1994, over 30 RJs (at approximately $17.5 million) had been delivered, and orders stood at 69.

In March 1994 Canadair announced the **Regional Jet 100LR**, a long-range version with its reach extended by a further 397 miles (640 km). First deliveries of this version will be made to Lauda Air, and the LR improvement package can be retrofitted. A stretched, re-engined 70-seat Regional Jet (**CRJ-X**) is under study, as is a hot-and-high version of existing models.

Cessna Citation, I, II, V and Citationjet

Having been a brand leader in supplying propeller-driven aircraft to the business community for many years, Cessna lagged behind its competitors when it came to introducing a jet-powered design. It was not until 15 September 1969 that the prototype of a new executive type known as the **Fanjet 500** made its first flight. Like the offerings from its contemporaries, the Cessna machine utilised pod-mounted engines attached to each side of the rear fuselage. Subsequently renamed as the **Citation**, deliveries of this Pratt & Whitney JT15D-1A turbofan-powered machine began just before the end of 1971, and it very quickly met with success. Refinement of the basic design next led to the **Model 500 Citation I** and **Model 501** (certified for single-pilot operation). A total of 691 Citation Is had been built when production ended in 1985.

By then the stretched **Model 550 Citation II** (and **Model 551**) had been available for a number of years, following its maiden flight in prototype form on 31 January 1977. Apart from having a longer fuselage, this also embodied an increase in wingspan and more powerful JT15D-4 turbofan engines. Further improvements, most notably to the wing structure, culminated in the **Citation S550 S/II** that became the basic production model in 1984, by which time more than 500 examples of all types had been built. By mid-1994, over 700 Citation IIs of all versions had been delivered, and the type is still in production alongside more recent developments.

Developed from the best-selling Model 500, the Cessna Citation II has been in production for almost 20 years and is still in demand.

Continued development of the straight-winged design resulted in the **Model 560 Citation V** with a further fuselage stretch and seating for eight. An engineering prototype made its first flight in August 1987, with a pre-production prototype following in early 1988. FAA certification was achieved in December 1988 and deliveries began in April 1989, with production surpassing the 250-mark in 1994. In June 1994 Cessna received certification for the **Citation V Ultra**, fitted with JT15D-5D engines and Honeywell Primus 1000 EFIS cockpit.

The most recent variation on the Citation theme to appear has been the **Model 525 CitationJet**. Cessna announced this version in 1989, specifically as a replacement for the original production models. A prototype was flown for the first time on 29 April 1991, and the first delivery was made on 30 March 1993. Easily the smallest member of the range, it is a six/seven-seater, other key features being its T-tail layout, supercritical wing and Williams International/Rolls-Royce FJ44 engines rated at 1,950 lb (8.4 kN). By mid-1994, orders for the CitationJet stood at over 100, with 60 delivered.

Cessna's latest light business jet is the Citationjet. With this aircraft, Cessna hopes to entice operators who previously had not considered buying a jet.

SPECIFICATION:
Cessna Model 560 Citation V
Powerplant: two 2,900-lb (12.89-kN) Pratt & Whitney Canada JT15D-5A turbofans
Accommodation: two (flight deck), up to eight passengers
Dimensions: span 52 ft 2½ in (15.90 m); height 15 ft (4.75 m); length 47 ft 2½ in (14.39 m)
Weights: empty, equipped 8,059 lb (3655 kg); maximum take-off 15,100 lb (6849 kg)
Performance: maximum operating speed 318 mph (511 km/h); maximum operating altitude 43,000 ft (13105 m); maximum range, with maximum fuel 2,300 miles (3701 km)

Cessna Citation III, VI, VII and X

A much more radical redesign effort undertaken in the latter half of the 1970s resulted in the advent of a very different-looking addition to the growing Citation family, shortly before the end of the decade. This was the **Model 650 Citation III**, which took to the skies for its initial flight on 30 May 1979 and which was a much more aesthetically pleasing machine.

Gone was the familiar straight-winged layout, abandoned in favour of a slightly swept, supercritical wing of increased span. At the same time, the fuselage was significantly longer, with space for two crew and up to 13 passengers, while the fin was also greatly altered to a much more sharply swept configuration capped by a T-tail.

Customer deliveries started in spring 1983, with the 100th example being handed over just three years later. Production was eventually to continue until 1992, by which time 187 Citation IIIs had been completed. Since then, the **Citation VI** and **Citation VII** (both retain the Model 650 designation) derivatives have been the standard models, with the former being a six/nine-seat, simplified, lower-cost version, while the latter is basically similar apart from using more powerful TFE731 engines. Cessna first made public its plans to switch production to these models in 1990 and development proceeded

Production of the Model 650 Citation III, Cessna's first 'large' business jet, ended in 1991 with 201 delivered. Current versions improve on its design.

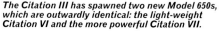

The Citation III has spawned two new Model 650s, which are outwardly identical: the light-weight Citation VI and the more powerful Citation VII.

simultaneously, with first flights occurring early in 1991 and initial deliveries from 1992. By mid-1994, 37 Citation VIs had been delivered. Construction numbers for this version continue directly on from the Citation III. Not so the Citation VII, 40 of which have been delivered.

Cessna has high hopes of capturing a substantial share of the long-range, high-speed, biz-jet market with the **Model 750 Citation X**. The existence of this new 12-seat addition to the Cessna line was revealed in October 1990 and the prototype made a successful maiden flight on 21 December 1993, some months later than originally scheduled. According to the manufacturer, initial flight tests staged from the company's Wichita airfield reveal good handling as well as impressive acceleration. Powered by a pair of 6,000-lb (26.69-kN) Allison AE3007C turbofans (formerly GMA3007s), the Citation X boasts Mach 0.9 performance and a range of 3,800 miles (6115 km).

Despite the delay in starting the flight development effort, Cessna remains optimistic that deliveries to customers will begin during the course of 1995. However, with a fully-equipped and furnished price tag that approaches the $13-million mark, it is unlikely that the Citation X will sell quite as briskly as other versions of the family have.

SPECIFICATION:
Cessna Model 650 Citation VI
Powerplant: two 3,650-lb (16.24-kN) Garrett TFE731-3B-100S turbofans
Accommodation: two (flight deck), six passengers
Dimensions: span 53 ft 6 in (16.31 m); height 16 ft 9½ in (5.12 m); length 55 ft 5½ in (16.90 m)
Weights: empty, standard 11,811 lb (5357kg); maximum take-off 22,000 lb (9979 kg)
Performance: maximum operating speed 320 mph (515 km/h); maximum operating altitude 43,000 ft (13106 m); maximum range, with reserves 2,701miles (4348 km)

One of a number of aircraft designed to replace the irreplaceable Douglas DC-3, Convair's **Model 240** evolved in response to a 1945 American Airlines requirement and flew for the first time on 16 March 1947. Entering scheduled service just over a year later, in June 1948, it could hold 40 passengers in pressurised comfort.

Subsequent developments aimed at the large commercial market led to two more versions being produced by Convair. The first of these was the stretched **Model 340** with capacity for 44 passengers, which entered service with United Air Lines in 1952. Next came the high-density **Model 440** that could carry up to 52 passengers.

In addition to the civil versions, large numbers of the military **T-29** navigation trainer and **C-131** transport derivatives were delivered to the US armed forces during the late 1940s and 1950s. Canada obtained 10 examples of the **Canadair CL-66 Cosmopolitan (CC-109)**, which was powered by British-built Napier Eland turboprops.

In fact, the first turboprop conversion was undertaken as early as 1954, when Napier fitted two Eland engines to a Convair 340. Making its maiden flight in this guise on 9 February 1955, the aircraft paved the way for the **Convair 540** that served with Allegheny Airlines for several years. At a later date, other conversions of the piston-powered versions were undertaken by several companies. According to preference, these used either Allison 501 or Rolls-Royce Dart engines. Those with the former

Small numbers of the early piston-engined Convair airliners are still in use. One operator still flying passenger services is Trans Florida Airways.

powerplant were known as **Model 580**s, while Dart-powered examples became either the **Model 600** (based on the 240) or the **Model 640** (based on the 340/440). Approximately 240 conversions were undertaken in the 1960s.

Despite its age, the twin-engined Convair remains active in some numbers and is still a candidate for updating, with the most recent initiative originating from the Kelowna Flightcraft company of British Columbia. Now known as the **Convair 5800**, this stretched version flew for the first time on 11 February 1992. Canadian certification was secured in December 1993, with the first cargo-carrying aircraft entering service in January 1994. A passenger-carrying version is to be offered. Changes include extensive revision of the cockpit using Honeywell electronic flight instruments, insertion of a 13-ft 11-in (4.25-m) fuselage section, provision of new wiring throughout and major structural strengthening. Approximately 160 Convairs, largely turboprop-powered aircraft and including several reconditioned military examples, are still active as freighters in Europe, South America, Africa and the USA.

Convair 340s and 440s were candidates for re-engining with Allison turboprops, to become CV-580s or 'Super Convairs'.

SPECIFICATION:
Convair CV 580
Powerplant: two 3,750-hp (2796-kW) Allison 501-D13H turboprops
Accommodation: two (flight deck)
Dimensions: span 105 ft 4 in (32.12 m); height 29 ft 2 in (8.89 m); length 81 ft 6 in (24.84 m)
Weights: operating, empty 30,275 lb (13732 kg); maximum payload 8,870 lb (4023 kg); maximum take-off 58,140 lb (26371 kg)
Performance: cruising speed 340 mph (550 km/h); maximum range, with maximum fuel 2965 miles (4773 km/h)

Curtiss C-46 Commando

riginally conceived as a 36-seat passenger airliner and flown for the first time on 26 March 1940, the **Curtiss-Wright CW-20** very quickly attracted the attention of the US Army Air Corps, which was searching for a new general-purpose transport. As a consequence, a specialised military freighter version with the basic designation **C-46 Commando** was ordered into production, and this began to enter service in the summer of 1942. At the time of its introduction, it was the largest and heaviest twin-engined aircraft in USAAC service and it proved of particular value in the Pacific theatre of war, playing a key role in the movement of men and materiel throughout this region. Nowhere was this more apparent than in operations 'over the hump' of the eastern Himalayas between India and China, where the C-46's superior performance at high altitude clearly gave it the edge over the Douglas C-47 Skytrain. In general, though, it was less popular than the immortal 'Dak', by virtue of its dismal single-engined performance characteristics.

Major variants in USAAC service were the **C-46A**, **C-46D**, **C-46E** and **C-46F**, while a much smaller number were also used by the US Marine Corps as the **R5C-1**. By the time production ended, successive orders for the improved versions eventually resulted in some 3,180 Commandos being built.

Despite its age and a marked airline preference for the DC-3/C-47, over 20 C-46s soldier on, from the snows of Alaska to the tropics of South America.

Along with a handful of others, Alaska-based Everts Air Fuel still flies the C-46. Everts operates four Commandos as freighters/fuel tankers.

Many war-surplus examples were eventually passed on to friendly nations in South East Asia and Latin America, with some of these continuing in use until well into the 1980s.

In the closing stages of World War II, Curtiss-Wright again began considering a commercial version. Given the company designation **CW-20E**, it was to be a 36-seater. Design was launched during 1944 and construction of a mock-up generated considerable interest, resulting in at least two major US airlines placing contracts by the end of 1944. At a later date, the ready availability of war surplus aircraft meant that a large number of redundant Commandos were disposed of to civil operators.

The type proved popular for hauling cargo through harsh terrain, where the type's good load, sturdy structure and low-speed handling made it ideal for operating from semi-prepared strips. Many carried meat in South America, and a few got into the hands of drug smugglers. A modest number of these veteran machines are still active around the world, most notably in Bolivia (Air Beni, Frigorifico Santa Rita, NEBA, SAC, TAVIC), Canada (Buffalo Air Cargo), Colombia (Coral, Selva, Tala and Transoceana), the Dominican Republic (Aerotim Cargo and AMSA), Nicaragua (Aero Pac) and the United States (Everts Air Fuel).

SPECIFICATION:
Curtiss C-46 Commando
Powerplant: two 2,000-hp (1492-kW) Pratt & Whitney R-2800-51 radial piston engines
Accommodation: two (flight deck)
Dimensions: span 108 ft (32.31 m); height 21 ft 9 in (6.62 m); length 76 ft 4 in (23.26 m)
Weights: empty 30,00 lb (13608 kg); maximum take-off 45,000 lb (20412 kg)
Performance: maximum speed 270mph (435 km/h); service ceiling 24,500 ft (7470 m); maximum range 3,150 miles (5069 km/h)

Dassault Falcon 10, 20, 100 and 200

France
Light business jets

One of a crop of twin-engined executive jets that appeared during the early 1960s, the 10/12- seat **Falcon 20** (originally flown as the **Mystère XX** on 4 May 1963) made its maiden flight in its definitive form on New Year's Day 1965. Powered by General Electric CF700 engines, the baseline model was designated the **Falcon 20C**. It was followed by the **Falcon 20D** (with extra fuel and CF700-2D turbofans), **Falcon 20E** (with increased weights, modified rudder and starter/generator) and the **Falcon 20F** (with extra fuel and full leading-edge slats). The **Falcon 20G** was a specialised maritime surveillance version (named Gardian/Guardian). Dassault has never acknowledged designations such as 'Da.20', and commonly refers to the Falcon family as Mystères.

Production of the original Falcon 20 terminated in 1983, with 480 of all versions built, following introduction of the **Falcon 200** in 1981. At the time of its debut, the Falcon 200 was known as the **Falcon 20H**, and the main alteration was the fitment of Garrett ATF-3-6-2C turbofans in place of CF700s. Other, less visible variations concerned the provision of a larger integral fuel tank in the aft fuselage, redesigned wingroot fairing and automatic slats. Thirty-six Falcon 200s were built when production ended in 1988. In 1989, Garrett, in association with Dassault, began offering TFE731-5AR refits to existing Falcons under the 'Dash-5' programme. Thus modified, aircraft become known as **Falcon 20C-5**, **Falcon 20D-5** etc.

Dassault built several versions of the 10/12-seat Falcon 20, with a variety of engines. All were referred to by the manufacturer as the Mystère 20.

Following the success of the Falcon 20, Dassault turned its attention to building a smaller biz-jet. This was the seven/nine-seat **Falcon 10** (originally known as the **Mini-Falcon** and powered by Turboméca Larzac turbofans), which made its first flight on 1 December 1970. Customer deliveries started shortly before the end of 1973. Unlike its larger brother, the Falcon 10 relied on Garrett turbofans from the outset, with a pair of 3,230-lb (14.4-kN) TFE731-2s fitted as standard. The Falcon 10 was built without sub-types, although the French navy flies a number of modified aircraft (some with ventral radars) as **Falcon 10MER**s.

By 1985, over 193 examples of the smaller jet had been been sold when production ended in favour of the improved **Falcon 100**. Although dimensionally identical, the latter version featured a 496-lb (225-kg) increase in MTOW, a fourth cabin window to starboard, and a larger unpressurised baggage compartment in the rear fuselage. Production of the Falcon 10/100 (and with it all of Dassault's smaller jets) ended with the delivery of the 226th aircraft in September 1990.

Appearing some years after the Falcon 20, the Falcon 10 (or 'Mini-Falcon') is a super-sleek seven/nine-seat bizjet, which led to the Falcon 100.

SPECIFICATION:
Dassault Falcon 20
Powerplant: two 5,200-lb (23.13-kN) Garrett ATF3-6A-4C turbofans
Accommodation: two (flight deck), maximum of 12 passengers (nine standard)
Dimensions: span 53 ft 6½ in (16.32 m); height 17 ft 5 in (5.32 m); length 56 ft 3 in (17.15 m)
Weights: empty, equipped 18,190 lb (8250 kg); maximum take-off 32,000 lb (14515 kg)
Performance: maximum speed 402 mph (648 km/h); service ceiling 45,000 ft (13715 m); maximum range, with reserves 2,890 miles (4650 km/h)

Dassault Falcon 50 and 900

Continued development of the highly successful Dassault family of executive jets led to the first flight of a prototype three-engined, intercontinental derivative known as the **Falcon 50 (Mystère 50)** on 7 November 1976. Although this featured the same external fuselage cross-section as the twin-engined Falcon 200, it was a brand new design incorporating area ruling and advanced wing aerodynamics.

Flight testing of two prototypes and a pre-production Falcon 50 paved the way for French certification in February 1979, with US type approval following in March. Deliveries commenced in July 1979 and the Falcon 50 proved a popular addition to Dassault's product line, with orders being placed by civil and military customers around the world. The Falcon 50 remains in production, and in June 1991 Dassault announced an agreement with MiG whereby the Russian firm would supply tail surfaces for the French assembly line. By mid-1994, 245 Falcon 50s had been sold.

Less than four years after the first Falcon 50 was handed over, Dassault announced that it was to proceed with development of a new longer-range jet, the **Falcon 900**. News of this programme was first made public at the 1983 Paris air show, and the prototype was rolled out less than a year later, on 18 May 1984. In the event, this did not fly for

Dassault's first intercontinental biz-jet design was the Falcon 50 of 1976. It remains in production alongside the stretched Falcon 900.

the first time until 21 September, being joined in the flight test effort by a second prototype at the end of August 1985. French and US certification was obtained in March 1986.

In general, the Falcon 900 bears a strong family resemblance to the Falcon 50, although the fuselage is redesigned as a 'wide-body'. This gives the cabin almost twice the volume of the Falcon 50 (and 12 windows), and can accommodate up to 19 passengers. It also has slightly greater range, with the transatlantic capability of the Falcon 900 being demonstrated in fine style in September 1985 when the second aircraft made a non-stop flight of 4,954 miles (7973 km) from Paris to Little Rock, Arkansas, in order to appear at the NBAA show.

Since 1991 Dassault has been offering its customers the improved **Falcon 900B**. Featuring 4,750-lb (21.13-kN) Garrett TFE731-5BR turbofans, (limited) rough-field capability, improved landing aids, higher cruising altitude (39,000 ft/11855 m) and increased range (4,600 miles/7402 km), the Falcon 900B has superseded the previous model. The 900B modifications are also available for retro-fit, and by mid-1994 101 Falcon 900s and 39 Falcon 900Bs were in service. In June 1988 a Falcon 900 became the 1,000th Dassault Falcon executive jet to be delivered.

Although the Falcon 900 resembles the Falcon 50, it is a much larger aircraft, with a reprofiled fuselage, advanced avionics and more powerful engines.

SPECIFICATION:
Dassault Falcon 900
Powerplant: three 4,500-lb (20-kN) Garrett TFE731-5AR-1C turbofans
Accommodation: two (flight deck), maximum of 19 passengers
Dimensions: span 63 ft 5 in (19.33 m); height 24 ft 9¼ in (7.55 m); length 66 ft 3¾ in (20.21 m)
Weights: empty, equipped 22,575 lb (10240 kg); maximum take-off 45,500 lb (20640 kg)
Performance: maximum operating speed Mach 0.87; maximum cruising altitude 51,000 ft (15550 m); maximum range, with reserves and eight passengers 4,491 miles (7227 km)

Dassault Falcon 2000

Intended as a follow-on to the highly successful Falcon 20/200 series, the latest addition to the expanding family of Dassault business jets was announced as the Falcon X at the 1989 Paris air show and launched as the **Falcon 2000** in October 1990. Four months later, in February 1991, Alenia of Italy entered the project as a partner, taking 25 per cent of the risk and bearing responsibility for manufacture of the aft fuselage and the engine nacelles.

Powered by two General Electric/Garrett CFE738 turbofan engines, the sole prototype flew for the first time on 3 March 1993. Roll-out of the second example occurred at Bordeaux in December 1993, and this is eventually earmarked for use as a demonstrator on completion of test work connected with the powerplants. The second Falcon 2000 to fly got airborne in the early summer of 1994, and was actually the third to be completed. It is due to go to the USA for demonstration purposes. Dassault anticipates achieving near-simultaneous French and US certification to the JAR/FAR Pt 25 Transport Category Aircraft standard during December 1994.

Although it is a twin-engined machine, many of the physical attributes of the Falcon 2000 approximate more closely to the Falcon 900. For instance, it shares wide-body characteristics with the Falcon 900, although it has transcontinental rather than transatlantic range capability. In fact, it features an identical fuselage cross section, but is 6 ft 6 in

While nominally a Falcon 20/200 replacement, the Falcon 2000 is a much larger aircraft, essentially a twin-engined Falcon 900.

(1.98 m) shorter, which results in a cabin length that measures almost exactly two-thirds that of the three-engined aircraft. In addition, the Falcon 2000 utilises the same basic wing structure as the Falcon 900, albeit in slightly modified form, since it has a revised leading edge and lacks the inboard slats of the latter version.

Initial orders for the Falcon 2000 were actually received in advance of the decision to proceed with final design, development and production, and Dassault's research indicates that the market for an aircraft in this class is estimated as lying somewhere in the region of 300-400 over a 10-year period. By early 1993, the French manufacturer was in possession of a total of 50 commitments, although this figure included just 15 firm orders. The third and fourth aircraft will be delivered to the US, while Swiss-based executive jet operator Aeroleasing, long a Dassault Falcon customer, will be another early operator. In view of the company's past record in promotion, there is every reason to believe that the Falcon 2000 will be just as successful as its predecessors.

The wide-bodied Falcon 2000 began life as the Falcon X in 1989, and the prototype was rolled out in its definitive form in early 1993.

SPECIFICATION:
Dassault Falcon 2000
Powerplant: two 6,000-lb (26.7-kN) GE/Garrett CFE738 turbofans
Accommodation: two (flight deck), maximum of 12 passengers
Dimensions: span 63 ft 5 in (19.33 m); height 22 ft 10¾ in (7.55 m); length 66 ft 4½ in (20.23m)
Weights: empty, equipped 19,522 lb (8855 kg); maximum take-off 35,000 lb (15875 kg)
Performance: maximum operating speed Mach 0.85; maximum cruising altitude 47,000 ft (14330 m); maximum range, with reserves and eight passengers 3,448 miles (5550 km)

de Havilland Canada DHC-6

Building on experience gained with earlier short take-off and landing (STOL) aircraft such as the **DHC-2 Beaver**, **DHC-3 Otter** and **DHC-4 Caribou**, de Havilland Canada began work on a new design in 1964, aiming this firmly at the large market that existed for a 20-seater that possessed good field performance characteristics. The result was the **DHC-6 Twin Otter**, and work on construction of a batch of five aircraft started in November 1964.

Powered by 579-ehp (432-kW) PT6A-6 engines, the first of these machines made its maiden flight on 20 May 1965, and the ensuing flight test programme culminated in type certification being achieved in the early summer of 1966. Not long after, the initial production example was delivered to Ontario's Department of Lands and Forests in July, with this **DHC-6-100** aircraft being fitted with PT6A-20 powerplants in place of the PT6A-6 that was used by the first four Twin Otters. The main benefit arising from this change concerned reliability, for the later version of the engine possessed an identical power rating.

By the time that production was terminated in December 1988, slightly more than 830 Twin Otters had been completed for civil and military operators worldwide. Three basic models were eventually built, with the Series 100 leading the

Las Vegas-based Scenic Airlines flies 18 DHC-6s, modified with large windows as 'Vistaliners', on sightseeing tours of the nearby Grand Canyon.

The four highly-distinctive DHC-6-310 Twin Otters of the British Antarctic Survey operate from Rothera Base, on the polar ice cap.

way. Just over 100 had been produced when the improved **DHC-6-200** made its debut. This had increased luggage capacity in an extended nose section, and some 115 were completed before the **DHC-6-300** version was introduced by the 231st example to roll from the Downsview factory. This eventually became by far the most numerous derivative and deliveries got under way in the spring of 1969. A development of this was the **DHC-6-300S**, fitted with upper wing spoilers and other STOL improvements, six of which undertook test operations in the mid-1970s. Military utility DHC-6s were designated **DHC-6-300M** or **DHC-6-300MR**.

The main differences between the final production model and its predecessors centred around extra power and greater payload/range capability. In the case of the former, this stemmed from replacement of the PT6A-20 by the PT6A-27 version of Pratt & Whitney Canada's successful turboprop. This in turn allowed the take-off weight to be increased by some 2,000 lb (907 kg), which resulted in worthwhile payload benefits.

In addition to the land-based Twin Otters, all three basic versions were available as floatplanes. In this configuration, however, aerodynamic factors dictated use of the shorter nose. DHC-6s still serve in considerable numbers.

SPECIFICATION:
DHC-6-300 Twin Otter
Type: twin-engined STOL transport
Powerplant: two 620-hp (462-kW) Pratt & Whitney Canada PT6A-27 turboprops
Accommodation: two (flight deck), maximum of 20 passengers
Dimensions: span 65 ft (19.81 m); height 19 ft 6 in (5.94 m); length 51 ft 9 in (19.77 m)
Weights: operating empty 7,415 lb (3363 kg); maximum take-off 12,500 lb (5670 kg)
Performance: maximum cruising speed 210 mph (338 km/h); service ceiling 26,700 ft (8140 m); maximum range, with reserves 805 miles (1297 km)

de Havilland Canada DHC-7

After achieving considerable success with its previous designs de Havilland Canada initiated design of a large four-engined STOL aircraft that would provide the capacity and comfort to operators who regularly operated from very short fields. These comprised both airlines flying from austere locations in mountainous or jungle terrains, and those flying from small city airports.

With aid from the Canadian government, de Havilland Canada began work on two **DHC-7 Dash 7** prototypes in 1972, the first of which flew on 27 March 1975. The layout drew heavily on that of the Buffalo, featuring a high-set wing with large double-slotted flaps, four sets of spoilers and small ailerons. The four Pratt & Whitney PT6A-50 turbo-props drove slow-turning four-bladed propellers, providing high power, low noise levels and a measure of slipstream blowing for the flaps. The tail surfaces were mounted high on the large upswept fin, keeping the tailplane well away from the engine exhaust blast. The tricycle undercarriage tucked neatly away into the forward fuselage and inboard engine nacelles.

Internally, the Dash 7 is routinely configured for 46-50 passengers in 2+2 seating, and is flown by a flight crew of two. Access to the main cabin is via a port-side door just aft of the wing, which features an integral airstair. Baggage is accommodated at the rear of the cabin, the compartment served by a starboard-side door. The toilet and galley facilities are also located at the back.

Plymouth-based Brymon European (now owned by British Airways as Brymon Airways) operates an all-de Havilland fleet that includes five DHC-7s.

Rocky Mountain Airways was the first recipient of a Dash 7, acquiring its initial aircraft on 3 February 1978. Many customers followed, the aircraft selling in fair numbers to carriers requiring its unique capabilities. Among the best-known were carriers such as Brymon Airways, as the Dash 7 was initially the only type allowed to land at London City.

Production was initially of the **Dash 7 Series 100** and **Series 101**, the latter being a freighter version with an upward-hinging cargo door on the port side of the forward fuselage. These were followed in 1986 by the **Series 150** and **151**, featuring higher weight and greater fuel capacity. A specialist variant was the **Dash 7 IR Ranger**, a specialised ice reconnaissance variant for the Canadian government that had an observation blister behind the flight deck and a side-mounted surveillance radar.

Production ended in 1988 with 114 aircraft built, following the take-over of DHC by Boeing, which decided to concentrate on Dash 8 manufacture. The company has since revived the de Havilland name, although it is now part of the Bombardier Group.

The exotically-named Paradise Island Airways operates seven Dash 7s on services to the Caribbean from Ft Lauderdale and Miami airports.

SPECIFICATION:
de Havilland Canada DHC-7 Series 150
Powerplant: four 1,120-shp (835-kW) Pratt & Whitney Canada PT6A-50 turboprops
Accommodation: two (flight deck), standard layout for 50 passengers
Dimensions: span 93 ft (28.35 m); length 80 ft 6 in (24.54 m); height 26 ft 2 in (7.98 m)
Weights: empty 27,480 lb (12465 kg); maximum take-off 47,000 lb (21319 kg)
Performance: maximum cruising speed 266 mph (428 km/h); service ceiling 21,000 ft (6400 m); range with 50 passengers and typical reserves 1,313 miles (2112 km)

de Havilland DHC-8 Dash 8

Twin-engined advanced STOL airliner

Increasing demand for 30/40-seat regional aircraft in the late 1970s encouraged de Havilland Canada to build a twin-engined turboprop as a follow-on from its four-engined DHC-7. The resultant aircraft was a scaled-down version of the Dash 7 with a similar high-wing and T-tail, a major element of the design being the provision of good STOL performance in keeping with the company's tradition. The 36/39-seat **DHC-8 Dash 8** design incorporated a two-element rudder and powerful single-slotted flaps, and Pratt & Whitney Canada PW100 series engines. The prototype **DHC-8-100** made its maiden flight on 20 June 1983 and the first production aircraft entered revenue-earning service with Canada's NorOntair on 19 December 1984.

The initial Series 100, powered by two 1,800-shp (1342-kW) PW120s, was supplemented by the larger **DHC-8-300**, which first flew on 15 May 1987. Time Air accepted the initial aircraft on 27 February 1989. The Series 300 provides a 40 per cent increase in capacity to 50-56 passengers. To accommodate the extra seats, two extensions totalling 11 ft 3 in (3.43m) were added fore and aft of the wing, the wingspan was increased by 5 ft (1.52 m) and the landing gear was beefed up to handle the 6,600-lb (2994-kg) increase in gross weight. The Series 300 also featured uprated 2,380-shp (1775-kW) PW123

Widerøe is one of Norway's major domestic airlines and counts the DHC-6, -7 and -8 in its current fleet. This is one of its 10 DHC-8-103s, with more on order.

engines and a high level of commonality with the Series 100. Product enhancements, including higher gross weights, have been incorporated in both series and these are known as the **DHC-8-100A** and **DHC-8-300A**, powered by the improved PW120A and PW123A engines, but with the same take-off rating. The new **DHC-8-100B** has two PW121 engines, providing a take-off power of 2,150 shp (1603 kW) for better airfield and climb performance. The optional 43,000-lb (19505-kg) gross weight of the -300A is standard on the latest **DHC-8-300B**, which also incorporates more powerful 2,500-shp (1865-kW) PW123B engines and better airfield performance.

In 1992, Bombardier Aerospace, which had acquired de Havilland Canada from Boeing in 1992, announced the (renamed) **de Havilland DHC-8-200** for improved hot-and-high performance. Identical in size to the Series 100, the 200 will have a faster cruise speed of 345 mph (555 km/h) and better single-engined performance. Powerplant will be the 2,150-shp (1603-kW) PW123C in the **DHC-8-200A** and the equivalent PW123D in the **DHC-8-200B**. The first aircraft is scheduled to fly in October 1994. Plans to produce a stretched 60-70 seat **DHC-8-400** are in abeyance. The order book for the Dash 8 had reached 401 by May 1994.

In 1989, Hamburg Airlines became a DHC-8 operator. It currently flies three 36-seat DHC-8-102s and a pair of 50-seat DHC-8-311s.

SPECIFICATION:
de Havilland DHC-8-300B
Powerplant: two 2,500-hp (1865-kW) Pratt & Whitney PW123B turboprops
Accommodation: two (flight deck), with a maximum of 56 passengers
Dimensions: span 90 ft 9 in (27.43 m); height 24 ft 7 in (7.49 m); length 84 ft 3 in (25.68 m)
Weights: operating empty 25,700 lb (11657 kg); maximum ramp 43,000 lb (19505 kg)
Performance: maximum operating speed 327 mph (527 km/h); service ceiling 25,000 ft (7620 m); range with maximum payload and typical reserves 954 miles (1540 km)

Dornier Do 228

L aunched at the start of the 1980s, two versions of the **Do 228** were made available virtually from the outset of the programme, with the **Do 228-100** prototype being the first derivative to fly. That milestone was successfully negotiated on 28 March 1981 and the **Do 228-200** prototype, with a 5-ft (1.52-m) longer fuselage, followed suit barely six weeks later, on 9 May. UK and US certification was achieved in the first half of 1984, with deliveries commencing at about the same time. By 1986, production was running at a rate of just under four aircraft per month and orders had been secured from almost 40 customers.

A licence agreement covering production of as many as 150 aircraft was also concluded in 1983 with the Kanpur Division of Hindustan Aeronautics. Indian manufacture of the Do 228 began with assembly of major component parts supplied by Dornier, but later aircraft built there have incorporated a greater indigenous contribution. In more recent times, Dornier has been negotiating with China over the matter of licence-manufacture, but the details of this programme have still to be settled. However, it is hoped to launch Chinese production in 1996-97.

Production of the 15-seat Series 100 and 19-seat Series 200 continued in Germany until 1993, by which time a combined total of over 200 had been delivered worldwide. Variations on the theme included the **Dornier Do 228-101**, **Do 228-201** and **Do 228 Maritime Patrol**. The first two were more

Druk Air is the Kingdom of Bhutan's sole airline, which selected the Do 228 as the ideal type for STOL operations in its mountainous home.

or less identical to the original models, save for having a reinforced fuselage structure and different mainwheel tyres so as to allow greater operating weights to be achieved. Manufacture of both was started in 1984, but the only version presently being built by the parent company is the **Do 228-212**, which won German certification in 1989.

Standard features embodied in the Do 228-212 include more powerful AlliedSignal (formerly Garrett) TPE331s, strengthened wing box and fuselage structure and the addition of underfuselage strakes to enhance short-field capability. The opportunity has also been taken to fit updated avionics. In normal passenger-carrying configuration, the Do 228-212 has 19 seats and is able to carry a 4,850-lb (2200-kg) payload some 175 miles (280 km) further than the Do 228-202 that it replaced. Dornier has also developed a double door-equipped **Do 228 Cargo** freighter, based on the Do 228-212, and the **Do 228 Ambulance** that can accommodate up to six stretchers. By January 1993, when the most recent (Indian) example was delivered, 248 Do 228s had been completed.

Holmstroem Air, of Sweden, operates two Dornier Do 228-100s and two Do 228-200s (as seen here) on commuter services from its Hultsfred home.

SPECIFICATION:
Dornier Do 228-200
Powerplant: two 715-hp (533-kW) AlliedSignal (Garrett) TPE331-5-252D turboprops
Accommodation: two (flight deck), maximum of 19 passengers
Dimensions: span 55 ft 8 in (16.97 m); height 15 ft 11½ in (4.86 m); length 54 ft 4 in (16.56 m)
Weights: operating empty 7,820 lb (3547 kg); maximum take-off 12,566 lb (5700 kg)
Performance: maximum cruising speed 265 mph (428 km/h); service ceiling 28,000 ft (8535 m); maximum range, with reserves 1680 miles (2704 km)

Dornier Do 328

ollowing a successful maiden flight at Oberpfaffenhofen near Munich in December 1991, a decision to go ahead with quantity production of the **Dornier Do 328** 30-seat twin-turboprop regional airliner was reached at the beginning of 1993. European and US certification was achieved in the autumn of that same year, clearing the path for the first aircraft to be delivered to Air Engiadina of Switzerland on 21 October 1993. Initial deliveries to the first US customer followed in November 1993, when two of the 20 examples ordered by Horizon were formally handed over. The Do 328 comes equipped with a Honeywell Primus 2000 EFIS cockpit, featuring five colour multi-function displays and also fibre-optic laser gyros and Primus 650 colour weather radar. GPS, MLS and TCAS (mandatory in the USA) are also available as optional equipment.

Generally speaking, sales of the Do 328 have been disappointingly slow, even though the aircraft has demonstrated a commendable despatch reliability level of about 98 per cent since entering service in late 1993. As a consequence of the low level of interest, by the summer of 1994 only 43 firm orders had been placed, with a further 50 forming the subject of existing options. This is still some way short of the 150 aircraft that Dornier must sell

Launch customer for the Do 328 was Horizon Air, which ordered 35 (with 25 options) for use on its services as Alaska Airlines Commuter from Seattle.

The Do 328 mates the Do 228's TNT supercritical wing with a wide and largely composite fuselage, and has a five-screen EFIS cockpit.

before it can begin to recoup some of its $675 million investment in development.

In the meantime, efforts to improve performance are in hand and these should result in benefits to climb rate, short-field performance and cruising altitude, which may yet succeed in attracting more orders. Dornier is also presently in the process of developing a new variant that will feature an improved performance kit (IPK). This will be known as the **Do 328-200** and is expected to fly for the first time in the middle of 1995, with certification to follow soon afterwards. Plans to build and market a stretched 50-seater derivative have now been shelved, despite earlier company studies suggesting that an increased-capacity version might generate extra interest in the Do 328, even though it would have been in direct competition with the Fokker 50 (DASA now has a controlling stake in Fokker).

Although final assembly is centred upon the Munich factory of Deutsche Aerospace, much of the manufacturing process is split between aerospace concerns located in Europe and elsewhere, and the Do 328 most definitely merits description as a co-production venture. By way of illustration, fuselage sections are produced by Aermacchi in Italy, using sub-assemblies that originate from South Korea's Daewoo Heavy Industries.

SPECIFICATION:
Dornier Do 328-200
Powerplant: two 1,850-hp (1380-kW) Pratt & Whitney PW119B turboprops
Accommodation: two (flight deck), maximum of 19 passengers
Dimensions: span 55 ft 8 in (16.97 m); height 15 ft 11½ in (4.86 m); length 54 ft 3 in (16.55 m)
Weights: operating empty 7,820 lb (3547 kg); maximum take-off 12,566 lb (5700 kg)
Performance: maximum cruising speed 265 mph (428 km/h); service ceiling 28,000 ft (8535 m); maximum range, with reserves 1680 miles (2704 km)

Douglas DC-3

The illustrious line of Douglas commercial transports began in 1932, when TWA announced that it needed an aircraft similar to the Boeing 247 (the airline asked for a 12-seat, three-engined design) more quickly than Boeing could provide it. Donald W. Douglas produced the **DC-1**, which first flew on 1 July 1933, followed by the refined **DC-2**, which was chiefly bought by US domestic airlines. All these were eclipsed by the immortal **DC-3** (originally the 14-berth **DST** – Douglas Sleeper Transport) which first flew on 17 December 1935. In its 24-seat day version, this all-metal aircraft, powered by a pair of ultra-reliable Pratt & Whitney radial piston engines, revolutionised air transport.

The type is perhaps best known by its World War II appellation of **C-47** (**Skytrain** in the US, but **Dakota** to the RAF). Eisenhower ranked its as one of the five weapons crucial to Allied success and by 1945 10,692 had been built, in addition to over 2,000 unlicensed **Lisunov Li-2** copies in the USSR. The availability of such a quantity of aircraft at the war's end, in addition to its established reputation and ease of operation, ensured that the DC-3 (known everywhere beyond the US as the Dakota) would become the classic airliner design and an irreplaceable asset to companies around the world.

Many manufacturers have sought, with varying degrees of success, to find a 'DC-3 replacement'. It has long been mooted that the only replacement for a DC-3 is another DC-3, and to this end several conversions of the type have been produced over

Vintage Airways is a collaboration between Virgin Atlantic and Vintage Air Tours, operating two DC-3s on nostalgia flights from Kissimee, Florida.

the years. Today two major modifications are on offer, both adding turboprop engines as an alternative to the ageing piston powerplants. In the United States, Basler Turbo Conversions Inc. (based at Oshkosh, Winsconsin) will refit and re-engine an aircraft with 1,220-shp (910-kW) Pratt & Whitney Canada PT6A-67R turboprops, stretching the fuselage by 8 ft 4 in (2.54 m) to counteract the resultant change in the centre of gravity. Christened the **Basler T-67**, over 20 aircraft had been delivered by mid-1994, primarily to military customers, in Central and Southern America.

In South Africa, conversions are undertaken by Professional Aviation, who use 1,424-shp (1062-kW) PT6A-65ARs to produce the **Jet Prop DC-3 AMI**. These aircraft are zero-timed and stretched by 3 ft 4in (1.02 m), can seat up to 40 and are refitted with new hydraulics, electrics and avionics. The programme began in 1991, with the South African Air Force as its first customer. Hundreds of original DC-3/C-47s survive in commercial service around the world, chiefly as freighters, although there are many in passenger service also.

Oshkosh-based Basler Aviation is offering turbine conversions for the DC-3 by adding Pratt & Whitney PT6A-67R engines and stretching the fuselage.

SPECIFICATION:
Douglas C-47 (typical post-war conversion)
Powerplant: two 1,200-hp (895-kW) Pratt & Whitney R-1830-S1C3G Twin Wasp radial piston engines
Accommodation: two (flight deck), with a maximum of 24 passengers
Dimensions: span 95 ft (28.96 m); height 6 ft 11½ in (5.17 m); length 64 ft 5½ in (19.65 m)
Weights: empty 16,865 lb (7650 kg); maximum take-off 25,200 lb (11430 kg)
Performance: maximum cruising speed 230 mph (370 km/h); service ceiling 23,200 ft (7070 m); maximum range, with maximum payload 2,125 miles (3420 km)

Douglas DC-4, DC-6 and DC-7
USA
Four-engined transports

Even before the DC-3 had flown, Douglas was discussing a larger, more advanced development with US airlines. This resulted in the **DC-4E** (four-engined) of 1936. An almost complete redesign led to the definitive **DC-4**, which first flew on 14 February 1942. As the US was embroiled in war by then, the aircraft rapidly became a military transport, the **C-54 Skymaster**. Like the DC-3, the C-54 established a solid reputation as a long-range transport and by 1945 over 1,000 C-54s and 79 new-build DC-4s were available for commercial service. The basic 62-ft 6-in (19.05-m) long aircraft could carry 44 passengers, although high-density seating versions could increase this to a staggering 86. The search for greater capacity and range lead to the stretched **DC-6**, which could comfortably accommodate 52. The DC-6 first flew on 15 February 1946 (as the military-designated **XC-112A**) and entered airline service with American Airlines on 29 June of that year. The basic DC-6 was supplemented by the stretched (by 5 ft/1.52 m) **DC-6A** that featured two freight doors on the port side, no windows and a restressed floor. A similarly improved passenger version was dubbed **DC-6B**. Military versions were christened **C-118**, but the last civil DC-6 version built was the passenger/freight-convertible **DC-6C**. A total of 704 aircraft was built for all customers.

The Americas remain a haven for the big Douglases, with aircraft in regular service in the snows of Alaska or the tropics of Venezuela.

A life-sized cardboard cut-out of Marilyn Monroe rides in the third window from the rear on every flight by 'Tanker 152', a DC-4 fire-bomber of ARDCO.

The last and perhaps greatest of Douglas' classic 'propliners' was the **DC-7**. Prompted by American Airlines, Douglas designed a rival for the Lockheed Super Constellation, scaling up the DC-6B by 3 ft 4 in (1.02 m) and adding new 3,250-hp (2470-kW) Wright R-3350 Turbo Compound piston engines driving four-bladed props (as opposed to the DC-6's three). The **DC-7B** came next, offering optional saddle fuel tanks on the rear of the engine nacelles. The ultimate development was the long-range **DC-7C**, the **'Seven Seas'**, which could carry 107 passengers in style over 4,605 miles (7411 km). Its fuselage was further stretched to 112 ft 3 in (34.21 m), and 120 were built from a total of 457 DC-7s.

Many of these 'Douglas Dinosaurs' survive today. They include the DC-6 freighters of Air Atlantique in the UK, the DC-7 sprayers of T&G Aviation in the USA, the C-118s of Canada's Conifair, the DC-6s of Aerosol and Transamazonica in Colombia, the Dominican Republic-based DC-6s of Aeromar and Trado, and the fire-bombers operated in the United States by ARDCO (DC-4s), Macavia (DC-6s) and Central Air Services (DC-4s). Even two **Aviation Traders ATL.98 Carvairs** (a bulbous-nosed, UK-developed car freighter DC-4 conversion) are still active with Academy Airlines in the USA and Eclair in Zaïre.

SPECIFICATION:
Douglas DC-6B
Powerplant: four 2,500-hp (1864-kW) Pratt & Whitney R-2800-CB17 Double Wasp 18-cylinder two-row air-cooled radial piston engines
Accommodation: three (flight deck)
Dimensions: span 117 ft 6 in (35.81 m); height 29 ft 3 in (8.92 m); length 105 ft 7 in (32.18 m)
Weights: empty 62,000 lb (28123 kg); maximum payload 24,565 lb (11143 kg); maximum take-off 107,000 lb (48534 kg)
Performance: maximum cruising speed 316 mph (509 km/h); service ceiling 21,700 ft (6615 m); maximum range, with maximum payload 1,900 miles (3058 km)

EMBRAER EMB-110 Bandeirante

Brazil
Twin-engined light transport

Although initially designed to meet a Brazilian air force requirement for a multi-role transport, the 19-seat **Bandeirante** (Pioneer) was to play a key role in the foundation of Brazil's aerospace industry and the development of the country's internal air transport network. The first of three prototypes, built by the Institute for Research and Development, made its first flight on 26 October 1968. This led to the establishment of EMBRAER in August 1969 to handle production of the new aircraft at São Jose dos Campos, near São Paulo. The first production Bandeirante flew on 9 August 1972 and a total of 500 had been built by 1994.

Production started with the **C-95** for the Brazilian air force. This type shared the line with the initial commercial model, designated **EMB-110C**, which entered service with Transbrasil on 16 April 1973. The 110C provided accommodation for 15 passengers and was powered by two Pratt & Whitney PT6A-27 turboprops. It was operated by local airlines and gave way to the improved **EMB-110P** with higher gross weight for 18 passengers, first sold to TABA of Brazil in 1976. The major civil versions were the **EMB-110P1** and **EMB-110P2**, the last-named based on a military cargo version with a fuselage lengthened by a 9-in (85-cm) plug. The former had quick-change facilities and a cargo door for all-freight or mixed operation, while the P2, first flown on 3 May 1977, became the front-line commuter model with accommodation for up to 21 passengers. Powerplant was two 750-shp (559-kW) Pratt &

This late-production (1987 vintage) EMBRAER EMB-110P1A is seen wearing Brazilian test marks prior to its delivery to Angola.

Whitney Canada PT6A-34 turboprops.

In 1981, new **P1/41** and **P2/42** versions were introduced to meet US FAR Pt 41 certification for a maximum gross weight of 13,101 lb (5900 kg). First delivery of a P1/41 was made to PBA of Boston, in spring 1981. The updated **EMB-110P1A** and **P2A** incorporated several interior improvements and 10° tailplane dihedral, reducing vibration. The first two P1As entered service with PBA in December 1983. Also available from 1983 were the **P1A/41** and **P2A/41**, which replaced the P1/41 and P2/41 models.

The designation **EMB-110E(J)** referred to a seven-seat executive transport version of the Bandeirante. Another civil variant was the **EMB-110S1**, a geophysical survey version with additional wingtip tanks similar to those of the EMB-111, a maritime patrol version. Development work in the 1980s on a projected pressurised Bandeirante, the **EMB-110P3**, was discontinued in favour of the larger Brasilia. A total of 490 Bandeirantes of all versions had been delivered by the time production ceased in September 1990.

The Bandeirante still provides sterling service to smaller airlines around the world such as Sweden's Nyge-Aero, which operates four.

SPECIFICATION:
EMBRAER EMB-110P2A
Powerplant: two 750-shp (559-kW) Pratt & Whitney PT6A-34 turboprops
Accommodation: two (flight deck), maximum of 21 passengers
Dimensions: span 50 ft 3 in (15.33 m); height 16 ft 2 in (4.92 m); length 49 ft 6 in (15.10 m)
Weights: operating empty 7,751 lb (3516 kg); maximum ramp 12,566 lb (5700 kg)
Performance: maximum cruising speed 257 mph (413 km/h); service ceiling 22,500 ft (6860 m); maximum range with maximum fuel and reserves 1,244 miles (2010 km)

EMBRAER EMB-120 Brasilia

Brazil
Twin-engined regional airliner

The **EMB-120 Brasilia** grew out of a number of projects based on a pressurised Bandeirante and an increasing requirement for a larger 30-plus-seat aircraft. EMBRAER officially launched the new aircraft in September 1979. A twin-engined, low-wing design with a circular fuselage and a T-tail, the prototype EMB-120 made its initial flight on 27 July 1983 and received its Brazilian certification on 10 May 1985, followed by FAA type approval on 9 July 1985. The first customer, Atlantic Southeast Airlines of the USA, put the production Brasilia into revenue service in October 1985, having taken cere-monial delivery of the second prototype at the Paris air show on 1 June. By mid-1994, the EMB-120 Brasilia had logged a total of 318 orders, with deliveries to customers (including the Brazilian air force) in 14 countries standing at 279 aircraft.

Initial production aircraft were powered by two 1,590-shp (1185-kW) Pratt & Whitney PW115 engines and had a maximum take-off weight of 23,810 lb (10800 kg), but the more powerful 1,800-shp (1342-kW) PW118 was adopted in early 1986 to improve performance at the higher gross weight of 25,353 lb (11500 kg) then being introduced. Maximum cruising speed was also increased to 360 mph (580 km/h). An 18-seat corporate model was handed over to United Technologies in the same

year. Late in 1987, a hot-and-high version became available. This was distinguished by improved PW118A engines which maintain maximum output up to a temperature of ISA+15° at sea level. Empty weight was also reduced by 858 lb (390 kg) through increased use of composites, which now make up 10 per cent of the basic equipped empty weight of the Brasilia. First customer was Utah-based Skywest.

In 1992 the increased-weight, extended range **EMB-120ER** appeared. Earlier models can be brought up to ER standard with a simple retrofit. The **EMB-120ER Advanced**, which became available from 1993, incorporates interchangeable leading edges on flying surfaces, improved flaps, new seals to cut interior noise, increased cargo capacity, and a number of cabin improvements. From August 1994, the standard production model will be the **EMB-120ERX** with further interior improve-ments and the deletion of the anti-icing boot on the tailfin's leading edge. Also now available are the **EMB-120QC** quick-change and the **EMB-120C** cargo and combi versions. The latter models have a payload of 7,715 lb (3500 kg). The QC is provided with floor plus side wall protection, fire detection, and a smoke curtain separating the cockpit from the cargo compartment.

An EMB-120ER of Skywest (another Delta Connection airline) demonstrates the dramatic start-up of its PW118A engines.

SPECIFICATION:
EMBRAER EMB-120 Brasilia
Powerplant: two 1,800-hp (1342-kW) Pratt & Whitney PW118 or 118A turboprops
Accommodation: two (flight deck), maximum of 30 passengers
Dimensions: span 64 ft 10½ in (19.78 m); height 20 ft 10 in (6.35 m); length 65 ft 7½ in (20 m)
Weights: operating, empty 16,457 lb (7465 kg); maximum take-off 25,353 lb (11500 kg)
Performance: maximum operating speed 313 mph (504 km/h); service ceiling PW118s, 30,000 ft (9150 m); maximum range, with maximum fuel 633 miles (1019 km)

Eurocopter Puma, Super Puma

This helicopter family was initially developed by Sud-Aviation (later to become Aérospatiale) to a 1962 French Army requirement for a medium transport helicopter. With development funds from the government, Sud-Aviation was able to proceed quickly, having already worked on a similar model, and the first of two prototypes, powered by twin 1,300-shp (970-kW) Turboméca Turmo IIIC4s, flew on 15 April 1965. The **SA 330 Puma** featured a fully-articulated main rotor with four aluminium blades and a five-bladed anti-torque tail rotor, and was capable of carrying up to 18 passengers. Initial customers were the French army and the UK Royal Air Force, the former taking delivery of the first production model in September 1968.

The **SA 330F** civil version, powered by the 1,290-shp (962-kW) Turmo IVA, flew for the first time in September 1969, and was superseded from 1976 by the **SA 330J**. Main differences were more powerful 1,580-shp (1177-kW) Turmo IVCs, composite main rotors and increased MTOW. Between 1970 and 1984, Aérospatiale sold 126 civil models. Design of a derivative, the **AS 332 Super Puma**, commenced in 1974, initially by refitting a Puma with two Turboméca Makila turboshafts and an uprated transmission as the **AS 331**. This modified experimental helicopter flew on 5 September 1977 and, after further changes to improve performance, led to the first flight of the AS 332 on 13 September 1978. Noticeable external differences include a lengthened nose, increased

Since 1983, Aberdeen-based Bond Helicopters has flown 10 suitably-registered AS 332L2 Super Pumas on oil rig support missions.

wheelbase, new landing gear and a ventral fin. The civil version, with seating for two crew and 19 passengers and two 1,877-shp (1400-kW) Makila 1A1 turboshaft engines, was given the suffix C. It was certificated on 24 April 1981, and this was followed on 2 December by the certification of the **AS 332L**. This version differed in having a cabin lengthened by 2 ft 6 in (0.76 m) to provide seating for up to 24.

The Super Puma Mk II, first flown on 6 September 1987, introduced new main and tail rotors and uprated transmission, without changing the Makila 1A1 powerplants. The rear fuselage was lengthened by 1 ft 6 in (0.45 m) to accommodate the slightly longer main rotor blades. Present production models (undertaken by Eurocopter France) are the AS 332L1 and AS 332L2, both for offshore work and VIP transportation. The latter, introduced in 1991, has more powerful 2,104-shp (1569-kW) Makila 1A2 engines, a higher gross weight of 22,046 lb (10000 kg) and enhanced performance. Maximum weight of the L1 is 20,615 lb (9350 kg) with external load. By the end of 1993, a total of 111 civil versions had been delivered.

The original AS 330 Puma, such as this radar-equipped AS 330J, also found favour with oil support companies such as PHI of the United States.

SPECIFICATION:
Eurocopter (Aérospatiale) AS 332L2
Powerplant: two 2,104-shp (1,569-kW) Turboméca Makila 1A2 turboshafts
Accommodation: two (flight deck), maximum of 24 passengers
Dimensions: main rotor diameter 53 ft 2 in (16.20 m); height 16 ft 3 in (4.97m); length 55 ft 1 in (16.78 m)
Weights: empty 10,270 lb (4660 kg), maximum take-off 20,172 lb (9150 kg)
Performance: maximum cruising speed 172 mph (277 km/h); service ceiling 16,995 ft (5180 m); maximum range 526 miles (850 km)

Fairchild Merlin and Metro

Twin-engined regional airliner/business-prop

The **Metro** had its origins in an eight-passenger corporate aircraft by Swearingen Aircraft, based at San Antonio, Texas. A rebuilt Beech Queen Air with a pressurised fuselage and two Lycoming piston engines became the **Merlin I**, but this was shelved in favour of the **SA-26T Merlin IIA**, which was the first production aircraft to fly on 13 April 1965. At the same time, the company began construction of a pressurised commuter aircraft, known as the **SA-226TC Metro**, which made its maiden flight on 26 August 1969 and received certification in June 1970. The first Metro was powered by two Garrett AiResearch TPE331s. Its circular fuselage could accommodate up to 20 passengers. Gross weight was restricted to 12,500 lb (5670 kg) to comply with US regulations for commuter aircraft. Production continued when Swearingen was taken over by Fairchild Industries in November 1971, but it delayed entry into service until 1973. The name Swearingen was later dropped.

In parallel, the company produced the **SA-226T Merlin III** also with Garrett engines, increased seating for 11 passengers, and several external changes. Further changes and improved performance led to the **Merlin IIIA**, powered by two 840-shp (626-kW) Garrett TPE331-3U-303G turboprops, and the **Merlin IIIB**. The original Metro was followed in

In production in one form or another for nearly 30 years the Fairchild Metro/Merlin family has proved a popular one, particularly in the United States.

The popular Metro/Merlin family earned the unattractive sobriquet 'the San Antonio sewer tube' by virtue of its very narrow fuselage.

1974 by the **Metro II**, which introduced larger 'squared' cabin windows and an optional rocket unit for improved hot-and-high performance. When the MTOW restriction was lifted, Fairchild next produced the **Metro IIA** in 1980 at a gross weight of 13,100 lb (5944 kg). The equivalent 12-seat corporate transport versions of these two models were the **SA-226AT Merlin IV** and the **SA-226AT Merlin IVA**.

Further significant changes, including an increase in wingspan and more powerful 1,000-shp (745-kW) TPE331-11U-601G turboprops, resulted in the **SA-227AC Metro III**, which was certificated on 23 June 1980. For airlines that preferred to standardise fleets on Pratt & Whitney engines, Fairchild produced the **Metro IIIA**. This model, with the 1,100-shp (820-kW) PT6A-45R engine and minor upgrades, first flew on 31 December 1981. The **SA-227AT Merlin IVC** is the corporate version. The **Expediter** was an all-cargo version of the Metro III with a rear cargo door, reinforced floor and a payload of 5,000 lb (2268 kg). Following the selection of the Metro III for the USAF **C-26** programme, many of the enhanced features were incorporated in the latest production model, the **Metro 23**, certificated in June 1990. By mid-1994, over 950 of all versions had been delivered.

SPECIFICATION: Fairchild Metro 23
Powerplant: two 1,000-shp (745-kW) AlliedSignal (Garrett) TPE331-12UA-701G turboprops
Accommodation: two (flight deck), with a maximum of 19 passengers
Dimensions: span 58 ft 1 in (17.70 m); height 16 ft 8 in (5.08 m); length 59 ft (18.09 m)
Weights: operating, empty 8,675 lb (3935 kg); maximum ramp 16,600 lb (7532 kg)
Performance: maximum cruising speed 331 mph (534 km/h); service ceiling 25,150 ft (7666 m); range with maximum payload and typical reserves 900 miles (1450 km)

Fokker F27 and FH227

Twin-engined regional airliner and utility transport

At the beginning of the 1950s, many aircraft manufacturers began searching for a successor to the ubiquitous Douglas DC-3. Some are still trying, but one of the most accomplished of the earlier designs was Fokker's **F27 Friendship**. The F27 began life with the Dutch firm as the 32-seat **P.275** in 1950. Taking advantage of the newly-developed Rolls-Royce Dart turboprop, and matching two with a modified, circular, high-winged fuselage, the **F27 Mk 100** emerged in its final form in 1953. At this point Fokker chose the F27's upbeat name, and entered into licence-production with Fairchild. The first Dutch-built aircraft flew on 24 November 1954, from Schipol, followed by a **Fairchild F27**, from Hagerstown, Maryland, on 12 April 1958.

Strangely, the first aircraft to enter airline service was a US-built one. West Coast Airways placed its first (modified 40-seat) F27 into service on 27 November 1958, while Aer Lingus followed with Dutch aircraft on 15 December. With uprated Dart Mk 532 engines, Fokker next flew the **F27 Mk 200** (**Fairchild F27A**) on 20 September 1962. This was followed by the **F27 Mk 300 Combiplane (F27B)**, a passenger/freight version with a reinforced floor and large cargo door forward in the port fuselage. Fokker alone built the **F27 Mk 400** (chiefly as the **Troopship** for the Dutch air force), which combined a freight door with further uprated engines.

The next major development came in the form of the stretched **F27 Mk 500**, seating between 52 and 60 (and 15 featuring freight doors on either

Jersey European Airways currently operates eight appropriately-registered Fokker F27 Mk 500s alongside Shorts 360s and BAe 146s.

side). This inspired Fairchild to come up with its own 'long' version. By 1966 the US manufacturer had become **Fairchild-Hiller**, and 79 of its **FH227** were eventually completed. Fairchild also built the corporate **F27F**, and higher-powered **F27J** and **F27M**. The final production version was Fokker's **F27 Mk 600**, which combined the short fuselage of the Mk 200 with the reinforced cabin and cargo door of the Mk 300/400 combiplanes. This was a true quick-change version with a roller floor, enabling the interior to be rapidly reconfigured.

Several military transport versions (with an 'M' suffix to the sub-type) and dedicated maritime patrol versions were built, but production of the F27 ended in favour of the Fokker 50 in June 1986. A total of 581 Dutch aircraft had been built, with a further 205 (128 F27s) completed in the United States, with sales to 168 customers in 63 countries. A sizeable proportion of these are still in use, with as many as 450 in regular service. The type has retained its market value (still approximately $1.1 million), and secondhand F27s are still much in demand, particularly as freighters.

FH227s, like this Belgian example, found their way to Europe. The last major user was France's TAT, which has now withdrawn its aircraft from use.

SPECIFICATION:
Fokker F27 Mk 500 Friendship
Powerplant: two 2,210-shp (1648-kW) Rolls-Royce Dart Mk 552 turboprops
Accommodation: two (flight deck), maximum of 60 passengers
Dimensions: span 95 ft 1¾ in (29.00 m); height 28 ft 7¼ in (8.71 m); length 82 ft 2¼ in (25.06 m)
Weights: operating empty 28,000 lb (12700 kg); maximum take-off 45,900 lb (20820 kg)
Performance: normal cruising speed 298 mph (480 km/h); service ceiling 29,500 ft (8990 m); range with 52 passengers and reserves 1,082 miles (1741 km)

Fokker F28 Fellowship

The success of the Fokker F27 convinced the Dutch firm that there was a market for a comparable, jet-powered, 32-seat design with a range of approximately 575 miles (926 km). As with the F27, Dutch governmental backing was sought, and Fokker also entered into a contract with Germany's VFW and HFB to build the rear fuselage and tail sections. Shorts, in Northern Ireland, was then selected to build the wings. In keeping with the precedent set by the F27, the new design was named **F28 Fellowship**. Rolls-Royce Spey Mk 555 turbofans were chosen as the sole powerplant. The F28 was launched with an order from LTU in November 1965, but by the time the first example had flown, on 9 May 1967, this was the only firm interest shown in the new airliner.

Norway's Braathens SAFE next placed an order early in the flight test programme, and by the time the F28 was certified, in February 1969, a total of 22 orders had been received. The initial production version was the 65-seat, 89-ft 11-in (27.16-m) **F28 Mk 1000** and 100 of these were built before production of this version ceased in 1977. Throughout its life the Mk 1000's maximum weight was steadily increased, improving its range to 1,150 miles (1852 km). In 1972 Fokker launched the next model, the **F28 Mk 2000**, which was

KLM Cityhopper, formerly NLM, has long been a Fokker operator and its current fleet includes four F28 Mk 4000s in addition to 10 Fokker 50s.

After TAT's acquisition by British Airways, several of its F28s (and Fokker 100s) began to operate in the latter's colours, using British Airways callsigns.

stretched to accommodate 79 passengers but had its maximum range reduced to 805 miles (1296 km). Chronologically, the next version was the **F28 Mk 6000** of 1975. This combined a slatted wing (to improve take-off performance) with the Mk 2000's fuselage, but airline interest was weak, with only two aircraft ever delivered to individual customers.

Fokker instead turned its attention to the **F28 Mk 4000**, the most popular version. Instigated by a requirement from Swedish domestic carrier Linjeflyg, the Mk 4000 first flew on 20 October 1976. This was the same length as the Mk 2000, but featured an increased wingspan, 85 seats and optional extra fuel. One hundred and eleven Mk 4000s were built, with the last example (also the last F28) delivered on 7 August 1987. The final version to be developed was the **F28 Mk 3000**. This incorporated all the new design features of the Mks 4000 and 6000, but used the short fuselage of the F28 Mk 1000. The first example flew on 23 December 1976, and initial deliveries were made to Garuda. A water/methanol injection version, the **F28 Mk 3000R**, was developed for hot-and-high operations; so too was a cargo door-equipped version, the **F28 Mk 3000C**, in 1978. Twenty-one Mk 3000s were completed, and in total 248 F28s were delivered before production was halted.

SPECIFICATION:
Fokker F28 Mk 4000
Powerplant: two 9,900-lb (44-kN) Rolls-Royce Spey Mk 555-1P turbofans
Accommodation: two (flight deck), maximum of 85 passengers
Dimensions: span 82 ft 3 in (25.07 m); height 27 ft 9½ in (8.47 m); length 97 ft 1¾ in (29.61 m)
Weights: operating, empty 38,900 lb (17465 kg); maximum take-off 73,000 lb (33113 kg)
Performance: maximum operating speed 380 mph (612 km/h); service ceiling 35,000 ft (10675 m); maximum range, with maximum load 1,295 miles (2085 km)

Fokker 50 and 60

With the success of the F27 Friendship, which has almost become a household name, there was never any doubt that Fokker would launch a successor, taking advantage of all the technological advances that had occurred in the intervening years. On the F27's 25th anniversary in service, in 1983, Fokker announced the **Fokker 50** (**F50**). Similar in size and configuration to the F27, the F50 (so-called because of its seating configuration) features new Pratt & Whitney PW120 series engines with six-bladed propellers, hydraulic gear and flap systems, substantial use of composite materials, and a completely redesigned Honeywell EFIS cockpit. The wing also has been much improved and features small 'Fokklets' (or winglets). From a passenger's point of view, one less satisfactory change is the removal of the F27's large windows in favour of an increased number of smaller ones.

The first two prototypes were modified from F27s, and Fokker's official documentation and some registration certificates still refer to the F50 as the **F27-050**. Ansett Transport Industries, of Australia, placed the launch order for 15 aircraft. The first flight took place from the Fokker plant at Schipol on 28 December 1985, followed by the first production F50 on 13 February 1987. Deliveries commenced to Lufthansa Cityline on 7 August 1987, although the first revenue service was made by DLT. The baseline model is the **Fokker 50 Series 100**, powered by PW125B engines. Depending on the seating configuration, which can range from 46 to 68, the

In 1989 Sudan Airways took delivery of a pair of Fokker 50s, which it operates alongside DHC-6s, 737-200s, an A320, 707-300Cs and A310-300s.

Series 100 is further divided into **Fokker 50-100** (with four doors) and **Fokker 50-120** (three doors).

By early 1993, Fokker was delivering the **F50 Series 300**. This PW127B-powered, hot-and-high version was first ordered by Avianca, and is again available in **F50-300** and **F50-320** models. Fokker has also considered a stretched version, the **Fokker 50 Series 400**, with a 68-seat cabin and an overall increase in length of 7 ft 10½ in (2.40 m). By mid-1994, 198 Fokker 50s (including some military versions) had been delivered, with a further 26 on option. At the end of 1993, Fokker had an unsold backlog of 32 'white tail' F50s, but these have now largely been disposed of.

The **Fokker 50 Utility** (**F50U**) is a primarily military variant that can be configured for a wide variety of transport missions; however, it is also available in corporate or oil support versions. In February 1994 the Dutch air force launched a new development, the **Fokker 60 Utility** (**F60U**), ordering 12 to replace its existing F27 Troopships. The F60U is stretched by 5 ft 4 in (1.6 m) and is fitted with a large cargo door to starboard.

Rio Sul is a subsidiary of VARIG, which flies domestic and regional services from Rio de Janeiro with Brasilias, 737-500s and six Fokker 50s.

SPECIFICATION:
Fokker 50-100
Powerplant: two 2,500-hp (1864-kW) Pratt & Whitney Canada PW125B turboprops
Accommodation: two (flight deck), maximum of 30 passengers
Dimensions: span 64 ft 10½ in (19.78 m); height 20 ft 10 in (6.35 m); length 65 ft 7½ in (20 m)
Weights: operating, empty 16,457 lb (7465 kg); maximum take-off 25,353 lb (11500 kg)
Performance: maximum operating speed 313 mph (504 km/h); service ceiling 30,000 ft (9150 m); maximum range, with maximum fuel 633 miles (1019 km)

Fokker 70 and 100

Fokker began the search for an F28 replacement with the 110/130-seat **'Super F28'**, for service entry in 1984. This became the **Fokker F29**, and the manufacturer even considered using Boeing 737 fuselages for a maximum of 180 seats. This did not succeed and, along with McDonnell Douglas, Fokker next drew up the 150-seat, 737-lookalike **MDF 100**, before finally returning to the proven F28. Stretching the original aircraft, and adding a pair of new Rolls-Royce Tay engines, Fokker launched the **Fokker 100**, simultaneously with the F50, in November 1983.

To build the 107-seat aircraft, Fokker entered into a partnership with MBB (now DASA) to build the mid-section and tail, and Shorts Bros to build the wing. The F100 achieved its first order in 1984, 10 for Swissair – but it was to be almost three more years until another airline signed for the type. A major boost came in 1986 with the signing of an agreement between Ireland-based lessors GPA and Fokker, which established GPA Fokker 100 Ltd to purchase and place aircraft with airlines around the world. The first aircraft took to the air on 30 November of that year. Swissair took delivery of its first F100 on 29 February 1988, entering service on the Zürich-Vienna route on 3 April.

On 8 June 1988, Fokker flew an uprated Tay

The single Fokker 70 prototype has shouldered the flight test programme. It will be joined in the air by the first production F70 at the end of 1994.

Air Gabon was one of several airlines that contracted to lease F100s from GPA Fokker 100, receiving this single example in 1989.

650-powered version of which American Airlines ordered 75, with 75 options. Deliveries of this version began, to USAir, in 1989. The 75th aircraft for American was also the 250th F100 to be delivered, in early June 1994. The F100 is also available in an 88-seat **Fokker 100QC** (Quick Change) cargo version and the VIP-configured **Fokker 100 Corporate**. By mid-1994, orders for the Fokker 100 (at $22 million) stood at 379 from 18 countries.

In 1992 Fokker gave the go-ahead to a short-fuselage variant of the F100, the 79-seat, Tay 620-powered **Fokker 70**. Modification of the second prototype F100 to this configuration began in October 1992, and this aircraft flew on 4 April 1993. Measuring 101 ft 4¾ in (30.91 m), the Fokker 70 will be built on the same line as the F100 and customers will be able to switch between either version with only 12 months' notice. The two aircraft are being marketed as the 'Fokker Jetline'.

Launch orders for the F70 came from Pelita and Sempati Air in Indonesia, followed by British Midland and Mesa Airlines, in the USA. By mid-1994, over 300 hours of test flying had been successfully undertaken. On 12 July 1994 the first production aircraft flew at the Schipol plant. Pending certification in October, deliveries are scheduled to commence at the end of 1994.

SPECIFICATION:
Fokker F100
Powerplant: two 9,900-lb (44-kN) Rolls-Royce Tay Mk 620-15 turbofans
Accommodation: two (flight deck), maximum of 107 passengers (standard 97)
Dimensions: span 92 ft 1½ in (28.08 m); height 27 ft 10½ in (8.5 m); length 115 ft 10¼ in (35.31 m)
Weights: operating, empty 51,260 lb (23250 kg); maximum take-off 91,500 lb (41500 kg)
Performance: maximum operating speed 367 mph (592 km/h); maximum cruising altitude 35,000 ft (10670 m); maximum range, with maximum load 2,222 miles (1380 km)

Gulfstream I, II, III, IV and V

Twin-engined long-range business aircraft

In the early 1950s Leroy Grumman, chief of the Grumman Aircraft Corporation, saw the market for a purpose-built executive aircraft, rather than just a conversion of a World War II-vintage type. Using a pair of the newly developed Rolls-Royce Dart turboprops, Grumman started planning a high-wing, S-2 Tracker anti-submarine aircraft derivative. This proved an unsatisfactory starting point and instead the low-wing **G.159** emerged in 1957. Christened the **Gulfstream** (later **Gulfstream I**), it first flew, from Bethpage, on 14 August 1958.

Although the first generation of biz-jets was entering production simultaneously, none could rival the Gulfstream. Even so, Grumman began to consider a swept-wing jet version, which would retain the Gulfstream I's short-field capability. The T-tailed **G.1159 Gulfstream II** was launched in 1964 and the prototype flew on 2 October 1966. G.159 production ended in 1969 at 200 aircraft, as Gulfstream II orders began to mount. The jet-powered aircraft, which soon became known simply as the **'GII'**, had a maximum range of 3,670 miles (5907 km) as compared to the Gulfstream I's 2,540 miles (4088 km), but Grumman sensed there was room for improvement.

At the same time that the company was reorganised as the Gulfstream American Aviation Co. (in 1973), the **Gulfstream III** was launched. The original, very ambitious plans for a supercritical-winged aircraft were scaled back to produce a stretched GII, with 'winglets'. The definitive 4,686-mile

The GIV-SP boosts the payload of the baseline GIV with no increase in empty weight. From September 1992, all Gulfstream IVs are to this standard.

(6732-km) capable Gulfstream III first flew on 2 December 1979, replacing the GII, of which 258 had been sold. The GII benefited from GIII technology and a refit programme added winglets to existing GIIs. Forty-three examples were thus transformed into **Gulfstream IIB**s. The Gulfstream II, somewhat awkwardly, then became the **G.1159A**, and the GIII, the **G.1159B**. Gulfstream IIs fitted with new blended winglets developed by Seattle's Aviation Partners are designated **Gulfstream IIW**s.

The latest development came in 1983 with the launch of the **G.1159C Gulfstream IV**. This replaced the GIII, 198 of which had been built by 1988. The long-range GIV first flew on 11 September 1985. By mid-1994, 241 GIVs had been ordered. In 1992 Gulfstream launched the **GIV-SP** (Special Performance), further increasing the version's remarkable payload/range capability. on 28 November 1995 Gulfstream (now Gulfstream Aerospace) flew the prototype **Gulfstream V**, an ultra-long-range (7,250 miles/11667 km) biz-jet. The 'GV' is powered by two BMW/Rolls-Royce BR710 turbofans and deliveries will begin in 1997.

The Gulfstream III's (and II's) Rolls-Royce Spey engines are threatened by engine noise regulations, hence the GIV's much quieter Tay turbofans.

SPECIFICATION:
Gulfstream IV
Powerplant: two 13,859-lb (61.6-kN) Rolls-Royce Tay Mk 611-8 turbofans
Accommodation: two (flight deck), standard seating for 14 to 19
Dimensions: span 90 ft 8 in (27.68 m); height 24 ft 3 in (7.4 m); length 92 ft 2 in (28.05 m)
Weights: operating, empty 45,500 lb (20640 kg); maximum take-off 85,000 lb (38500 kg)
Performance: maximum cruising speed speed 582 mph (629 km/h); maximum operating altitude 45,000 ft (13715 m); maximum range, with maximum load 7,239 miles (11650 km)

The 17-passenger **Y-12** (or **Yunshuji-12** – transport aircraft 12) traces its origins to the 9/10-seat **Y-11**, designed and developed by Harbin Aircraft Manufacturing Corporation in China's Heilongjiang Province. Studies to improve the payload/range capabilities of the Y-11 resulted in an initial development version, designated the **Y-12 I** (originally **Y-11T1**), replacing the 285-shp (213-kW) Huosai-6A piston engines with two higher-powered Pratt & Whitney PT6A-11 turboprop engines, rated at 500 shp (373 kW) each. The more powerful engines enabled the basic Y-11 airframe to be scaled up in diameter and from 39 ft 5 in (12.02 m) to 48 ft 9 in (14.86 m) in length, to provide increased seating for 17 passengers. Other changes from the Y-11 included a 9-in (0.23-m) increase in wingspan, a new supercritical aerofoil section, integral fuel tanks and bonded construction.

Two prototypes and a static test airframe were built, and the Y-12 I made its first flight on 14 July 1982. The two flying models were later modified for geological survey work in the Harbin area. About 30 production models of the Y-12 I were also built, for domestic use. Three further development aircraft followed in 1983. Designated the **Y-12 II** (originally **Y-11T2**), these introduced yet more powerful PT6A-27 turboprops, each flat rated

The 1984-vintage Harbin Y-12 I was built in small numbers and owed much to the earlier Y-11 DHC-6 Twin Otter lookalike.

The Y-12 II differs only slightly from preceding or subsequent versions. It has a simpler wing and a smaller ventral fin.

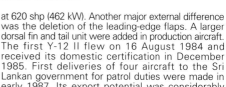

at 620 shp (462 kW). Another major external difference was the deletion of the leading-edge flaps. A larger dorsal fin and tail unit were added in production aircraft. The first Y-12 II flew on 16 August 1984 and received its domestic certification in December 1985. First deliveries of four aircraft to the Sri Lankan government for patrol duties were made in early 1987. Its export potential was considerably improved when it obtained certification from the UK Civil Aviation Authority on 20 June 1990. FAA approval is still being sought. Around 75 Y-12 IIs are believed to have been built by mid-1994. The type has been exported in small numbers to Gabon, Iran, Laos, Malaysia, Mongolia, Sudan, Zambia and Zimbabwe. Five aircraft were delivered to Nepal Airways, but two were quickly lost in 1992 and 1993, the type proving inferior to the airline's DHC-6 Twin Otters in the demanding mountainous operating environment.

Under development is an improved version, under the designation **Y-12 IV**. This will incorporate modifications to the wingtips, control surface actuation, main gear and brakes, rear baggage door, and a redesigned interior for 18 to 19 passengers. Maximum take-off weight would be 12,500 lb (5671 kg). Longer-term plans envisage a stretched version and one with a pressurised cabin.

SPECIFICATION:
Harbin Y-12 II
Powerplant: two 680-shp (507-kW) Pratt & Whitney Canada PT6A-27 turboprops
Accommodation: two (flight deck), maximum of 17 passengers
Dimensions: span 56 ft 7 in (17.24 m); height 17 ft 4 in (5.28 m); length 48 ft 9 in (4.86 m)
Weights: operating empty 6,614 lb (3000 kg); maximum ramp 11,747 lb (5330 kg)
Performance: maximum cruising speed 201 mph (325 km/h); service ceiling 22,965 ft (7000 m); range with maximum passenger load 254 miles (410 km)

Handley Page Herald

Originally designed as a replacement for the immortal DC-3, and powered by four piston engines (600-hp/447-kW Alvis Leonides radials), the **Handley Page Herald** was subsequently reworked with two 2,105-shp (1568-kW) Rolls-Royce Dart 527 turboprops after the 25 August 1955 first flight of the prototype. In making this change, Handley Page recognised the reliability and economy shown by the Dart in the Viscount airliner, and realised that this more than compensated for the simplicity, familiarity and maintainability of the piston engine. The resulting aircraft was very similar to the Fokker F27 in configuration, although it proved slower, but was cheaper and had better short-field performance and better-designed freight doors for loading a truck-bead height.

The prototype was converted to Dart power and reflew on 11 March 1958, with many detail changes. This changed the aircraft's designation from **HPR.3** to **HPR.4**, and led to the revised name of **Dart Herald**.

A 42-in (107-cm) fuselage extension and an increased MTOW led to the **HPR.7 Dart Herald Series 200**, with the original short-bodied aircraft being retrospectively redesignated **Series 100**. Malaysia took eight **Series 400**s with a strengthened floor and a flight-openable door for paratrooping or freight dropping. Proposed jet-engined derivatives, specialist car-carriers and a rear-loading military freighter came to nothing. Fifty Heralds were built, 36 of them Series 200s, before Handley Page went

To Channel Express the Herald is an unrivalled asset, and its ease of operation as a freighter ensures the type will be active for years to come.

into liquidation in 1969. The aircraft served mainly with UK domestic airlines, especially on the Channel Islands routes, but 29 went new to operators in Brazil, Canada, Germany, Israel, Italy, Jordan and the Philippines.

Today the Herald is a rarity. Eight fly as pure freighters with Bournemouth-based Channel Express (six of these having been converted to **'Super Dart Herald'** standard, after an extensive overhaul and the addition of the strengthened floor of the military Series 400), with another aircraft held for spares recovery. The Channel Express aircraft fly flowers and other perishable goods from the Channel Islands to the British mainland, and also fly a wide range of general freight and night mail within the UK and Europe. One more Herald (the only aircraft still flying passengers) flies with Guatemalan operator Aerovias, from its base at Guatemala City airport, where two more Heralds act as spares ships. Compared with some other types the Herald shares the sky with, it is still young. The oldest aircraft is near its 35th birthday and has chalked up over 38,220 flying hours.

South America was one of the islands of Herald activity into the early 1990s. Now, only Guatemala's Aerovias counts the type among its fleet.

SPECIFICATION:
Handley Page HPR-7 Dart Herald 200
Powerplant: two 2,105-shp (1570-kW) Rolls-Royce Dart Mk 527 turboprops
Accommodation: two (flight deck), maximum of 56 passengers
Dimensions: span 94 ft 9 in (28.88 m); height 24 ft 1 in (7.34 m); length 75 ft 6 in (23.01 m)
Weights: operating empty 25,800 lb (11703 kg); maximum payload 11,700 lb (5307 kg); maximum take off 43,000 lb (19505 kg)
Performance: 275 mph (443km/h); service ceiling 27,900 ft (8505 m); range with maximum payload 700 miles (1127 km)

Hawker Siddeley HS 748

The 748 turboprop airliner was the result of a decision by the Avro company to re-enter the commercial market in the late 1950s with a competitor to the Fokker Friendship and a replacement for such types as the DC-3 and Vickers Viking. Early designs envisaged a 20-seat, high-wing aircraft, but this evolved into a larger 36-seat, low-wing model in response to market demand. Known at first as the **Avro 748**, it became the **HS 748** when Avro was absorbed into the Hawker Siddeley Group in 1963, and the **BAe 748** after Hawker Siddeley became part of the new British Aerospace in April 1977. The first of two prototypes took to the air on 24 June 1960, and the type received its certification on 7 December 1961. When production finally closed in 1989, a total of 379 748s had been built both in the UK and under licence by Hindustan Aeronautics Limited (HAL) in India, including 31 military **Andover C.Mk 1**s for the Royal Air Force.

The first production batch was the **Series 1**, which flew on 30 August 1961 and was powered by two Rolls-Royce Dart RDa6 Mk 514 turboprop engines rated at 1,880 shp (1402 kW). The Series 1 also differed from the prototype in having an increased wingspan of 98 ft 6 in (30.04 m). Next came the **Series 2** with higher-rated 1,910-shp (1425-kW) RDa7 Mk 531 engines; later 2,105-shp

LIAT (Leeward Islands Air Transport), the Antiguan flag carrier, flies four 44-seat HS 748 Series 2As from its base at Antigua-V.C. Bird International.

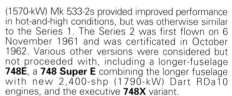

The HS 748 has served in a variety of roles, but one of the most spectacular is this Turbine Tanker firebomber conversion produced for Macavia.

(1570-kW) Mk 533-2s provided improved performance in hot-and-high conditions, but was otherwise similar to the Series 1. The Series 2 was first flown on 6 November 1961 and was certificated in October 1962. Various other versions were considered but not proceeded with, including a longer-fuselage **748E**, a **748 Super E** combining the longer fuselage with new 2,400-shp (1790-kW) Dart RDa10 engines, and the executive **748X** variant.

The Series 2 was superseded by the **Series 2A** with uprated Darts for improved performance. First flown on 5 September 1967, the 2A introduced two versions of the Dart: the 2,280-shp (1700-kW) RDa.7 Mk 535-2 (originally designated 532-2S), and the 2,230-shp (1663-kW) Mk 534-2 (originally 532-2L). Most of the Series 2 models were modified to the 2A standard. As part of a continual updating process, the company developed the **Series 2B**, which made its first flight on 22 June 1979. New features included the latest Mk 536-2 engines with the same rating as the Mk 535-2 but had improved single-engined performance, a 4-ft (1.22-m) increase in wingspan, modified tail surfaces, an optional hush-kit and interior enhancements. The final variant was the **Super 748**, based on the 2B but with a completely new flight deck, Mk 552 engines with hush-kit and water-methanol injection.

SPECIFICATION:
BAe (Hawker Siddeley) Super 748
Powerplant: two 2,280-shp (1700-kW) Rolls-Royce Dart RDa7 Mk 552 turboprops
Accommodation: two (flight deck), with a maximum of 58 passengers
Dimensions: span 102 ft 6 in (31.24 m); height 24 ft 10 in (7.57 m); length 67 ft (20.42 m)
Weights: operating empty 27,060 lb (12278 kg); maximum ramp 46,500 lb (21098 kg)
Performance: maximum cruising speed 280 mph (452 km/h); service ceiling 25,000 ft (7620 m); range with maximum payload and typical reserves 1,155 miles (1865 km)

Hawker 800 and 1000

USA (UK)
Twin-engined medium- to long-range business jets

The family of business jets known as the Hawker 800 and 1000 are the latest variants of a long line of aircraft that began life as the **de Havilland D.H.125 Jet Dragon**. The D.H.125 was designed to succeed the popular Dove in the executive transport market and featured a pressurised cabin for six to eight passengers. The moderately-swept wing gave good range performance, and power came from a pair of Rolls-Royce Viper 20 turbojets. The tailplane was set high up the fin to keep it out of disturbed air. The prototype flew on 13 August 1962. Soon after, de Havilland became part of Hawker Siddeley and the aircraft was redesignated the **HS 125**.

Initial **Series 1** production accounted for eight aircraft, followed by 77 **Series 1A**s (the A suffix being for North American aircraft) and **1B**s (the B for customers in the rest of the world), these featuring uprated engines. Twenty **Series 2**s were built for the RAF as the **Dominie T.Mk 1**. Production continued with 39 **Series 3**, **3A** and **3B**s, powered by Viper 522s and with numerous refinements. The 36 **3A-RA**s and **3B-RA**s had longer range. Following was the **HS 125-400**, with uprated engine, standardised cabin for seven passengers and flight deck improvements. A total of 116 was sold.

On 21 January 1971 the first **HS 125 Series 600** flew. This introduced a 3-ft 1-in (0.95-m) fuselage stretch to seat eight in executive layout or 14 in high-density seating, and Viper 601-22 engines. Production of this model amounted to 72, before

The 15-seat long-range Hawker 1000 (formerly the BAe 125-1000) is the latest version of a design that first flew in 1962.

the **Series 700** was introduced. This marked a major change, as it introduced Garrett AiResearch TFE731 turbofans, offering dramatically improved performance. A total of 215 was built, followed by the **Series 800** with many improvements including a 'glass' cockpit and curved windscreen. This variant offers non-stop, American coast-to-coast or transatlantic performance. By then, the aircraft was known as the **British Aerospace BAe 125-800**.

In response to the challenge of the Falcon 50 and 2000, BAe developed the **BAe 1000**, based on the 125-800 but with a 2-ft 9-in (0.84-m) fuselage stretch, greater cabin height, Pratt & Whitney Canada PW305 turbofans and extra fuel for true intercontinental range. First flown on 16 June 1990, initial deliveries began in December 1991.

In 1993 BAe sold its Corporate Jets division to Raytheon (which also owns Beech) and the two production 125s were renamed **Hawker 800** and **Hawker 1000**. In September 1994 the US firm announced that it was suspending production of the 1000 and would soon move the 800 line to the United States, closing Hatfield and Chester in the UK.

The Hawker 800 (or BAe 125-800) has proved to be the most popular of the 125-derived family, with sales now exceeding 200.

SPECIFICATION:
Hawker 800
Powerplant: two 4,300-lb (19.13-kN) Garrett TFE731-5R-1H turbofans
Accommodation: two (flight deck), maximum of 14 passengers
Dimensions: span 51 ft 4½ in (15.66 m); length 51 ft 2 in (15.60 m); height 17 ft 7 in (5.36 m)
Weights: empty 14,720 lb (6676 kg); maximum take-off 27,400 lb (12430 kg)
Performance: maximum cruising speed 525 mph (845 km/h); service ceiling 43,000 ft (13100 m); maximum range with maximum payload 3,305 miles (5318 km)

IAI Westwind and Astra

Twin-engined, medium- to long-range biz-jets

Another executive jet with a convoluted history, the Westwind/Astra family was originally a design of the Aero Commander company and known as the **Model 1121 Jet Commander**. First flying on 27 January 1963, the aircraft had a mid-mounted wing, pod-mounted General Electric CJ610 turbojets, high-set tail and a pressurised cabin for up to eight passengers. Production aircraft had a lengthened fuselage compared to the prototype.

In 1967 Rockwell, which was Aero Commander's parent company, acquired North American, which produced the Sabreliner. US anti-trust laws forbade Rockwell having two business jet production lines, so the Jet Commander programme was sold to Israel Aircraft Industries.

IAI initially produced an unchanged Jet Commander, but introduced the **1121A** with more fuel and the **1121B** with uprated engines. The **1123 Commodore Jet** followed, with a lengthened fuselage to accommodate 10 passengers. The first 1123 flew on 28 September 1970, and was later renamed the **Westwind 1123**. Like most executive jets, the design was reworked with fuel-efficient turbofans (Garrett AiResearch TFE731) as the **Westwind 1124**. Minor improvements led to the **1124 Westwind 1**, with optional extra fuel tank in the forward baggage compartment, and a military

The Westwind II was the final version of the Jet Commander family built by IAI and was distinguished by its tip-tank-mounted winglets.

From the Westwind family, IAI developed the sleek Astra biz-jet. It has gone on to offer the improved Astra SP and the latest Astra IV.

version (**1124N Sea Scan**) was also produced. On 24 April 1979 the first prototype of the **1124 Westwind 2** made its maiden flight, this version featuring an all-new 'Sigma' wing with drag-reducing winglets and various seating options for seven to 10 passengers. Like its predecessors, the Westwind 2 sold well in the United States, production ending in 1987 in favour of the **1125 Astra**.

The new aircraft retained little of the 1124, although it emerged with some similar features, such as the tail and engine pods. The 'Sigma 2' wing was low-set and swept back, and the new cabin was much deeper to allow for standing room. The first flight was made on 19 March 1984, and the aircraft soon demonstrated outstanding range performance. Power comes from Garrett TFE731-3A-200G turbofans. In 1989 IAI announced the **Astra SP**, an improved version with Collins digital autopilot and EFIS 'glass' cockpit, new interior and further refined aerodynamics.

In the early 1990s, IAI was working on the **Astra IV**, an enlarged version with wings based on those of the Astra but having winglets. This aircraft has a wider, deeper fuselage for use in either the eight-passenger executive transport role or as a 19-seat feederliner, a rapid-change interior being one of the features. The first flight was expected in late 1994.

SPECIFICATION:
IAI 1125 Astra
Powerplant: two 3,700-lb (16.46-kN) Garrett TFE731-3A-200G turbofans
Accommodation: two (flight deck), standard layout for six passengers
Dimensions: span 52 ft 8 in (16.05 m); length 55 ft 7 in (16.94 m); height 18 ft 2 in (5.54 m)
Weights: empty 13,225 lb (6999 kg); maximum take-off 23,500 lb (10659 kg)
Performance: maximum cruising speed 533 mph (858 km/h); maximum operating altitude 45,000 ft (13715 m); maximum range with four passengers and reserves 3,241 miles (5215 km)

The **Ilyushin Il-18 'Coot'** was designed to meet an Aeroflot requirement for a medium-range transport aircraft for at least 75 passengers, and for operations from primitive unpaved airfields. It featured a conventional low-wing monoplane configuration with a pressurised circular fuselage and retractable tricycle landing gear. The prototype, named 'Moskva', first flew on 4 July 1957, powered by four wing-mounted Kuznetsov NK-4 turboprop engines that each developed 4,000 shp (2983 kW). The five development aircraft in a trials batch of 20 were also fitted with the NK-4, while others had the refined Ivchenko AI-20K with the same rating. Aeroflot put the type into service on routes from Moscow to Adler and Alma Ata on 20 April 1959.

The Ivchenko powerplant was adopted as standard on subsequent aircraft, beginning with the **Il-18B**. Maximum take-off weight was also increased from 126,100 lb (57200 kg) to 130,514 lb (59200 kg) and the cabin rearranged to seat up to 84 passengers. The Il-18B gave way in 1961 to the **Il-18V**, which differed primarily in a revised interior layout for 90 to 100 passengers. This required repositioning of some cabin windows. Further development work resulted in the **Il-18I**, put into production in 1964 as the **Il-18D**. This new version introduced the more powerful AI-20M turboprop engines, rated at 4,250 shp (3170 kW) and increased fuel capacity through the installation of extra fuel cells in the centre-section to add an additional 1,386 Imp gal (6300 litres). In

Operating from Warsaw-Okecie airport, Polnippon cargo is a joint Japanese/Polish-funded company that flies a pair of former Interflug Il-18Ds.

addition, an extensive internal redesign involved the moving aft of the pressure bulkhead, deletion of the rear cargo hold and increase of the passenger capacity to 110. In the summer months, this could be increased to 122 by removing the coat stowage space required in the winter period. The extra fuel provided the aircraft with a long-range capability, serving Aeroflot in the interim period before the arrival of the turbofan-powered Il-62, and found success in the export market. The **Il-18E**, produced in parallel, was identical except for the absence of the additional fuel cells. Both versions entered service with Aeroflot during 1965.

Retired from mainline service, the Il-18 proved useful in a cargo role and remains in limited service. The cargo modifications are distinguished by a large rear cargo door and strengthening of the floor. Production finished in 1970 and is believed to have totalled around 800 units. The demand for secondhand aircraft is strong and over 70 Il-18s are in regular service, chiefly as freighters, in Eastern Europe, the former Soviet Union, the Middle East and Far East.

A single passenger-configured Il-18D, once flown by Air Mauritanie, is operated by Vietnam Airlines (formerly Hang Khong Viet Nam) from Hanoi.

SPECIFICATION:
Ilyushin Il-18D
Powerplant: four 4,250-shp (3170-kW) Ivchenko AI-20M turboprops
Accommodation: five (flight deck), with a maximum of 122 passengers
Dimensions: span 122 ft 8 in (37.40 m); height 33 ft 4 in (10.17 m); length 117 ft 9 in (35.90 m)
Weights: operating empty 77,140 lb (35000 kg); maximum take-off 141,056 lb (64000 kg)
Performance: maximum cruising speed 418 mph (675 km/h); range with maximum payload and reserves 4,025 miles (6500 km)

Ilyushin Il-62

Russia
Four-engined medium- to long-range airliner

The **Il-62 'Classic'** was developed as a long-haul jetliner for Aeroflot's International Directorate, primarily as a replacement for the turboprop-powered Tu-114. With its T-tail and pairs of side-by-side turbofans mounted on each side of the rear fuselage, the Il-62 was of a configuration broadly similar to Britain's VC-10. AL-7 turbojet-engined prototypes flew from January 1963, while production aircraft, powered by 22,273-lb (99-kN) NK-8-4 turbofans, were built at Kazan and entered service in March 1967. In high-density configuration, the Il-62 seated 72 in the forward cabin and 114 in the rear, separated by the galley. Seats were six abreast, split into threes by the central aisle.

The availability of the new Soloviev D-30KU engine allowed a redesign as the **Il-62M**, with a new fuel tank in the fin, clamshell-type thrust reversers, and completely new avionics. The cabin was redesigned to seat up to 174, and the aircraft incorporated containerised underfloor baggage and cargo holds. First flying in 1970, the Il-62M entered Aeroflot service during 1974.

Further improvement of the Il-62 design resulted in the **Il-62MK**, externally indistinguishable from the Il-62 but with a completely restressed structure and a redesigned low-pressure undercarriage allowing take-off at higher weights. Payload was

Dwindling numbers of Il-62s survive with Eastern European airlines. Despite the advent of the A310, TAROM is one of those still flying the type.

Aeroflot still relies on the Il-62M and Il-62MK for its long-haul services, as the Il-86 is too short-legged and other types are not available in quantity.

increased from 25.4 tons (23 tonnes) to 27.6 tons (25 tonnes) and the cabin was completely redesigned, with provision for up to 195 seats, despite a wider aisle and overhead luggage lockers.

A total of 244 Il-62s of all types had been delivered when production finally ended in 1990, many having been updated with a triplex INS and new engine nacelles that reduce noise and emissions. The break-up of the USSR has led to the replacement of many Il-62s by more efficient, newer Western wide-bodies like the A310 and Boeing 767, but retired Il-62s often find new customers. For example, Il-62s withdrawn by LOT and Interflug have been eagerly snapped up by Air Ukraine and Uzbekistan Airways.

The type remains in use with Aeroflot Russian International Airlines, especially on longer-range routes and for VIP flights, for which some are modified with extra communications equipment in an extended dorsal spine. Il-62s (for which there is a strong second-hand market) remain in use with a variety of new airlines created after the break-up of the USSR. Elsewhere, Il-62s and Il-62Ms serve in Angola (TAAG), Cuba (Cubana), the Czech Republic (CSA, Ensor Air and Georgia Air), North Korea (Air Koryo, formerly Chosonminhang Korean Airways) and Romania (TAROM).

SPECIFICATION:
Ilyushin Il-162M
Powerplant: four 24,250-lb (107.9-kN) Soloviev D-30KU turbofans
Accommodation: five (flight deck), with 186 passengers standard
Dimensions: span 141 ft 9 in (43.20 m); height 40 ft 6¼ in (12.35 m); length 174 ft 3½ in (53.12 m)
Weights: operating empty 157,520 lb (71600 kg); maximum take-off 363,760 lb (165000 kg)
Performance: maximum cruising speed 571 mph (920 km/h); range with maximum payload and typical reserves 4,846 miles (7800 km)

Ilyushin Il-76

The **Il-76 'Candid'** was developed to meet a joint Aeroflot/air forces' requirement for a long-range heavy freighter/transport to replace the piston-engined Antonov An-12. Of T-tailed, high-wing configuration, with four turbofan engines in underslung pods, the aircraft was of similar layout to the US Lockheed C-141. The aircraft's military role dictated the use of a low-pressure landing gear and a modestly swept wing to ensure good short-field/semi-prepared runway capability. The aircraft has a weather radar in the nose and a mapping radar below it, but is also provided with a glazed navigator's compartment (especially useful in military paradropping missions and for tactical off-airways navigation). The aircraft has a cargo floor made up of titanium panels, with overhead hoists of 2.8- and 3.3-ton (2.5- and 3-tonne) capacity and with provision for optional rollers in the floor. In an improvement over the An-12, the entire fuselage is pressurised.

The prototype Il-76 made its maiden flight on 25 March 1971, and has been followed by a number of variants. The higher-payload **Il-76T** introduced extra fuel tankage in the centre-section, as did the military **Il-76M**, which also has ECM equipment, provision for chaff/flare dispensers and a gun turret in the tail, with two GSh-23L twin-barrelled machine-guns. Large numbers of 'military' Il-76s have been delivered to Aeroflot.

Introduction of the D-30KP-2 turbofan with better hot-and-high performance resulted in the civil **Il-76TD** and the military **Il-76MD**, each of which had

The Il-76T is the civilian 'Candid', with no gun turret. Surprisingly few of this version have been exported, one customer being Syrianair.

greater fuel capacity, higher payload and higher MTOW. A new variant with CFM56 turbofan engines is under development, as is the stretched **Il-76MF**, which is intended to use Russian Aviadvigatel PS-90AN turbofans. Specialised fire-fighting (**Il-76DMP**), inflight-refuelling (**Il-78 'Midas'**) and AEW (**A-50 'Mainstay'**) versions have also been produced. Production of all variants by mid-1994 totals more than 700.

Large numbers of Il-76s were delivered to Aeroflot and the military VTA, and with the break-up of Aeroflot into separate companies the type has gained a large number of new operators in addition to Aeroflot's old International and Cargo Directorate. Outside the former Soviet Union, the Il-76 remains in service with a number of civil and military operators. Cubana has a pair of Il-76MDs, North Korea has three more, and Syrianair operates four Il-76Ms. Iraq's sizeable fleet is believed to have been largely grounded. Although it remains on the Russian civil register, one Il-76 is operated by Britain's Heavylift Air Cargo as a rapid-response transport for oil spills at sea.

The Il-76's military origins are underlined by the tail turret of the Il-76M, as seen on this Iraqi Airways example. Some aircraft have this position faired over.

SPECIFICATION:
Ilyushin Il-76T
Powerplant: four 26,455-lb (117.7-kN) Soloviev D-30KP turbofans
Accommodation: five (flight deck)
Dimensions: span 165 ft 8 in (50.5 m); height 57 ft 7 in (17.5 m); length 181 ft 7 in (55.3 m)
Weights: maximum payload 88,185 lb (40000 kg); maximum take-off 374,784 lb (170000 kg)
Performance: maximum level speed 528 mph (850 km/h); range with maximum payload and typical reserves 2,265 miles (3650 km)

Ilyushin Il-86 and Il-96

Intended as a successor to the Il-62 on Aeroflot's international routes, the **Il-86 'Camber'** was developed in response to the Boeing 747, and intended to be broadly equivalent, despite the fact that the USSR had no high bypass ratio turbofan engines. Originally designed as a wide-bodied Il-62, retaining the same T-tail and engines but redesigned with a conventional low-set tailplane and with new Kuznetsov NK-86 engines in underwing pods, the prototype Il-86 made its maiden flight on 22 December 1976. The extra power of the NK-86 allowed fuel capacity and MTOW to be increased. The Il-86 has two decks, with passengers carrying on their own luggage and coats, stowing them on the lower deck, before climbing upstairs to be seated. The type entered service in December 1980, but proved seriously deficient in range, resulting in the Il-62 remaining in service in large numbers for use on the longest-distance routes. Maximum accommodation is for up to 350 passengers (nine abreast) with twin aisles. Over 100 have been built.

Although it is outwardly similar to the Il-86, the **Il-96** is in every respect a new aircraft. Intended to overcome the deficiencies of the Il-86, the new aircraft introduced PS-90A turbofans, a new supercritical wing of greater span and slightly reduced sweep, and featured improved structure and mate-

The 'prestige' Il-86 was rushed in to service to coincide with Moscow's 1980 Olympics, but its performance since has been far from medal winning.

The Il-96 is intended to remedy the Il-86's shortcomings, and the prototype Il-96-300 has been modified to serve as the improved Il-96M testbed.

rials to give lower weight and longer life. New avionics and systems are provided, including a triplex fly-by-wire control system. Internal fuel capacity is doubled by comparison with the Il-86, while reduced drag also contributes to the new aircraft's dramatically increased range. The lower deck of the Il-96 is purely for cargo and luggage, and passengers enter only at cabin level. The basic production version seats up to 300 passengers and was designated **Il-96-300**, but the mixed-class layout that is normally used actually seats 235. The prototype made its maiden flight on 29 September 1988, and was converted to serve as the prototype of the stretched, 350-seat **Il-96MO** (originally designated **Il-96-350**), reflying in its new configuration on 6 April 1993. An **Il-96MK** with ducted engines is projected, while a freighter version of the Il-96MO is designated **Il-96T**. The **Il-90** is the designation of a study for a twin-engined derivative intended for short-range, high-density routes, which might be powered by Rolls-Royce Trent or Pratt & Whitney PW2337 engines. The **Il-96-550** would be a further-stretched 550-passenger aircraft with twin decks.

The Ilyushin Il-86 and Il-96 are in service with Aeroflot International Airlines and several Il-86s have been leased out particularly to airlines involved in Hadj pilgrimage charters.

SPECIFICATION:
Ilyushin Il-96-300
Powerplant: four 28,660-lb (127.5-kN) Kuznetsov NK-86 turbofans
Accommodation: five (flight deck), with a maximum of 350 seats
Dimensions: span 157 ft 8 in (48 m); height 51 ft 10 in (15.8 m); length 195 ft 4 in (59.4 m)
Weights: maximum take-off 458,560 lb (208000 kg)
Performance: maximum cruising speed at 36,000 ft (11000 m) 590 mph (950 km/h); range with maximum payload and typical reserves 2,235 miles (3600 km)

Jetstream 31 and 41

Twin-engined feederliner and regional airliner

The present **Jetstream** began as a Handley Page design for a 12/20-seat commuter aircraft, the **HP.137** – this was destined to become the last aircraft that the company built before its demise in 1969. The first of five prototypes, powered with Turboméca Astazou XIV turboprops, made its maiden flight on 18 August 1967. Other engines were tried, but 35 production aircraft with Astazous had been completed by 27 February 1970. Rights to the Jetstream were acquired by Scottish Aviation, which built 26 navigation-training versions for the RAF. The final version was the **Jetstream 200** with 969-shp (723-kW) Astazou XVID engines, and several earlier models were variously modified in the USA.

Following the incorporation of Scottish Aviation into the newly-established British Aerospace Group on 1 January 1978, BAe announced that it would relaunch the aircraft as the **Jetstream 31**. In its reincarnated form, with two 940-shp (701-kW) Garrett TPE331-10UF turboprops, new advanced-technology propellers and systems, revised cockpit layout and redesigned interior, the Jetstream 31 first flew on 18 March 1982. First deliveries were made to German airline Contactair on 15 December 1982, following UK certification the previous June. In addition to the 18-seat commuter versions, corporate and executive shuttle variants with nine- and 12-seat layouts, respectively, were available.

The first **Jetstream Super 31**, also referred to as the **Jetstream 32**, was certificated on 7 October 1988. This new variant provided significant

Even though sales of the Jetstream 31 series have slowed in recent times, it remains an effective and versatile commuter airliner.

improvements in performance and passenger comfort, derived from more powerful 1,020-shp (760-kW) TPE331-12UAR engines giving better hot-and-high performance, recontoured interior providing greater cabin width at head height, and reduced noise and vibration. By mid-1994, a total of 381 Jetstream 31s had been delivered. Plans for a stretched version came to fruition on 24 May 1989, when British Aerospace announced the go-ahead for the **Jetstream 41**. Although it retained the same fuselage cross-section, it had a 16-ft (4.88-m) longer fuselage to accommodate up to 29 passengers. Other major differences included 1,500-shp (1119-kW) TPE331-14GR/HR engines, a lowered wing to provide more baggage space and integral airstairs in the forward door. Flight testing began on 25 September 1991. Jetstream Aircraft, based at Prestwick, became a subsidiary of BAe, and is responsible for all Jetstream manufacture and marketing. A corporate Jetstream 41, fitted out in a 14-seat business shuttle configuration, took to the air on 18 May 1994. By mid-1994, 21 of 28 Jetstream 41s ordered had been delivered.

British Midland became the latest UK Jetstream 41 operator in May 1994, with the arrival of a leased aircraft from its sister company, Manx Airlines.

SPECIFICATION:
Jetstream 41
Powerplant: two 1,500-shp (1119-kW) AlliedSignal (Garrett) TPE331-14GR/HR turboprops
Accommodation: two (flight deck), with a maximum of 29 passengers
Dimensions: span 60 ft 5 in (18.42 m); height 18 ft 10 in (5.74 m); length 63 ft 2 in (19.25 m);
Weights: operating empty 14,040 lb (6370 kg); maximum ramp 23,110 lb (10485 kg)
Performance: maximum cruising speed 340 mph (547 km/h); service ceiling 26,000 ft (7925m); range with maximum payload and typical reserves 680 miles (1098 km)

Jetstream 61

Twin-engined regional airliner

British Aerospace announced on 1 March 1984 its intention to develop a larger advanced turboprop (**ATP**) regional transport, to succeed the Super 748. This, however, was not a new idea, Avro having considered various options, in its **748E** and **748 Super E** projects, some 20 years earlier. The ATP retains the same cabin cross-section of the Super 748, but has a longer fuselage to accommodate seating for 64 passengers in a standard configuration, with up to 72 seats possible. New fuel-efficient 2,150-shp (1604-kW) Pratt & Whitney Canada PW124 turboprop engines, driving slow-turning propellers with six composite blades, were later replaced by the more powerful 2,388-shp (1780-kW) PW126A model. Other major changes included the installation of the latest systems and equipment, comprising electrical, hydraulic, environmental control, carbon brakes and an advanced flight deck incorporating an electronic flight instrument system (EFIS) with four cathode-ray tube (CRT) displays. The ATP also introduced separate forward and rear passenger doors, with integral airstairs in the forward door, and separate forward and rear baggage doors.

The prototype ATP flew for the first time on 6 August 1986 and obtained its certification in March 1988. British Midland Airways became the first to

Manx Airlines is part of the Airlines of Britain Group and increased its own ATP fleet, to 14, by taking over aircraft from Scottish regional Loganair.

Indonesia's Merpati operates five ATPs alongside a varied fleet comprising DHC-6s, C-212s, CN-235s, F27s, F28s, Fk100s, DC-9s and L100s.

put the type into revenue service on 9 May that same year. In spite of good operating economics and the fact that sound measurements have shown the ATP to be the quietest aircraft in its class, its slow speed and early technical reliability problems have kept sales sluggish. By mid-1994, production at Prestwick had come to a virtual halt, with all 65 ordered aircraft delivered, though British Airways ordered one further aircraft that year.

The first production **Jetstream 61** took to the air on 11 May 1994. This is a major development in a last-ditch attempt to restimulate interest in the ATP and features more powerful Pratt & Whitney PW127D engines, each developing 2,750 shp (2051 kW) and providing improved airfield performance, especially in hot-and-high conditions. A completely new interior with new-style seats, better underseat stowage and larger overhead bins will considerably enhance passenger appeal. Certification is expected in the third quarter of 1994, with first deliveries soon after.

A go-ahead decision on the proposed 50-seat **Jetstream 51** and the 72-seat **Jetstream 71** is unlikely to be made before 1995 and is dependent on British Aerospace finding a suitable risk-sharing partner. This partner will probably come from the Asia/Pacific region.

SPECIFICATION:
Jetstream 61 (ATP)
Powerplant: two 2,388-shp (1,781-kW) Pratt & Whitney PW126A turboprops
Accommodation: two (flight deck), with a maximum of 72 passengers
Dimensions: span 100 ft 6 in (30.63 m); height 24 ft 11 in (7.59 m); length 85 ft 4 in (26.00 m)
Weights: operating empty 31,385 lb (14240 kg); maximum ramp 50,692 lb (23000 kg)
Performance: maximum cruising speed 305 mph (493 km/h); range with maximum payload and typical reserves 660 miles (1065 km)

LET 410 and 610

The **LET 410** (LET Akciová Spolecnost – LET aeronautical works) made its first flight on 16 April 1969, as the **XL-410**. While awaiting new Motorlet turboprop engines, the prototype and early models were fitted with 715-shp (533-kW) Pratt & Whitney PT6A-27s driving Hamilton Standard three-bladed props. Known as the **L-410A**, the first revenue service with Slov-Air in late 1971. One of the four prototypes became the **L-410AB** when tested with Hartzell four-bladed propellers. One **L-410AF** was built for Hungary in 1974 with a revised glazed nose for aerial survey work. A photo version was known as the **L-410FG**. A Soviet avionics fit produced the **L-410AS**.

When the Motorlet (Walter) engines became available, the **L-410M** entered production and was put into service in 1976. This model differed only in the installation of the 550-shp (410-kW) M 601A turboprop, but the L-410M soon gave way to the **L-410MA**, introducing M 601Bs rated at 730 shp (554 kW). The **L-410MU** was an MA specifically for Aeroflot, seating up to 17 passengers. The **L-410UVP**, first flown on 1 November 1977, introduced a number of major changes to comply with new Soviet airworthiness regulations and stringent Aeroflot requirements that required operations in temperatures of -50 to +45°C. Major external differences were an increased wingspan and tail area, dihedral tailplane, spoilers and new flaps. Soviet certification was obtained in 1980, and most of the 495 L-410UVPs produced went to Aeroflot.

Czech-based Skoda Air, which has just announced an order for Saab 340s, currently operates four LET 410s (including this L-410UVP-E8) from Pilsen.

The improved **L-410UVP-E**, earlier designated **L-410E** and **L-420**, with five-bladed Avia propellers, wingtip tanks and more powerful 750-shp (559-kW) M 601E engines, made its first flight on 30 December 1984 and entered Aeroflot service in 1985. Various suffixes denoted VIP, paramilitary, photomapping and other uses. The L-420 designation has been resurrected in a proposed export version with new M-601F engines.

More than 1,000 L-410s have been produced to date, but LET is now concentrating on the larger 40-seat **L-610**, initially denoted the **L-410G** and developed from the mid-1980s to an Aeroflot requirement. With the collapse of the Soviet market, progress has been slow. Similar in appearance, the L-610 is an entirely new design with a pressurised cabin, auxiliary power unit and 1,822-shp (1358-kW) M-602 turboprops. It first flew on 28 December 1988. With an eye on the Western market, LET produced the **L-610G** in a joint venture with General Electric. This version, powered by two 1,745-shp (1300-kW) General Electric CT7-9D turboprops, first flew on 18 December 1992.

The L-410 was delivered in large numbers to the former Soviet Union. Other countries' airlines, such as Guatemala's Tikal Jets, also took some.

SPECIFICATION:
LET L-410UVP-E
Powerplant: two 750-shp (559-kW) Motorlet (Walter) M 601E turboprops
Accommodation: one or two flight crew and up to 19 passengers
Dimensions: span 63 ft 11 in (19.48 m); height 19 ft 1 in (5.83 m), length 47 ft 4 in (14.4 3 m)
Weights: operating empty 9,171 lb (4160 kg); maximum ramp 14,154 lb (6420 kg)
Performance: maximum cruising speed 236 mph (380 km/h); service ceiling 23,125 ft (7050 m); range with maximum payload and typical reserves 339 miles (546 km)

Learjet 23, 24 and 25

William P. 'Bill' Lear's **Learjet** family has its origins in Switzerland in 1955, when the Swiss air force rejected the indigenous **FFA P-1604** single-seat fighter. Already fabulously wealthy, having founded Motorola and the Lear Siegler Corporation, Bill Lear had retired to Switzerland in the late 1950s with a track record of executive aircraft conversions (such as the Lockheed Lodestar to Learstar modification) behind him. In 1959 he picked up the P-1604 design and began preliminary development of a new executive jet derivative at St Gallen.

Christened the **Swiss-American Aircraft Corporation (SAAC) Learjet 23**, the company moved work to Wichita, Kansas, where the first aircraft flew on 7 October 1963. The type's high speed and striking good looks, plus the fact that it could be flown by a single pilot (not to mention its lower price), ensured success in the face of competition from aircraft such as the Falcon 20. The 43-ft 3-in (13.18-m) Learjet 23 was a five/seven-seat aircraft, powered by a pair of 2,850-lb (12.68-kN) General Electric CJ610-4 turbojets (though the first 30 relied on lower-powered CJ610-1s). Initially, several Learjet 23s were lost, leading to a series of modifications to improve its demanding handling characteristics.

Now named the Lear Jet Corporation, in 1965 the manufacturer began work on a similar but heavier

The Learjet 25D was fitted with quieter CJ610-8A engines and a new wing to improve its take-off and low-speed performance.

Original short-bodied Learjet 23s (Gates' 'pocket rocket') are becoming increasingly rare but, as over 350 were built, many remain in the USA and Mexico.

second model that would seat up to eight passengers and fly at a higher cruising altitude. The **Learjet 24** first flew on 24 February 1966. It was followed by the up-engined **Learjet 24B** and longer-range **Learjet 24D**, which was the first aircraft to do away with Learjet's trademark bullet fin fairing and to introduce square windows. A lightweight **Learjet 24D/A** was succeeded by the **Learjet 24E** and **Learjet 24F**, both of which boasted refined interiors and aerodynamics, while the latter had additional fuel for further increased range.

In 1966 the company was renamed Lear Jet Industries but, in April of the following year, was taken over by the Gates Rubber Company, becoming the Gates Learjet Corp. 1966 also saw the first major development of the basic design, the stretched, 10-seat **Learjet 25**. First flying on 12 August 1966, the improved **Learjet 25B** and longer-range **Learjet 25C** came next. In 1976 a new cambered wing led to the **Learjet 25D** and **Learjet 25F**. Every version still relied on the CJ610 engine. The Learjet 25 led to the **Learjet 28** and **Learjet 29 Longhorn**, the first wingletted Learjets (although they shared the same cabin size as the Learjet 25, they are more fully described under the Learjet 55 entry). Between 1964 and 1982, 105 Learjet 23s, 255 Learjet 24s and 368 Learjet 25s were delivered.

SPECIFICATION:
Learjet 24F
Powerplant: two 2,850-lb (12.68-kN) General Electric CJ610-8A turbojets
Accommodation: two (flight deck), with a maximum of eight passengers
Dimensions: span 35 ft 7 in (10.85 m); height 12 ft 3 in (3.73 m); length 43 ft 3 in (14.18 m)
Weights: operating empty 7,064 lb (3204 kg); maximum take-off 15,000 lb (6804 kg)
Performance: maximum speed 549 mph (884 km/h); service ceiling 51,000 ft (15545 m); range with four passengers and typical reserves 1,584 miles (2549 km)

Learjet 35, 36, 31 and 45

USA

Twin-engined medium- to long-range biz-jets

Increased competition and the availability of newer, more economical and quieter turbofan engines lead Gates Lear Jet to introduce the most popular development of the family so far. The eight-seat **Learjet 35** was a stretched (by 13 in/33 cm) Learjet 25 with a slightly larger wing. The complimentary **Learjet 36** was a six-seat, longer-range version with more fuel for a transatlantic crossing. Both were powered by a pair of Garrett TFE731-2 turbofans. After a test programme involving re-engined Learjet 25s, the first Learjet 35 flew on 22 August 1973. Certification was gained the following year. As with previous models, development of an improved wing brought new versions, the **Learjet 35A** and **Learjet 36A** – the latter with a further increased MTOW of 18,000 lb (8162 kg). Many special variants have been developed for military duties such as target-towing, electronic warfare and photo/maritime reconnaissance. The USAF is a substantial Learjet 35A operator, flying 85 aircraft as the **C-21A**. The Learjet 36 has been hugely outsold by the Learjet 35, as most operators do not require its five-hour endurance. In 1976 golfer Arnold Palmer set a new round-the-world speed record in a Learjet 36, covering 22,984 miles (36990 km) in 57 hours, 25 minutes and 42 seconds. In mid-1994, the Learjet 35A/36A remain in production, with over 740 sold (including 66 Learjet 35s, 17 Learjet 36s and 46 Learjet 36As).

By the mid-1980s, Gates Lear Jet was in serious financial trouble and looking for a buyer. Several failed deals and changes of factory location led to

The 10-seat Learjet 31, seen here in its current Lear 31A form, is an advanced Lear 35/36 replacement readily identified by its winglets and rear delta fins.

the acquisition in 1990 of the firm by Canada's Bombardier, and a new name of Learjet Inc.

This change in fortunes ensured the future of the **Learjet 31**, which first flew on 11 May 1987. Wedding the wing of the Learjet 55 to the Learjet 35 fuselage, this longer-range aircraft was still powered by TFE731s but featured distinctive delta fins beneath the tail. Capable of carrying two crew and seven passengers over 1,911 miles (3076 km), it was superseded, in 1991, by the current-production, EFIS-equipped **Learjet 31A** that cruises at Mach 0.81, and by the longer-range (1756 miles/ 2826 km) **Learjet 31A/ER**. By mid-1994, 85 of all versions had been delivered.

The latest short- to medium-range Learjet is the **Learjet 45**, which first flew on 7 October 1995. This 10/12-seat design, based on the Learjet 31 and unveiled in 1992, offers much improved efficiency courtesy of its newly developed AlliedSignal 3,500-lb (15.57-kN) TFE731-20 turbofans and NASA-designed wing. Shorts, another Bombardier subsidiary, is supplying components. Joint JAR/FAA certification and first deliveries are due in late 1996.

Sales of the best-selling Lear 35A and 36A are still steady, if small, and far in excess of its successor, the Learjet 31 series.

SPECIFICATION:
Learjet 35A
Powerplant: two 3,500-lb (15.65-kN) AlliedSignal (Garrett) TFE731-2-28 turbofans
Accommodation: two (flight deck), with a maximum of eight passengers
Dimensions: span, over tip tanks 39 ft 6 in (12.04 m); height 12 ft 3 in (3.73 m); length 48 ft 8 in (14.83 m)
Weights: empty, equipped 10,119 lb (4590 kg); maximum take-off 18,300 lb (8300 kg)
Performance: maximum speed Mach 0.81; service ceiling 41,000 ft (12500 m); range with four passengers and typical reserves 2,528 miles (4069 km)

Learjet 55, 55C and 60

The origins of the wingletted Learjets lie in the development by Gates Lear Jet of the NASA-designed, supercritical 'Longhorn' wing in the late 1970s. This new wing (so called because its Whitcomb winglets resembled the horns of Longhorn cattle) was applied to the Learjet 25D-derived, 10-seat **Learjet 28**, which first flew on 21 August 1978, and to the eight-seat **Learjet 29 Longhorn**, which traded passengers for extra fuel. Both aircraft proved unpopular; they were too small and too expensive for their performance benefits to be of any use. Only five and two, respectively, had been built by 1982. Mating the wing with a new stretched fuselage (and Lear Jet's first 'stand-up' cabin) resulted in the **Learjet 55 Longhorn**.

The 10-seat Learjet 55 first flew on 19 April 1979, powered by 3,700-lb (16.65-kN) TFE731-3-100B turbofans. Two other models – the **Learjet 54** (smaller) and **56** (larger) – were later abandoned. Certification and first deliveries were achieved by April 1981. The seven-seat, long-range **Learjet 55LR** featured a fuel capacity of some 1,141 US gal (4319 litres), while the **Learjet 55XLR** was an even longer-range version with a total of 1,231 US gal (4569 litres) of fuel. An improved-performance, glass-cockpit-equipped **Learjet 55B** was introduced in September 1986. One year later the **Learjet 55C**

The Learjet 55C combined all the features of the Lear 55 Longhorn with a pair of distinctive rear delta fins. Production ended in December 1990.

The medium-range Learjet 60 is the largest Learjet ever built, with a wide cabin, gold-film-covered windscreen and a Collins ProLine 4 EFIS cockpit.

appeared, with its distinctive rear delta fins, the first time these had appeared on any Learjet design. The fins improved directional stability and did away with the need for a 'stick pusher' by reducing the type's landing speed. The **Learjet 55C/LR** was fitted with additional tankage in the tailcone and could cover 2,361 miles (3800 km), while the **Learjet 55C/ER** boasted even longer range by adding yet more fuel. Production of all Learjet 55s ended in 1992, with a 147 delivered.

A replacement for the Longhorns has come in the form of the **Learjet 60**, which first flew (as a proof-of-concept airframe) on 18 October 1990. This aircraft was powered by a Garrett TFE331-3A and a Pratt & Whitney Canada PW305 engine, with the latter chosen as the production powerplant. The first production standard aircraft flew on 13 June 1991. The Learjet 60 is the largest Learjet ever built and features the now standard winglets and delta fins, a Collins-equipped EFIS cockpit and a wide (5-ft 11-in/1.80-m), well-equipped, stand-up (5-ft 7½-in/1.71-m) cabin. Thrust reversers and a 'steer-by-wire' nosewheel are standard. Certification was obtained on 15 January 1993 and deliveries began almost immediately. By mid-1994, 27 aircraft had been delivered to customers, chiefly in the United States but also in Brazil, Turkey and Switzerland.

SPECIFICATION:
Learjet 60
Powerplant: two 4,600-lb (20.46-kN) Pratt & Whitney Canada 305 turbofans
Accommodation: two (flight deck), with a maximum of nine passengers
Dimensions: span 43 ft 9 in (13.38 m); height 14 ft 8 in (4.47 m); length 58 ft 8 in (17.88 m)
Weights: empty, equipped 13,922 lb (6315 kg); maximum take-off 22,750 lb (10319 kg)
Performance: maximum speed 533 mph (858 km/h); maximum operating altitude 51,000 ft (15545 m); range with typical reserves 3,155 miles (5078 km)

Lockheed L-100 Hercules

When Lockheed flew the first **YC-130A Hercules** (actually the second aircraft to be completed) at Burbank on 23 August 1954, few could have guessed quite what an important aircraft was making its first steps. So unorthodox was its boxy and uncompromising shape (which had been designed and built in secret) that one company onlooker could only remark, "well, it's got a great paint scheme." The Hercules has gone on to become the definitive tactical military airlifter and in 1993 passed the 2,000 sales mark. From the outset, Lockheed was not blind to the type's commercial potential and worked hard to sell it to US airlines.

In 1959 Lockheed announced the sale of 12 **GL-207 Super Hercules** to Pan American, followed by six for Slick Airways, all for delivery in 1962. Powered by four Allison T61 engines, the Super Hercules was to be 23 ft 4 in (7.11 m) longer than the then production standard **C-130B**. Versions with alternative powerplants, even jet engines, were proposed, but the GL-207 was cancelled, leaving the standard military Hercules as the only version available. Commercially designated **L-100**, the first civil Hercules (**Lockheed Model 382**) made its 25-hour record maiden flight on 20/21 April 1964. Twenty-one production aircraft (**Model 382B**) were sold in the USA. The first commercial operator was Alaska Airlines, from March 1965.

Next came the stretched **L-100-200 (Model 382E)**, which was 8 ft 4 in (2.54 m) longer than its predecessor. This model entered service with Interior

Southern Air Transport has a fleet of 15 L-100s (the world's largest), which is active worldwide on a multitude of charters for a variety of customers.

Airways on 11 October 1968. Thirty-four were completed, including nine L-100 conversions.

The main commercial Hercules variant entered service in 1970 with Saturn Airways and is still in production. The **L-100-30 (Model 382G)** Hercules is stretched by an additional 6 ft 8 in (2.03 m), which accords it a fuselage volume of 6,057 cu ft (171.5 m³). The stretched Hercules have all attracted military orders, and the line between the legitimate civil and clandestine (even outright) military operations of some users has at times been more than blurred. A total of 112 L-100s has been delivered by mid-1994 (including 67 L-100-30s), of which 31 have been lost – some of these shot down or destroyed by groundfire.

For the Saudi Air Force/Saudia Special Services division, Lockheed built five **L-100-30HS** hospital aircraft that boast X-ray and intensive care facilities, operating theatres and fully independent electrical generators. The future of the L-100 lies with the **Advanced L-100** that will incorporate the advances of the 'new-generation' **C-130J**, including its Allison GMA 2100 turboprops.

Since 1981 Air Algerie has flown a pair of L-100-30s on freight operations from its base at Algiers. The Algerian air force is a Hercules operator also.

SPECIFICATION:
Lockheed L-100-30 Hercules
Powerplant: four 3,362-ehp (4508-kW) Allison 501-D22A (T56-A-15) turboprops
Accommodation: three (flight deck)
Dimensions: span 132 ft 7 in (40.41 m); height 38 ft 3 in (11.66 m); length 112 ft 9 in (34.37 m)
Weights: empty 77,736 lb (35,260 kg); maximum payload 51,054 lb (23,158 kg); maximum take-off 155,000 lb (70,308 kg)
Performance: maximum level speed 355 mph (571 km/h): service ceiling 33,500 ft (10,200 m): maximum range, with maximum payload 1,536 miles (2472 km)

Lockheed L188 Electra

In 1954 American Airlines issued a specification for a turboprop-powered airliner, with a greater passenger capacity than the Vickers Viscount, for its short- to medium-haul domestic routes. The Viscount was winning substantial orders in the US at that time and Vickers, along with Lockheed, bid for the new design. Lockheed's attempts proved unsuccessful at first, but in 1955 American revised its requirement and Lockheed got the go-ahead for the 75/100-seat **L188A Electra**. That same year saw the launch of the Boeing 707 and DC-8. In addition to American's interest, Lockheed secured a second launch order from Eastern Airlines for a combined total of 75 Electras.

The Electra was the first turboprop airliner to be built in the United States, and the prototype aircraft took to the air on 19 May 1958. Deliveries commenced to Eastern Airlines in October, with services beginning the following year. Two versions were available: the L188A and **L188C**, with additional fuel. This was a period just prior to the arrival of first short- to medium-range jets, and many operators believed that aircraft like the Electra would be more economical to run, in any case, so orders mounted. However, the 'prestige' to be had in operating jets, and the fact that they could operate profitably, whittled away the Electra's market.

Perhaps the last scheduled passenger operator of the Electra is Reeve Aleutian Airways, which flies three aircraft from Anchorage-International.

Channel Express is one of several modern UK Electra freighter operators, carrying everything from car parts to the Royal Mail.

More damaging was a series of accidents that occurred in the L188's first 15 months of operations when an American aircraft, then a Braniff example and finally a Northwest Airlines' Electra all crashed. Modifications undertaken to the propellers and engine nacelles cured the dangerous resonance problems, but the L188's fate was sealed and production abruptly ceased in January 1961 as orders disappeared. Production ended at just 170 aircraft, including 55 L188Cs.

From 1968 the Lockheed Aircraft Service Co. began to modify Electras as freighters (**L188AF** and **L188CF**) with reinforced floors and cargo doors on one or either side of the fuselage. Too late, several airlines (such as Eastern) realised what a great design the Electra was, as its early problems never resurfaced and the survivors continued to provide sterling service into the 1980s and even the 1990s. VARIG's famous airbridge between Rio de Janeiro and São Paulo ended in favour of Boeing 737s in 1992, leaving the bulk of approximately 70 remaining Electras in cargo operation. Sizeable populations of L188s are now active in Africa, Europe and the United States, chiefly in the hands of overnight freight carriers who appreciate the type's ability to carry a load superior to that of many jets, without any of the latter's noise restrictions.

SPECIFICATION:
Lockheed L188AF Electra
Powerplant: four 3,750-ehp (2800-kW) Allison 501D-13A turboprops
Accommodation: three (flight deck)
Dimensions: span 99 ft (30.18 m); height 32 ft 10 in (10 m); length 104 ft 6 in (31.81 m)
Weights: empty 27,895 lb (61500 kg); maximum payload 26,500 lb (12020 kg); maximum take-off 116,000 lb (526648 kg)
Performance: maximum cruising speed 405 mph (652 km/h); service ceiling 27,000 ft (8230 m); maximum range, with max payload 2,200 miles (3540 km)

Lockheed L1011 TriStar

Three-engined medium- to long-range airliner

Joining battle in what would become dubbed the 'wide-body war' of the late 1960s and early 1970s, the Lockheed-California Company answered a requirement from American Airlines for a twin-engined aircraft to serve on its Los Angeles-Chicago route. Lockheed launched the three-engined, medium-haul **L1011 TriStar** on 1 April 1968 with orders for 144 aircraft, although none came from American. As the first TriStar began assembly at Palmdale, the project was badly affected by Lockheed's severe financial difficulties caused by the C-5 Galaxy military airlifter. Then, in 1971, the sole engine supplier, Rolls-Royce, collapsed. New engines could not be accommodated by the design and the TriStar was saved only when Rolls-Royce was effectively nationalised and the RB 211 turbofan was saved from oblivion.

Despite this, the first **L1011-1 TriStar** flew on 16 November 1970, and Eastern flew the first service on 26 April 1972. One hundred and sixty of this version were built until 1983, though 119 of these were sold between 1973 and 1975. Essentially a US domestic version, the L1011-1 (**TriStar 1**), was followed by the higher gross weight **L1011-100 TriStar**, with additional fuel improving its range by 20 per cent. The first of these was delivered to Cathay Pacific in 1975. In 1974 Saudi placed orders for the **L1011-200**, a hot-and-high TriStar powered by RB211-524 engines. Twenty-four L1011-200s were built, followed by 14 conversions. British Airways inspired the final production version, the

Air Transat is Canada's largest charter airline and operates four TriStar 150s and a single TriStar 100 from Montreal-Mirabel, in Quebec.

L1011-500 TriStar. A long-range development to compete with the DC-10-30 that had won substantial orders, the L1011-500 was powered by RB211-524B engines. The **TriStar 500** is shorter than previous aircraft – 164 ft 2 in (50.09 m) compared to 177 ft 8½ in (54.17 m) – and has a greater wingspan. TriStar production ceased in 1983 at a total of 249 (with some unsold aircraft), the majority still in regular airline service.

Lockheed began to offer a series of conversions for existing aircraft. Beginning in 1981, 28 L1011-1s became **L1011-50**s through an increase in maximum weight from 430,000 lb (195048 kg) to 450,000 lb (204120 kg). A small number of **L1011-150** conversions were undertaken, increasing the range of a Tristar 1 by 10 per cent, slightly better than the marginally transatlantic TriStar 50. In 1986 Delta Airlines pioneered the **L1011-250** conversion. This substantially increases the TriStar 1's MTOW and refits more powerful RB211-524 engines. Apart from military conversions undertaken for the RAF, attempts at building a commercial TriStar freighter have not yet proved successful.

Illustrating the ties that still exist between Angola and Portugal, TAAG Angola Airlines flies this 250-seat L1011-500 leased from TAP Air Portugal.

SPECIFICATION:
Lockheed L1011-500 TriStar
Powerplant: three 50,000-lb (222.5-kN) Rolls-Royce RB211-524B4 turbofans
Accommodation: three (flight deck), maximum of 315 passengers (standard 280)
Dimensions: span 164 ft 6 in (50.09 m); height 55 ft 4 in (16.87 m); length 164 ft 2½ in (50.05 m)
Weights: operating, empty 245,400 lb (111312 kg); maximum take-off 510,000 lb (231330 kg)
Performance: cruising speed 595 mph (959 km/h); service ceiling 43,000 ft (13100 m); maximum range, with maximum fuel 7012 miles (11286 km)

McDonnell Douglas DC-8

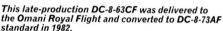

This late-production DC-8-63CF was delivered to the Omani Royal Flight and converted to DC-8-73AF standard in 1982.

One of the great civil aircraft manufacturers, the Douglas Aircraft Coprporation (which was taken over by McDonnell in 1967), launched its first jet age competitor, the **DC-8**, in 1955. Boeing was already well advanced with its Model 707 (Dash 80) and, as a result, the DC-8's launch order (from Pan Am) in October 1955 had to be split with the rival Boeing aircraft. The first Pratt & Whitney JT3C-6 turbojet-powered **DC-8-10** made its maiden flight, at Edwards AFB, on 30 May 1958. The first aircraft entered service with United Airlines and Delta Air Lines on 18 September 1959. The 150-ft 6-in (45.9-m) DC-8-10 was offered as the **DC-8-11** and **DC-8-12** with increased weights and wing modifications.

On 20 November 1958 Douglas flew the first **DC-8-21**, powered by JT4A-9 engines. A far more important version was the DC-8-30 family, an intercontinental development of the Series 20. The first aircraft flew on 21 February 1959. Both the **DC-8-31** and **DC-8-32** featured increased MTOWs, while the **DC-8-33** had modified flaps and JT4A-11/12 turbojets. Rolls-Royce Conway RCO.12 engines replaced Pratt & Whitney units on the **DC-8-40**, which was delivered to Air Canada, Alitalia and Canadian Pacific from 1960.

Turbojets were replaced by JT3D turbofans in the **DC-8-50**s. Combined with the DC-8-21 airframe,

Many passenger-configured DC-8s are still in use. Miami-based Rich International flies a trio of 189-seat DC-8-62s and this 250-seat DC-8-63.

this resulted in the DC-8-51, which first flew on 20 December 1960. Five versions were eventually produced, including the **DC-8-52, -53, -54** and **-55** with a range of JT3D engines and MTOWs. In 1961 Douglas announced the **DC-8F Combi (DC-8-54CF)** freighter, followed by an all-freight **DC-8-54AF**.

With the **DC-8-60**, Douglas stretched the original airframe by 36 ft 8 in (11.2 m). The first **DC-8-61** flew on 14 March 1966 and was followed by the **DC-8-62** (a DC-8-50 stretched by only 3 ft 3 in/1 m and a more efficient wing) and long-range **DC-8-63** (a DC-8-61 with a much improved wing). Combi (CF) and all-freight (AF) versions were made available, in addition to a passenger freighter (**PF**) stressed for future cargo operations but not initially fitted with a cargo door. DC-8 production ended in May 1972 after 556 aircraft had been completed.

Since then, 110 DC-8-60s have been re-engined with CFM56 turbofans (by Cammacorp) to produce the **DC-8-70** family. Converted aircraft retain their original sub-type, so a re-engined DC-8-63AF becomes a DC-8-73AF. Italy's Aeronavali Venezia has undertaken many freighter conversions. UPS is fitting its DC-8s with EFIS cockpits. A number of hush-kits are available for the type, ensuring the current fleet of approximately 250 DC-8-5-/-60/-70s will remain active for many years.

SPECIFICATION:
McDonnell Douglas DC-8-73CF
Powerplant: four CFM International CFM56-2-C5 turbofans
Accommodation: three (flight deck)
Dimensions: span 148 ft 5 in (45.20 m); height 43 ft (13.11 m); length 187 ft 5 in (57.12 m)
Weights: operating, empty 141,100 lb (64000 kg); maximum payload 94,000 lb (58410 kg); maximum take-off 355,000 lb (161025 kg)
Performance: maximum cruising speed 551 mph (887 km/h); service ceiling 36,000 ft (10972 m); maximum range, with maximum payload and reserves 5,561 miles (8950 km)

McDonnell Douglas DC-9 Twin-engined short- to medium-range airliner

The search for a smaller companion for the DC-8 led the Douglas Aircraft Company to first propose a four-engined aircraft, two-thirds the size of a DC-8, before scaling back their plans even further to arrive at the **Model 2086** of 1962. Delta Air Lines placed the first orders for this twin-engined type, now known as the DC-9, in April 1963. The initial model of the DC-9, the **DC-9-10**, was 104 ft 5 in (31.85 m) long, powered by a pair of Pratt & Whitney JT8D-7 turbofans and able to seat up to 109 passengers; it first flew on 25 February 1965. Two main sub-variants were built, the **DC-9-14** and **DC-9-15** (both with progressively increased MTOWs). Cargo versions included the **DC-9-15MC** (multiple change) and **DC-9-15RC** (rapid change), the latter with a roller floor allowing quick changes in configuration.

Eastern Airlines launched the advanced **DC-9-30** in February 1965, the same month the DC-9-10 flew. The fuselage was increased by 9 ft 6 in (2.92 m), with a 4-ft (1.2-m) increase in wingspan. The first example flew on 1 August 1966 and deliveries began to Eastern in February 1967. This proved to be the most popular DC-9 variant (661 built) and appeared in several versions. The **DC-9-31** and **DC-9-32** were increased maximum weight aircraft, (usually) powered by JT8D-7 and -9 engines, respectively. Freighter versions included the **DC-9-32LWF** (lightweight freight), which retained full passenger capability, the **DC-9-32CF** (convertible freighter) with no cargo door for small package use, and the windowless **DC-9-32AF** (all freight).

The vast majority of active DC-9s (of which there are approximately 740) serve in the USA. Hawaiian Air maintains a fleet of nine DC-9-51s.

In 1966 SAS asked McDonnell Douglas to produce a version that could operate from short runways. The result was the **DC-9-21**, which combined the fuselage of the DC-9-10 with the wing of the DC-9-30 and two uprated JT8D-11 turbofan engines. The first aircraft flew on 18 September 1968, and 10 were built for SAS alone. At the same time (1966), SAS also ordered the **DC-9-40**, which first flew on 28 November 1967. A high-density, short-range version, the DC-9-40, was further stretched by 6 ft 2 in (1.88 m), and could seat up to 128. Seventy-one were built.

Swissair launched the final 'original' DC-9, the **DC-9-50**. This was stretched by 8 ft (2.43 m) to seat up to 139 passengers, and featured new brakes and redesigned thrust reversers. Ninety-six of this version were completed (from a total of 976 DC-9s) by April 1981, when McDonnell Douglas moved on to the 'Super Stretch' **DC-9-80** (**MD-80**), described separately. McDD is currently trying to raise enough airline interest to proceed with the multiphased **DC-9X** upgrade, featuring hush-kits, a new EFIS cockpit and even potential re-engining.

The DC-9 is still an important part of many European airline fleets, albeit in smaller numbers now. Alitalia flies 29 107-seat DC-9-32s.

SPECIFICATION:
McDonnell Douglas DC-9-30
Powerplant: two 14,500-lb (64.4-kN) Pratt & Whitney JT8D-15 turbofans
Accommodation: two (flight deck), maximum of 115 passengers (standard 105)
Dimensions: span 93 ft 5 in (28.47 m); height 27 ft 6 in (8.38 m); length 119 ft 3½ in (36.37 m)
Weights: operating, empty 57,190 lb (25940 kg); maximum take-off 121,000 lb (54885 kg)
Performance: max cruising speed, at 25,000 ft (7620 m) 563 mph, (907 km/h); max cruising altitude 35,000 ft (10670 m); max range, with 80 passengers 1,923 miles (3095 km)

McDonnell Douglas DC-10

USA
Three-engined long-range airliner

The USAF's 1965 CX-HLS programme brought the **DC-10** into being. McDonnell Douglas refined a proposal for a 650-seat aircraft to suit the same 250-seat market (and proposed American Airlines requirement) at which the TriStar was aimed. The DC-10 was launched in February 1968 with 50 orders, soon increasing to over 100.

The first **DC-10-10** flew on 29 August 1970, with to United and American Airlines in August. Essentially for the US domestic market, 122 DC-10-10s, including combi **DC-10-10CF** freighters with side cargo doors, were built – 87 of these in the first four years of production. Up to 380 passengers can be carried. The DC-10-10 is powered by three CF6-6D engines, and has a fuselage length of 182 ft 3 in (55.5 m). Pratt & Whitney JT9D-20s featured on the next version, the **DC-10-40**, at the insistence of Northwest Orient. The longer-legged DC-10-40 first flew on 28 February 1972, and 42 went to Northwest Orient and JAL (with JT9D-59A engines).

In 1969 KLM, Swissair, SAS and UTA (the KSSU Group) launched the penultimate production DC-10, the long-range **DC-10-30**. Developed alongside the DC-10-40, the DC-10-30 first flew on 21 June 1972 and entered service on Swissair's transatlantic routes on 15 December. Operating at higher weights the DC-10-30 has an additional undercarriage

'Mont Ngaliema' was Air Zaïre's sole DC-10-30, flying alongside two Boeing 737-200Cs and a DC-8 freighter from Kinshasa-Ndiji airport.

Since 1983, this DC-10-30 has been Ghana Airway's flagship, flying chiefly on the airline's services from Accra to London-Heathrow.

leg on the centreline, an increased wingspan and more powerful engines. The next chapter in the DC-10 story was an unpleasant one, when the type was grounded after an accident involving an American Airlines DC-10-10 at Chicago in June 1979. The FAA took the unusual move of withdrawing the type certificate and the DC-10's reputation suffered undeservedly. A small number of extended-range **DC-10-30ER**s were delivered from 1982 to 1988, with extra fuel and CF6-50C2Bs. Seven aircraft were later converted to this standard. Twenty-eight **DC-10-30CF** freighters were built, in addition to nine all-cargo **DC-10-30AF**s, primarily for Federal Express.

The final version was the hot-and-high **DC-10-15**, powered by General Electric CF6-50C2Fs and ordered by Mexicana and Aeromexico. Only seven were built. Plans for a stretched wingletted **DC-10-60** series lead to the MD-11. McDonnell Douglas won orders from the USAF for 60 **KC-10A Extender** tanker/transports (between 1978 and 1982), ensuring that DC-10 production continued into the late 1980s. Two Martinair DC-10s have been acquired by the Dutch air force for conversion to military tanker/transport standard in 1995. The last aircraft off the line was a DC-10-30 delivered to Nigerian Airlines in 1989, the 266th Series 30 and the 446th KC-/DC-10. Approximately 360 are still in service.

SPECIFICATION:
McDonnell Douglas DC-10-30
Powerplant: three General Electric CF6-50A/
-50C/-50C1/-50C2/-50C2B turbofans, rated
between 49,000 lb (218 kN) and 54,000 lb (240 kN)
Accommodation: three (flight deck),
maximum of 380 passengers (standard 300)
Dimensions: span 165 ft 4 in (50.40 m); height
58 ft 1 in (17.70 m); length 182 ft 1 in (55.50 m)
Weights: operating, empty 267,197 lb (121198 kg);
maximum take-off 572,000 lb (259450 kg)
Performance: cruising speed 564 mph (908 km/h);
service ceiling 33,400 ft (10810 m); maximum
range, with maximum fuel 7490 miles
(12055 km)

McDonnell Douglas MD-80

McDonnell Douglas realised that the 'stretch' potential of the DC-9 had only begun to be tapped with the -30 and -50. Further improved Pratt & Whitney JT8D turbofans, coupled with intense customer interest, prompted the study of new larger versions, perhaps fitted with a supercritical wing. Designations such as the **DC-9-60**, **DC-9-55RSS** (Refanned Super Stretch) or **DC-9-55** lead to the **DC-9-80**, launched in August 1977. The 147-ft 10-in (44.8-m) long aircraft was so named to reflect its proposed in-service date (1980), and early customers included Swissair (15 orders, five options) and Austrian Airways (eight orders, four options).

From the outset, the DC-9-80 was offered as a family with three specific sub-types. The **DC-9-81** was the basic 135-seat, JT8D-209-powered aircraft, which first flew on 18 October 1979. First deliveries commenced to Swissair on 13 September 1980. Announced in April 1979, the **DC-9-82** was powered by higher-thrust JT8D-217s, for hot-and-high operations or improved payload/range in normal conditions. The DC-9-82 made its maiden flight on 8 January 1981, and the first deliveries were made to Aeromexico in August 1981.

In June 1983 McDonnell Douglas dropped its illustrious DC (Douglas Commercial) prefix in favour of the current MD designation. Thus, the DC-9-80 family became the **MD-80** family: the **MD-81** and **MD-82**. This meant that the third development of the standard MD-80, launched in January 1983, rapidly became the **MD-83**.

Reno Air is a recent addition to American skies, operating a fleet of 17 140-seat MD-82s and MD-83s from its Nevada home.

Featuring increased range, and more powerful JT8D-219 engines, the MD-83 came with two additional fuel tanks fore and aft of its centre-section. Its floor and wings, along with the landing gear, have all been modified to cope with the extra weight. The first MD-83 flew on 17 December 1984 and deliveries commenced to Alaska Airlines in February 1985.

The next member of the MD-80 family is the short-fuselage (DC-9-50 equivalent) **MD-87**, which was launched in January 1987. Seating between 109 and 130, this aircraft takes advantage of all the structural and avionics improvements of the MD-80 series. The first aircraft flew on 4 December 1986 and the type entered service with Finnair and Austrian Airlines in November 1987.

In answer to an order for 80 aircraft from Delta Air Lines in 1986, McDonnell Douglas produced the **MD-88**. Similar to the MD-82 or -83, this version boasts a full EFIS 'glass' cockpit and was certified by the FAA on 8 December 1987, entering service on 5 January 1988. By mid-1994, 1,113 MD-80s of all versions had been delivered.

The short-fuselage MD-87 is readily identifiable by its revised fintip and tapered tailcone, a redesign now being applied to the larger, later-model MD-80s.

SPECIFICATION:
McDonnell Douglas MD-83
Powerplant: two 21,000-lb (93.4-kN) Pratt & Whitney JT8D-219 turbofans
Accommodation: two (flight deck), maximum of 172 passengers (standard 150)
Dimensions: span 107 ft 10¼ in (32.87 m); height 30 ft 2 in (9.19 m); length 135 ft 6 in (41.30 m)
Weights: operating, empty 79,686 lb (36145 kg); maximum take-off 160,000 lb (72575 kg)
Performance: maximum cruising speed Mach 0.76; maximum cruising altitude 35,000 ft (10670 m); maximum range, with 155 passengers 3,014 miles (4851 km)

McDonnell Douglas MD-11

Three-engined long-range airliner

While outwardly appearing to be a DC-10 derivative, the **MD-11** is an advanced design featuring a new 'wingletted' wing, tail and choice of power-plants. By the late 1970s, McDonnell Douglas was examining ways to stretch and improve the DC-10. Initial proposals for a stretched, rewinged **DC-10-61**, **-62** and **-63** series of varying payload range capabilities were shelved by the recession of the early 1980. The design re-emerged as the **MD-100** in 1982, becoming the **MD-XXX** and finally the **MD-11X**. In July 1985 the MD-11 as its exists today was announced, for delivery in late 1989. Some 18 ft 7 in (5.69 m) longer than the DC-10-30, and powered by either General Electric CF6-80C2 or Pratt & Whitney PW4000 series engines, the MD-11 was formally launched on 30 December 1986 with 92 commitments. Other current versions include the **MD-11Combi** freighter (launch customer Alitalia), the all-cargo **MD-11F** (launch customer Federal Express) and the **MD-11CF** convertible freighter (launched by Martinair Holland).

By the time assembly commenced in March 1988, only 47 firm orders had been received. The programme began to slip, so that the first flight took place eight months behind schedule, on 10 January 1990. This maiden voyage was undertaken by an MD-11F, destined for FedEx. Five aircraft

Like Korean Air, World Airways (based at Charleston, South Carolina) is a long-time DC-10 operator and now flies MD-11s and MD-11Fs.

In January 1991, the first of Korean Air's five PW4460-powered MD-11s entered service. The airline will soon be an A330 operator, too.

took part in the test programme (four GE-powered, one P&W), which saw certification obtained on 8 November 1990. The first delivery was made to Finnair on 29 November 1990, with the MD-11 entering revenue service on the airline's Helsinki-Tenerife route.

From the outset, the MD-11 was unable to meet its design range guarantees. McDonnell Douglas quickly introduced the **MD-11A-1 PIP** (performance improvement programme) on all new-build aircraft from 1993, and available as a refit. This makes changes to the MD-11's overall weight, aerodynamics, fuel capacity and wing slatting, in addition to improved engine performance. An optional belly fuel tank is available, with the result that by the end of 1993 the MD-11 could carry its advertised load some 7,940 miles (12778 km) – still about 100 miles (161 km) less than its design range. Further PIPs are now in the offing.

Future developments will include the **MD-11ER**, announced at the Asian Aerospace show of 1994 as 'the longest-range 300-seat airliner in revenue service' and planned to be available from 1996. Capable of carrying 298 passengers over 8,295 miles (13350 km), the MD-11ER is a direct competitor for the A340-300 and 777B. By mid-1994, McDonnell Douglas had delivered 129 MD-11s.

SPECIFICATION:
McDonnell Douglas MD-11
Powerplant: three Pratt & Whitney 60,000-lb (266.9-kN) PW4460 or 61,500-lb (273.57-kN) General Electric CF6-80C2D1F turbofans
Accommodation: two (flight deck), maximum of 410 passengers (standard 323)
Dimensions: span 169 ft 10 in (51.77 m); height 59 ft 7 in (17.60 m); length 192 ft 5 in (58.65 m)
Weights: operating, empty 288,880 lb (131035 kg); maximum take-off 625,500 lb (283725 kg)
Performance: maximum level speed at 31,000 ft (9449 m), 588 mph (945 km/h); maximum range, with 323 passengers 7810 miles (12566 km) and maximum fuel 7490 miles (12055 km)

McDonnell Douglas MD-90/95 Twin-engined medium-range airliners

Intended as an advanced-technology follow-on to the MD-80 series, the **MD-90** is most notable for its use of IAE V2500 turbofans, in place of the Pratt & Whitney JT8Ds that have powered every DC-9 and MD-80. The new aircraft was launched in November 1989, with an order for 50 from Delta Air Lines and a further 115 on option – these totals have now been revised significantly downwards. McDonnell Douglas has decreed that the aircraft should be referred to as the MD-90, but when dealing with specific sub-types the hyphen is omitted.

The basic **MD90-30** has the same fuselage length as a standard MD-80, with the enlarged tail of the MD-87. It will carry a maximum of 172 and be powered by V2525-D5s. The **MD90-50** is an extended-range version, accommodating fewer passengers (153) but powered by more powerful 28,000-lb (124.55-kN) V2528-D5 engines, developed specifically for the MD90-50. The **MD90-55** will be almost identical to the previous model, but with additional exit doors to allow 187 passengers to be carried.

The first MD-90 flew on 22 February 1993 and two aircraft were engaged in the flight test programme that led to certification in November 1994. Assembly of the first production example began at Long Beach in February 1994, and deliveries should commence to Delta exactly 12 months later. By mid-1994, 141 MD-90s were on order or option, with 35 to be in service by the end of 1995.

Since April 1986 the Shanghai Aircraft Manufacturing Factory (SAMF) has assembled 35

The MD-90 is a stretched MD-80, powered by a pair of new IAE V2525 turbofans in place of the DC-9/MD-80's faithful Pratt & Whitney JT8Ds.

MD-82s and MD-83s for the Chinese airline market. SAMF had previously been manufacturing MD-80 components for McDonnell Douglas, and is poised to play a major part in the MD-90 story. In 1992 both companies announced the signing of the Trunkliner agreement. The **MD90-30T Trunkliner** is specially modified with dual main landing gear for operations from rugged Chinese airfields, and 20 will be built initially, entirely in China, for delivery in 1997. Up to 130 further aircraft are a possibility, for China's rapidly expanding air transport scene.

SAMF was also proposed as the builder of the 95/124-seat **MD-95**, which was launched at the Paris air show of 1991. The project was shelved in favour of securing the MD90T deal, but now McDonnell Douglas is looking for partners outside China to commence development. In March 1994 the 18,500-lb (82-kN) BMW Rolls-Royce BR715 turbofan was chosen as the new powerplant. In July 1994 the formal MD-95 go-ahead was given and the MD-95 was launched in October 1995 with an order from US low-cost carrier Valujet, in the face of stiff competition from Airbus and Boeing.

The MD-95 will combine the short fuselage of the MD-87 (comparable to a DC-9-50) with the wing of the MD-80 and the avionics of the MD-90.

SPECIFICATION:
McDonnell Douglas MD90-30
Powerplant: two 25,000-lb (111.21-kN) IAE V2525-D5 turbofans
Accommodation: two (flight deck), maximum of 172 passengers (standard 153)
Dimensions: span 107 ft 10 in (32.87 m); height 30 ft 7¼ in (9.33 m); length 152 ft 7 in (46.51 m)
Weights: operating, empty 88,200 lb (40007 kg); maximum take-off 156,000 lb (70760 kg)
Performance: maximum cruising speed at 35,000 ft (10670 m), 503 mph (809 km/h); maximum range, with 153 passengers and reserves 2,610 miles (4200 km)

Development of the turbine-powered **Mi-8 'Hip'**, derived from the **Mi-4 'Hound'**, began in 1960. Then known as the **V-8**, the prototype was a much larger helicopter with a single, much more powerful 2,700-shp (2013-kW) Soloviev turboshaft, but retaining the four-bladed main rotor, transmission and tail boom of the Mi-4. The Mi-8 was first seen by the public at the 1961 Soviet Aviation Day display. A second twin-engined prototype flew for the first time on 17 September 1962, and this introduced the standard 1,500-shp (1119k-W) Isotov TV2-117 turboshafts and a five-bladed rotor system adopted in 1966 for the first production aircraft. The 1,700-shp (1268-kW) TV2-117A was fitted later. Production was initiated and is continuing at two locations, the Kazan Helicopter Plant and the Ulan-Ude Aviation Industrial Association.

The Mi-8 is of typical pod-and-boom construction, which provides accommodation for 28 passengers and two or three crew. Without coat stowage, seating can be increased to 32 passengers. Large clamshell doors at the rear facilitate the loading of bulky freight. The basic utility version was the **Mi-8T** for both civil and military use, distinguished by circular windows, aluminium cargo floor, hook-on ramps, electric winch, and optional rescue electric hoist and 24 tip-up seats along the walls. In an ambu-

Large square cabin windows mark this Polish-registered Mi-8 as the passenger transport Salon version, known by its NATO codename of 'Hip-C'.

The Mi-8 and Mi-17 are versatile types in regular commercial service worldwide. These Aeroflot examples wear a non-standard 'high-viz' scheme.

lance role, the Mi-8 can accommodate 12 stretchers and attendant. The **Mi-8P** passenger version differs in having rectangular windows, airstairs in the clamshell doors and comfortably furnished accommodation and toilet for up to 32 passengers. Range is around 215 miles (350 km). A nine/11-seat deluxe version had the designation **Mi-8 Salon**, but is now referred to as the **Mi-8 VIP**.

First displayed at the Paris air show of 1981, the **Mi-17** combined the airframe of the Mi-8 with uprated Isotov TV3-117MT turboshafts as fitted to the Mi-14. With a take-off rating of 1,900 shp (1417 kW), the **Mi-17MT** has much enhanced performance. Various improvements have been incorporated since, and other versions being offered include the latest **Mi-17VM** with two 2,000-shp (1491-kW) TV3-117VM engines to improve hot-and-high performance and payload capacity to 8,816 lb (4000 kg); and the **Mi-171**, which has the same engines and payload, but minor differences. The former is produced by the Mil Moscow Helicopter Plant and the latter by the Ulan-Ude plant. An **Mi-17 Mk 30** upgrade, produced by South Korea's Daewoo, is due to fly in November 1994. The Mi-8MT is also still in production for export customers. Total production of the Mi-8/Mi-17 series is believed to have exceeded 10,000 units by 1994.

SPECIFICATION:
Mil Mi-17VM
Powerplant: two 2,000-shp (1491-kW) Isotov TV3-117VM turboshafts
Accommodation: three (flight deck), with a maximum of 32 passengers
Dimensions: main rotor diameter 69 ft 11 in (21.30 m); height 17 ft 7 in (5.35 m); length 83 ft 2 in (25.30 m)
Weights: empty 15,870 lb (7200 kg); maximum take-off 28,652 lb (13000 kg)
Performance: maximum cruising speed 155 mph (250 km/h); service ceiling 19,686 ft (6000 m); range with maximum payload and reserves 250 miles (400 km)

Mil Mi-26

Russia
Twin-engined heavylift helicopter

Design of the **Mi-26 'Halo'** began in the early 1970s in response to a requirement for a large helicopter for all-weather operations. The specification also stipulated an empty weight half of the take-off weight to maximise its payload capacity, and reliability for operations into unprepared landing sites. The achievement of the required performance parameters was entrusted to two powerful 11,240-shp (8380-kW) Lotarev D-136 turboshaft engines and the first-ever eight-bladed rotor system, with an aluminium rotor hub. The prototype Mi-26 flew for the first time on 14 December 1977, several pre-production models entered operational trials with the Soviet air force in 1983 and the type was fully operational by 1985. India took the first export deliveries in June 1986.

In February 1982, the Mi-26 set a number of impressive payload-to-height records. On 2 February, it lifted a 10000-kg payload to 6400 m, followed the next day by a 25000-kg load to 4100 m and a total 56769 kg to a height of 2000 m. On 4 February, more records were established when lifting a 15000-kg payload to 5600 m and 20000 kg to 4600 m. Everything about the Mi-26 is impressive. It has a massive maximum take-off weight of 123,425 lb (56000 kg) and is capably of lifting a payload of 44,080 lb (20000 kg), both internally or externally. Its cavernous hold is 49 ft 3 in (15.00 m) long, 10 ft 8 in (3.25 m) wide and up to 10 ft 5 in (3.17 m) high, adding up to a volume of 4,273 cu ft (121 m³). The hold is loaded via a hydraulically-actuated

The Mi-26's lifting ability is unrivalled, and underslung loads have ranged from artillery pieces to water-filled fire-fighting 'buckets'.

lower door with folding ramp, and two clamshell upper doors. Two electric overhead hoists with a capacity of 5,511 lb (2500 kg) each enable loads to be shifted along the cabin. In a typical cargo (**Mi-26T**) configuration, the Mi-26 has a crew of five: two pilots, flight engineer, navigator and loadmaster, and a four-seat passenger compartment behind. It can also accommodate 85 combat-ready troops, or up to 100 passengers in a civilian layout (**Mi-26P**).

An uprated **Mi-26M** (Modificatsirovanyi – modified) with substantially improved performance, particularly in hot-and-high conditions, is under development by the Mil Moscow Helicopter Plant. This will have new 14,000-hp (10440-kW) Lotarev D-127 turboshafts, composite main rotors with improved aerodynamics and upgraded flight control/navigation systems. The maximum payload is expected to be increased to 55,100 lb (25000 kg). Fly-by-wire controls could be introduced later. Also projected is a **Mi-26K** flying crane version to replace existing Mi-10s. Estimates of production to date vary, but the most likely figure is around 50 aircraft by 1994.

The Mi-26M, available in freight (Mi-26TM) or passenger (Mi-26PM) models, also forms the basis of a projected fire-fighting version, the Mi-26TZ.

SPECIFICATION: Mil Mi-26
Powerplant: two 11,240-shp (8380-kW) Lotarev D-136 turboshafts
Accommodation: four (flight deck) plus loadmaster and 44,091 lb (20000 kg) of freight or 100 passengers
Dimensions: main rotor diameter 110 ft 8 in (33.73 m); height 38 ft 1 in (11.60 m); length 131 ft 4 in (40.03 m)
Weights: empty 62,307 lb (28270 kg), maximum take-off 123,425 lb (56000 kg)
Performance: maximum cruising speed 158 mph (255 km/h); service ceiling 15,092 ft (4600 m); range with maximum payload and reserves 291 miles (470 km)

NAMC YS-11

Yet another aircraft designed in the hope of replacing the world's DC-3/C-47 fleet, the **NAMC YS-11** was a bold attempt by the Japanese aviation industry to satisfy its own airliner requirements. Launched in 1956, the YS-11 programme combined the talents of six established manufacturers, who were rebuilding their capability after World War II. The Nihon Aeroplane Manufacturing Company (NAMC) was in fact a consortium of Fuji, Kawasaki, Mitsubishi, Nippi, Shin Meiwa and Showa. The resulting aircraft was similar in layout to the Avro 748, with high aspect ratio wings with considerable dihedral, circular pressurised fuselage and Rolls-Royce Darts mounted in nacelles above the wing, the nacelle also housing the main undercarriage units. Where it differed was in being appreciably larger, able to accommodate 60 passengers.

The first YS-11 took to the air on 30 August 1962; the second followed it on 28 December. Japanese certification was awarded on 25 August 1964, while the FAA seal of approval came on 7 September 1965.

From the outset, the design of the YS-11 had been driven by the needs of the large Japanese domestic market, where the size of the aircraft was appreciated by the three major carriers. Toa Airways put the first **YS-11-100** into service on 1

Export sales of the robust YS-11 were hampered because the aircraft was tailored too closely to the needs of its original Japanese customers.

The oldest YS-11s are now approaching their 30th birthday but as many as 140 are still in use, chiefly in Japan and the United States.

April 1965. In May, Japan Domestic Airlines followed (soon to merge with Toa) and then All Nippon in July. Forty-eight YS-11s were built, the hoped-for foreign sales amounting to only seven.

To make the aircraft more attractive to foreign operators, it was redesigned with uprated Dart Mk 542 engines and an increase in payload as the **YS-11A**. The **YS-11A-200** was the most successful model, a 60-seat airliner that sold moderately in America, where Piedmont (22) and Cruzeiro (12) were notable customers. The **YS-11A-300CP** was a mixed passenger/freight carrier, while the **YS-11A-400** was a pure freighter with a rear cargo door that found favour with the Japanese air force. The final variants were the **YS-11A-500, -600** and **-700**, which were similar to the -200, -300 and -400 but had increased take-off weights. Only four -500s and five -600s were built, bringing total production of all variants to 182, the last aircraft being delivered in early 1974.

The YS-11 has proved to be a reliable workhorse and currently the largest fleets are those of the original operators, All Nippon flying seven and Japan Air System (formerly Toa Domestic) around 20. Several also serve with the air arms of Greece and Japan, and with a number of small civilian operators, mainly carrying freight in the USA.

SPECIFICATION:
NAMC YS-11A-200
Powerplant: two 3,060-ehp (2282-kW) Rolls-Royce Dart Mk 542-10K turboprops
Accommodation: two (flight deck), standard layout for 60 passengers
Dimensions: span 104 ft 11¾ in (32.00 m); length 86 ft 3½ in (26.30 m); height 29 ft 5½ in (8.98 m)
Weights: empty 33,993 lb (15419 kg); maximum take-off 54,010 lb (24500 kg)
Performance: maximum cruising speed 291 mph (469 km/h); service ceiling 22,900 ft (6980 m); range with maximum payload 680 miles (1090 km)

Rockwell Sabreliner

Twin-engined short- to medium-range business jet

Inspired by its famed F-86 Sabre fighter, in 1952 North American Aviation (NAA) began work on a twin turbojet-engined transport. Its early studies were rejuvenated when the USAF launched a competition in 1956 for an off-the-shelf transport and training aircraft. North American entered its earlier design as the **N.A.286 Sabreliner** (underlining its links with the F-86) and rolled out the first example on 8 May 1958, at Inglewood. This aircraft made its maiden flight from Palmdale on 16 September, and its successors won substantial orders from the USAF, USN and USMC as the **T-39 Sabre**.

While the first Sabreliners had been built for the military, by 1962 NAA began to turn its attention to commercial versions. The Sabreliner was already certified to CAR 4b jet transport standard, so NAA launched a version essentially similar to the USAF's **T-39A** transport, the **N.A.265**, so the Sabreliner 40 became the **N.A.265-40**. This version had its Pratt & Whitney JT12A-6A engines replaced by 3,300-lb (14.7-kN) JT12A-8 turbojets and featured an additional cabin window (for a total of three).

A single **Sabreliner 50** was built chiefly for test duties with NAA before the stretched **Sabreliner 60** was introduced in 1967. This version could seat 10 passengers and featured five cabin windows on each side. In September 1967 NAA merged with the Rockwell-Standard Corporation, and Sabreliner production became the responsibility of the Sabreliner Division of Rockwell International.

With its larger, bulbous cabin, the Sabre 75A lost some of the original design's sleek lines, but its new turbofan engines were a definite improvement.

On 17 June 1970 the **Sabreliner 70** was certified, with a 'stand-up' cabin, and square windows in place of the original triangular ones. This version was soon redesignated **Sabre 75**, and when mated with new General Electric CF 7002D-2 turbofans became the **Sabre 75A** (initially **Sabre 80**) from 1972. This re-engining greatly improved its sales performance. The final production Sabre was the **Sabre 65**, powered by Garret TFE731-3 engines. This transcontinental version first flew on 8 April 1979 and featured a new supercritical wing developed by the Reisbeck Group, of Seattle.

Reisbeck became heavily involved in modifying Sabres, retrofitting its new wing and 'Mark Five' aerodynamic improvement package to Sabre 75As (as the **Sabre 80A**) and TFE731 engines to the Sabre 60. Rockwell planned the stretched and improved **Sabre 85**, but production finally ceased on 1 January 1982 with a grand total of 441. Approximately 400 of these are still in use. Product support for all Sabreliners/T-39s is now undertaken by the St Louis-based Sabreliner Corporation, which acquired the production rights in 1983.

The Sabre 60 was the most numerous version to roll off the NAA production line, with 146 delivered. It retained the T-39's original triangular windows.

SPECIFICATION:
Rockwell (North American) Sabre 65
Powerplant: two 3,700-lb (16.46-kN) Garrett TFE731-3-D turbofans
Accommodation: two (flight deck), maximum of 12 passengers (nine standard)
Dimensions: span 55 ft 5¼ in (15.37 m); height 16 ft (4.88 m); length 46 ft 11 in (14.30 m)
Weights: empty 13,350 lb (6055 kg); maximum take-off 24,000 (10886 kg)
Performance: maximum speed Mach 0.85; service ceiling 45,000 ft (13715 m); maximum range, with maximum fuel 3351 miles (5393 km/h)

Saab 340

A unique US/European aviation collaboration was announced in January 1980 when Saab-Scania and Fairchild Industries announced a new jointly-developed, 35-seat, twin-turboprop design, the **Saab-Fairchild 340 (SF 340)**. Fairchild undertook to manufacture the wings, tail unit and engine nacelles, while Saab was responsible for 75 per cent of the development costs, systems integration and certification. Essentially an all-metal type, with selective use of composites and a NASA-developed low-drag wing, the SF 340 made its maiden flight on 25 January 1983. The launch customer was Switzerland's Crossair, to whom deliveries began in July 1984.

Two versions were initially on offer, the basic air transport configuration or an executive model. Teething troubles with the General Electric engines which caused inflight shut-downs led to a temporary grounding of the SF 340. These problems were soon rectified and at the 1985 Paris air show the manufacturers announced the next development, an increased MTOW (27,275 lb/12872 kg) version with uprated engines and larger Dowty propellers. This improvement was available for refit also.

Fairchild's ailing financial position forced it to withdraw from the project in October 1985, and production was gradually transferred to Saab's

Northwest Airlink incorporates Saab 340 operator Express Airlines, based at Memphis and Minneapolis, which feeds Northwest services.

*Founded in 1992, French carrier **Regional Airlines** began operations with Saab 340Bs and Jetstream 31s. By late 1994, it operated seven Saab 340s.*

Linköping home. The Swedish company next launched the **Saab 340QC**, a quick-change freighter aircraft, the first of which was sold to Finnaviation in 1987. That same year, as links were finally severed with Fairchild, the SF 340 became the **Saab 340**.

In 1987 Saab announced the **Saab 340B**, the current production version. Featuring higher-powered CT7-9B engines, a larger-span tailplane and a further increased maximum weight, Crossair was again the launch customer. The arrival of the Saab 340B invigorated sales that had slowed to around the 200 mark at that point. A substantial order was won from American Eagle, American Airline's commuter arm, for 100 Saab 340Bs (it already flew the SF 340). On 8 June 1993 the American Eagle's 100th aircraft, the 340th Saab 340, was handed over. By mid-1994, deliveries for the type stood at 355, with an order backlog of 52.

Saab is currently working to improve its hot-and-high and short-field performance by fitting a 1.96-ft (0.6-m) wingtip extension, known as the '1-g stall' modification. This increases the aircraft's take-off weight by 1,200 lb (544 kg), equivalent to six/seven passengers. Advances made in the Saab 2000 cabin design (including the active noise system) can now being applied to all new Saab 340Bs, the 'Generation 3' aircraft dubbed **Saab 340B Plus**.

SPECIFICATION:
Saab 340B
Powerplant: two 1,870-hp (1394-kW) General Electric CT7-9B turboprops
Accommodation: two (flight deck), standard load of 35 passengers
Dimensions: span 70 ft 4 in (9.50 m); height 22 ft 6½ in (6.87 m); length 64 ft 8 in (19.73 m)
Weights: operating, empty 17,715 lb (8035 kg); maximum ramp 28,800 lb (13063 kg)
Performance: maximum cruising speed 325 mph (522 km/h); service ceiling 25,000 ft (7620 m); maximum range, with 35 passengers, baggage and reserves 1,123 miles (1807 km)

Saab 2000

Experience with the Saab 340 convinced the Swedish manufacturer that there was a forseeable market for an advanced, high-speed regional airliner that could only be a turboprop design. Ignoring others attempts at regional jets, Saab laid down the **Saab 2000**. This 50-seat aircraft would be capable of matching jet performance and block times over a range of sectors, and the project was formally launched in December 1988, with an order for 25 (with 25 options) from Switzerland's Crossair.

Saab immediately began to spread the development burden of its new aircraft, entering into agreements with CASA, of Spain, to build the wing, Finland's Valmet to build the tail unit and elevators, and Westland to build the rear fuselage. A Collins Pro-line 4 avionics system was selected and a radical reduction in cabin noise became a major design goal. To this end, Allison GMA 2100 turboprops driving six-bladed propellers were selected. Saab also began work on an active noise reduction system that detects airflow and vibration noise and rebroadcasts an equal, opposite waveform, thus effectively 'switching off' cabin noise.

First metal was cut at Linköping in February 1990, and the prototype flew on 26 March 1992. A four-aircraft test programme was established, with the No. 2 aircraft undertaking much of the high-temperature and adverse weather flying. The third Saab 2000, the first full production standard example, undertook systems and avionics certification trials, while functional reliability was the responsibility of

The Saab 2000 offers a step forward for regional airlines, combining the performance benefits of a jet with the cost benefits of a turboprop.

Saab 2000 No. 4. Early in the programme, all Saab's performance requirements were met or exceeded. Underlining this, a Saab 2000 set a new time-to-climb record of 29527 ft (9000 m) in 8 minutes 8 seconds, bettering that set previously by an E-2 Hawkeye. Maximum cruise speed is well above the promised 360 kt (413 mph; 665 km/h) and in a dive the aircraft has attained 430 kt (493 mph; 794 km/h) with no ill effect.

The certification timetable was set back by problems with the aircraft's high-sped longitudinal stability, and a new Powered Elevator Control System (PECS) had to be initiated in late 1993. The delivery date was thus delayed into the fourth quarter of 1994 – 18 months behind schedule. European certification of the Saab 2000 was received on 31 March 1994, with a redesigned elevator spring tab. The full PECS modification is yet to be completed. FAA certification was achieved on 29 April 1994. Deliveries to Crossair finally began on 30 September 1994, and these will be followed by examples for Deutche BA. By mid-1994, firm orders for the $12.9-million aircraft stood at 36.

Moritz Suter's Crossair, already a firm Saab 340 operator, was the Saab 200 launch customer. Up to 50 of the high-speed Saabs could be acquired.

SPECIFICATION:
Saab 2000
Powerplant: two 4,152-hp (3096-kW) Allison GMA 2100 turboprops
Accommodation: two (flight deck), maximum of 58 passengers
Dimensions: span 81 ft 2¾ in (24.76 m); height 25 ft 4 in (7.73 m); length 88 ft 8¼ in (27.03 m)
Weights: operating, empty 29,762 lb (13500 kg); maximum take-off 48,500 lb (22000 kg)
Performance: maximum cruising speed 442 mph (680 km/h); service ceiling 31,000 ft (9450 m); maximum range, with 35 passengers, baggage and reserves 1,589 miles (2557 km)

Shorts Belfast

The **Short SC.5 Belfast** was designed as a strategic military freighter for the RAF, with a cavernous hold that could accommodate bulkier and more awkward loads than the Boeing 747 or Lockheed C-5 Galaxy, and with a removable 'stub deck' that could be installed in the roof of the hold for mixed freight/passenger duties. Drawing on Short's experience in licence-producing the Bristol Britannia, the company designed a high-winged freighter version, initially dubbed **Britannic**. A stretched centre-section was added (but wings and tail surfaces were still built in Britannia jigs) and the aircraft was formally named Belfast in 1959. Ten were built for the RAF, the first of these making its maiden flight on 5 January 1964, and the type entering service with No. 53 Squadron in 1966.

Short-sighted defence cuts led to a dramatic down-sizing of the RAF's transport fleet, and No.53 Sqn disbanded in 1977, its Belfasts put into storage at Kemble. A sale of all 10 to Pan African (possibly a CIA front company) fell through, but three aircraft continued to be modified for civil use (for Liberian certification) by Eurolatin. The other seven were sold to Rolls-Royce for recovery of their Tyne engines, for use on Aeritalia G.222 military transports – effectively a death sentence, after unsuccessful bids by Transmeridian Air Cargo, Tradewinds and

G-BEPE was the first civilian Belfast, and at its unveiling TAC Heavylift announced the "first aircraft that could carry a Hercules."

Today the Belfast is an asset unique to Stansted-based Heavylift Cargo Airlines, which (ominously) also operates L100s, An-124s and an Il-76.

IAS. One was presented to the RAF Museum by Rolls-Royce, and two were sold to Transmeridian, who had taken over the three Eurolatin aircraft and who became TAC Heavylift and eventually Heavylift Cargo Airlines.

Civil certification proved time-consuming and costly, but the aircraft began earning their keep in March 1980. The Belfasts were soon breaking records for bulk cargo moved by civil aircraft, especially for the oil, gas and mining industries. Flying BAC One-Eleven components to Romania, SEPECAT Jaguar sub-assemblies to India, and transporting components for Boeing 767s were all early jobs. MoD charters during the Falklands War alone reportedly cost the taxpayer more than would the cost of keeping every aircraft on in Royal Air Force service until 1990.

The end of the Cold War and the gradual change of Russia and other former USSR states into market economies has led to a flood of high-capacity transport aircraft (such as the An-22, An-124 and Il-76) and freighters entering the market, and the ageing Belfast has lost its unique selling point, although it continues to represent an extremely low-cost solution to bulk transport requirements. The Heavylift fleet is now down to two of these massive and reliable (if ponderous) giants.

SPECIFICATION:
Shorts S.C.5 Belfast
Powerplant: four 5,730-hp (4273-kW) Rolls-Royce Tyne Rty.12 turboprops
Accommodation: three or four (flight deck) plus a loadmaster
Dimensions: span 158 ft 9 in (48.40 m); height 47 ft (14.33 m); length 136 ft 5 in (41.48 m)
Weights: operating empty 127,000 lb (57606 kg); maximum take-off 230,000 lb (104326 kg)
Performance: maximum cruising speed 352 mph (566 km/h); service ceiling 30,000 ft (9145 m); range with maximum payload and typical reserves 1,000 miles (1609 km)

Shorts 330 and 360

Having perceived an emerging market for a 30-seat commuter aircraft, Shorts began to study a development of its 19-passenger Skyvan. The company decided to base the new aircraft, then known as the **SD3-30**, on the Skyvan. The same square fuselage cross-section, twin tail unit and outer wing panels were used, but the wingspan was increased, as was the fuselage length, and a retractable landing gear replaced the fixed gear of the Skyvan. The Garrett engines were changed to 1,156-shp (862-kW) Pratt & Whitney PT6A-45A turboprops. The first of two prototypes flew on 22 August 1974 and, after receiving UK and US certification, the type entered service with Time Air of Canada on 24 August 1976.

The **Shorts 330**, as it became known soon after, underwent a number of progressive upgrades. The first of these was the introduction of the PT6A-45B after 26 production aircraft, followed by the PT6A-45R with slightly greater power, which allowed a gross weight increase from 22,690 lb (10295 kg) to 22,900 lb (10390 kg). When the fuel capacity was increased in January 1985, the designation was changed to **330-200**. Earlier models then became known as the 330-100. A quick-change version was also available, and for military use Shorts produced the **330-UTT** (utility tactical transport) with a strengthened cabin floor, inward-opening rear door for paradropping, and some structural beefing-up. The **C-23A Sherpa** was basically a cargo version for the US forces.

During the 1980s, the Shorts 360 was a pre-eminent commuter airliner, gaining orders from prestige customers such as American Eagle.

The relaxation of US regulations, which prior to deregulation in 1978 had prohibited commuter airlines to use aircraft with more than 30 seats, led to the **Shorts 336**, distinguished by a lengthened and more streamlined fuselage that permitted six extra seats, a swept-back conventional tail and more powerful 1,327-shp (990-kW) PT6A-65Rs. By the time the prototype made its first flight on 1 June 1981, the aircraft had become known as the **Shorts 360**. The Shorts 360 entered service with Suburban Airlines of Reading, Pennsylvania, on 1 December 1982.

The **360 Advanced**, of 1986, introduced 1,425-shp (1062-kW) PT6A-65ARs. This was followed in 1987 by the final variant, the **360-300**, which featured PT6A-67ARs, an autopilot and substantially enhanced passenger comfort. Previous models were then redubbed the **Shorts 360-100** and **360-200**. By the time production of the 330/360 family ceased in 1991/92, Shorts had produced a total of 139 Shorts 330s, including military variants, and 164 Shorts 360s, although some of these remained unsold and in storage.

Many Shorts 330s now act as freighters, such as this Gill Air example, as the passenger versions are being replaced by more advanced types.

SPECIFICATION:
Shorts 360-300
Powerplant: two 1,424-shp (1062-kW) Pratt & Whitney PT6A-65AR turboprops
Accommodation: two (flight deck) with a maximum of 39 passengers
Dimensions: span 74 ft 9 in (22.80 m); height 23 ft 10 in (7.27 m); length 70 ft 9 in (21.58 m)
Weights: operating empty 17,356 lb (7875 kg); maximum ramp 27,198 lb (12340 kg)
Performance: maximum cruising speed 244 mph (343 km/h); range with maximum payload and typical reserves 460 miles (745 km)

Sikorsky S-61 Sea King

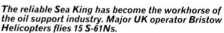

On 24 December 1957, the US Navy issued a contract for a new high-performance helicopter to replace the outdated S-58. Sikorsky submitted a design for a large twin-turbine aircraft with a boat-type hull and retractable undercarriage for amphibious operations. Given the Sikorsky model number **S-61**, the prototype made its first flight on 11 March 1959. This was followed by seven pre-production models, which began trials on 8 February 1961. First deliveries of the **S-61B** (Navy designation **HSS-2**, later **SH-3A Sea King**), for anti-submarine duties, were made in September that same year.

The S-61 was powered by two 1,250-shp (932-kW) General Electric T58-GE-18 turboshafts, driving a fully-articulated all-metal rotor system with five main interchangeable blades that could be folded. The specially-shaped fuselage was sealed to permit emergency landing on water, with the landing gear retracting hydraulically into stabilising floats on each side of the fuselage. The success of the naval trials, which proved the safety, survivability and reliability of the S-61, encouraged Sikorsky to develop a civil transport version. The first to be built was the **S-61L**, a non-amphibious model that first flew in prototype form on 6 December 1960.

The S-61L retained the rotor system of the military S-61s, but without the blade-folding feature.

KLM helicopters took delivery of its first S-61 in 1967 and currently operates six 24-seat S-61Ns from its base at Amsterdam.

The reliable Sea King has become the workhorse of the oil support industry. Major UK operator Bristow Helicopters flies 15 S-61Ns.

Other differences included a fixed landing gear and a longer fuselage to provide accommodation for up to 28 passengers. Powerplant was the 1,350-shp (1007-kW) CT58-140 turboshaft. The S-61L received its type certificate on 2 November 1961 and entered scheduled revenue passenger service with Los Angeles Airways on 1 March 1962.

The **S-61N**, which followed, was generally similar but had a sealed hull for amphibious operations, retractable undercarriage and stabilising floats. It was first flown on 7 August 1962. Later production aircraft introduced more powerful 1,500-shp (1119-kW) CT58-GE-140-1/2 engines, better baggage facilities and damping to reduce rotor-induced vibration. This model was designated **Sikorsky S-61N Mk II** and became highly popular in the offshore market, where it is still used by several operators. Sikorsky also produced a heavy-lift version, known as the **Payloader**. This reverted to a fixed landing gear and had all non-essential fittings and equipment stripped to increase the payload. Production of commercial Sea King versions ceased in June 1980, after the completion of a grand total of 13 S-61Ls and 123 S-61Ns. A potential successor, the General Electric T701-GE-401X-powered **S-92**, was demonstrated to prospective customers but shelved by Sikorsky in 1993.

SPECIFICATION:
Sikorsky S-61N Mk II
Powerplant: two 1,500-shp (1119-kW) General Electric CT58-GE-140-1/2 turboshafts
Accommodation: three (flight deck), with a maximum of 30 passengers
Dimensions: main rotor diameter 62 ft 0 in (18.90 m); height 17 ft 6 in (5.32 m); length 72 ft 10 in (22.20 m)
Weights: empty 12,510 lb (5676 kg); maximum take-off 20,500 lb (9300 kg)
Performance: maximum cruising speed 150 mph (241 km/h); service ceiling 12,500 ft (3810 m); range with maximum fuel and reserves 495 miles (797 km)

Sud-Est S.E.210 Caravelle Twin-engined short- to medium-range airliner

France's **Caravelle** was a pioneering design, the first short- to medium-range jet and the first rear-engined jet to be developed. It began life as a Sud-Est design, the 65/90-seat **X210**, and was launched as the **S.E.210 Caravelle** in January 1953. Rolls-Royce Avon turbojets were chosen and the Caravelle's nose section and cockpit were derived from the de Havilland Comet. The French government-funded prototype first flew, from Toulouse, on 27 May 1955 and soon afterwards the Caravelle attracted its first orders from Air France and SAS. The initial Avon Mk 522-powered **Caravelle I** was delivered the former on 2 April 1959, but entered revenue service with SAS on 26 April. A second version, the **Caravelle IA**, featured Mk 526 engines, but both aircraft shared the same 105-ft (32-m) fuselage and 79-seat layout. Thirty-four Caravelle I/IAs were built.

The second true production type was the **Caravelle III**, which first flew on 30 December 1959. This featured Avon Mk 527s and improved range. Seventy-nine were built and 31 Series I/IAs were later converted to this standard. The **Caravelle VI** was another up-engined development built in two variants. The **Caravelle VIN** was powered by Avon Mk 531 engines, while the **Caravelle VIR** was fitted with Mk 532s or Mk 533s with thrust reversers. The first Caravelle VI flew on 10 September 1960 and 109 were completed.

The **Caravelle 10B** (or **Super B**) of 1965 was a major development replacing the original noisy and

A single 99-seat Caravelle 10B still graces the Swiss register, as Aero Jet maintains a 1964-vintage example in service, flying from Zurich and Geneva.

thirsty engines with Pratt & Whitney JT8D turbofans. This version also had a fuselage stretch of 3 ft 3½ in (1.02 m) to accommodate 109 passengers. Many Caravelle VIRs were brought up to so-called **Caravelle 10R** standard through the refitting of JT8D-7 engines. Twenty-two Caravelle 10Bs and an equal number of 10Rs were built. Combi freight services could be undertaken by the **Caravelle 11R**, which first flew in June 1967. A fuselage stretch of 2 ft 4in (0.73 m) allowed the fitting of a forward cargo door to port, and six were built.

The final production version was the **Caravelle 12**, which was some 10 ft 6¼ in (3.23 m) longer than the Caravelle 10B. This could carry up to 140 passengers (though 128 was the norm) and the first aircraft flew on 29 October 1970. A total of 12 aircraft was built before production ended in 1973.

No Avon-powered Caravelles remain, although a handful of late-model aircraft remain in France and Switzerland, while Colombia's population is thriving. No Caravelle is Stage 3/Chapter 3 compliant and no hush-kit has been developed, so by 1999 all will have disappeared from the sky.

Air Provence still maintains a pair of Caravelle 12s, acquired from Sterling of Denmark in 1991. They are in regular operation from the base at Marseille.

SPECIFICATION:
Sud-Est S.E.210 Caravelle 10B
Powerplant: two 14,000-lb (62.3-kN) Pratt & Whitney JT8D-7 turbofans
Accommodation: two (flight deck), standard layout for 89 passengers
Dimensions: span 112 ft 6 in (34.30 m); height 28 ft 7 in (8.72 m); length 108 ft 3½ in (33.01 m)
Weights: operating, empty 66,259 lb (30055 kg); maximum take-off 123,457 lb (56000 kg)
Performance: maximum cruising speed, at 25,000 ft (7620 m) 512 mph (825 km/h); maximum cruising altitude 35,000 ft (10670 m); range, with max payload 1,668 miles (2685 km)

Tupolev Tu-134

The world's second turbofan-powered short-haul jetliner (after the **Tu-124**), the **Tu-134 'Crusty'** was Russia's first entirely new jet airliner, previous aircraft having been derived from the Tu-88 bomber (Tu-16 'Badger' prototype). The glazed navigator's compartment in the nose and Tupolev's trademark undercarriage fairings on the wing trailing edge gave the new aircraft a distinctively Soviet appearance. By comparison with the earlier Tu-124, the engines were moved to the sides of the rear fuselage (reducing cabin noise and allowing shorter, more efficient intake ducts). The aircraft also introduced a T-tail, while more powerful anti-skid brakes removed the need for a brake parachute. A redesigned wing allowed the aircraft to have a level cabin floor. The 11,905-lb (52.9-kN) Soloviev D-20P-engined prototype was originally designated **Tu-124A** and first flew in December 1963.

The more powerful 14,990-lb (66.7-kN) Soloviev D-30 turbofan was adopted on pre-production aircraft, which gained the new designation **Tu-134**. This basic version entered service in 1967, with a cabin accommodating 64 passengers in three cabins, typically 16 first class in the front, 20 tourist class in the middle, and 28 more tourist class at the rear. An APU and clamshell thrust reversers were added during production.

While early glass-nosed Tu-134s are becoming a rare sight, they are still to be found in service, as evidenced by this Estonian Air example.

Kampuchea Airlines flies two former Aeroflot Tu-134A-3s alongside two An-24s and a single ATR 72, from Phnom Penh-Pochentong airport.

In 1970 production switched to the **Tu-134A**. This was lengthened by 6 ft 10 in (2.1 m), mainly ahead of the wing, and retained the original 28-seat rear cabin, but new front/middle cabins gave a capacity of up to 80 or, exceptionally, 84 passengers. The Tu-134A also introduced the D-32 engine, which could maintain the same thrust ratings at higher temperatures and which had a higher take-off rating of 15,608 lb (69.4 kN). The wing structure was strengthened and the tailfin/tailplane bullet fairing was extended to house a new VHF antenna.

The Tu-134's glazed nose and chin radome were replaced with a more modern nose-mounted radar antenna at the 1971 suggestion of Yugoslav charter airline Aviogenex, for that carrier's second pair of aircraft. The new solid nose was subsequently made an option on all Tu-134As. The **Tu-134A-3** had lightweight seats allowing up to 96 passengers to be carried, while the **Tu-134B** had a revised flight deck with no navigator, and also introduced modified spoilers. At least 300 aircraft had been built by the time production ended in 1978.

In Russia and the former Soviet Union, the Tu-134 serves with many new airlines, and also with Malev and Air Service Hungary, Balkan Bulgarian and Hemus Air, CSA, Vietnam Airlines, Kampuchea Airlines and Syrianair.

SPECIFICATION:
Tupolev Tu-134A
Powerplant: two 14,990-lb (66.7-kN) Soloviev D-30 Series II turbofans
Accommodation: three (flight deck), maximum of 84 passengers (standard 76)
Dimensions: span 95 ft 1¾ in (29 m); height 30 ft (9.14 m); length 121 ft 6½ in (37.05 m)
Weights: operating, empty 64,045 lb (29050 kg); maximum take-off 103,600 lb (47000 kg)
Performance: max cruising speed, at 27,890 ft (8500 m) 558 mph (898 km/h); max cruising altitude 36,000 ft (10973 m); range, with maximum payload 1,174 miles (1890 km)

Tupolev Tu-154

The **Tupolev Tu-154 'Careless'** was designed as a replacement for the Tu-104 and Il-18 on Aeroflot's medium-range, medium-density routes. The new airliner had to seat at least 120 passengers, fly sectors of up to 3,728 miles (6000 km) and operate from short gravel or packed-earth runways. This contradictory requirement demanded a greater thrust-to-weight ratio than was expected of Western jetliners, such that although weight and seating capacity were lower than for the similar Boeing 727, the engines were more powerful. Resembling a three-engined Tu-134 in configuration, the Tu-154 copied the leading-edge slats and triple-slotted flaps of the Boeing 727 and the triplex hydraulic systems of the British Trident.

The prototype made its maiden flight on 4 October 1968, powered by 20,950-lb (93.2-kN) Kuznetsov NK-8-2 turbofans similar to those being developed for the Ilyushin Il-62. The **Tu-154A** introduced the 23,150-lb (103-kN) NK-8-2U which allowed operation at higher weights. The aircraft also introduced a new fuel storage tank in the centre-section. This could not be used in flight, and merely allowed an aircraft to take fuel with it for refuelling at its destination. Seating was increased to 168 and there were other minor improvements. Deliveries began in 1974.

The **Tu-154B**, introduced in 1977, gained two extra emergency exits to allow the carriage of up to 180 passengers, and had a higher MTOW. In the **Tu-154B-2** the centre-section fuel tank became

In addition to a redesigned wing and tail, the Tu-154M has gained an enlarged centre intake to improve the airflow to its new D-30KU engines.

part of the normal fuel system, and upgraded avionics and improved spoilers were also fitted.

The **Tu-154S** designation is applied to dedicated freighters, which feature a massive cargo door and a strengthened cargo floor with roller tracks. All were converted from Tu-154As and Tu-154Bs.

The **Tu-154M** was originally designated **Tu-164**, and switched to the 23,380-lb (104-kN) Soloviev D-30KU-154-II turbofans in redesigned nacelles with larger intakes. Slats and spoilers were redesigned, and the entire horizontal tail was redesigned with greater area. Most noticeably, the centrebody intake has been enlarged. The performance gains which might have been expected were negated by an increase in empty weight that reduces payload to a figure less than that of the original Tu-154. This shortcoming should be remedied in the proposed **Tu-154M2**, which is to be powered by a pair of Perm (formerly Soloviev) PS-90 turbofans. Deliveries of the Tu-154M began in December 1984, and have taken production beyond the 1,000 aircraft mark. During 1993, 32 Tu-154s were completed at Samara, with eight remaining uncompleted.

Since the break-up of the Soviet Union, Russian transport aircraft have become easily available. This is a Tu-154 of Turkish airline Greenair.

SPECIFICATION: Tupolev Tu-154M
Powerplant: three MKB Perm (Soloviev) 23,380-lb (104-kN) Soloviev D-30KU-154-II turbofans
Accommodation: three (flight deck), maximum of 180 passengers (standard 154)
Dimensions: span 123 ft 2½ in (37.55 m); height 37 ft 4¾ in (11.40 m); length 157 ft 1¾ in (47.90 m)
Weights: operating, empty 55,300 lb (121915 kg); maximum take-off 220,460 lb (100000 kg)
Performance: max cruising speed 590 mph, (950 km/h); max cruising altitude 39,000 ft (11900 m); range, with maximum payload 2,425 miles (3900 km)

Tupolev Tu-204

The **Tu-204** was developed as a replacement for the Tu-154 on Aeroflot's medium-range routes. The aircraft bears an astonishingly close resemblance to the Boeing 757, leading to inevitable accusations of plagiarism, but was originally planned with winglets. The Tu-204 is Tupolev's first truly modern airliner, with extensive use of composites (18 per cent by weight), a triplex digital fly-by-wire control system with analog fly-by-wire back-up, and an EFIS cockpit with colour MFDs for flight, navigation, engine and systems displays. A Tu-154 development hack even tested sidestick controllers, but these were rejected in favour of the central yokes now installed. The aircraft can be operated by two pilots, although Aeroflot has specified that provision also be made for a flight engineer and an instructor or observer. The Aeroflot requirement for the Tu-204 originally called for a total of up to 500 aircraft, but the advent of Western types into Aeroflot service calls such a total into question.

The basic PS-90AT-engined prototype made its maiden flight on 2 January 1989. Three identically sized versions were originally projected, the 206,125-lb (93498-kg) Tu-204, the 219,355-lb (99500-kg) **Tu-204-100** and the 50122-lb (110,500-kg) **Tu-204-200** on which current production versions are based. All versions offer the same three passenger

Domestic customers will still be offered the Tu-204 in its original PS-90-powered form, which made its first Western appearance at the 1991 Paris air show.

Tupolev announced the BRAVIA tie-up during the 1992 Farnborough air show, and its display aircraft was quickly repainted to herald the change.

seating configurations with 214 six-abreast tourist class seats, mixed-class layouts for 190, or 190 passengers in first/business/tourist classes.

The changed political situation has allowed Tupolev to offer the Tu-204 with a choice of Russian, American or British powerplants, these giving new designation suffixes. The **Tu-204-210** is the baseline Tu-204-200 derivative, powered by 35,260-lb (156.9-kN) Aviadvigatel (formerly Perm/Soloviev) PS-90AT turbofans and with extra fuel tankage by comparison with the original prototype. The **Tu-204-220** has 43,100-lb (191.7-kN) Rolls-Royce RB211-535F turbofans, a prototype having flown on 14 August 1992 with similar RB211-535E4s. This version is being funded and marketed by the British Russian Aviation Corporation (BRAVIA), which has announced over 20 orders for the type. JAR certification as the **BRAVIA Tu-204** was sought during in 1994. The **Tu-204-230** will have 41,700-lb (185.5-kN) Pratt & Whitney PW2240s. Total Tu-204 production at Ulyanovsk during 1993 was three aircraft out of six planned, with four unfinished.

Further projected versions from Tupolev include a Tu-204 powered by the Trud/Samara NK-93 propfan, while a new, more fuel-efficient version of the PS-90, the PS-90P is also being proposed for the aircraft.

SPECIFICATION:
(BRAVIA) Tupolev Tu-202-220
Powerplant: two 43,100-lb (191.7-kN) Rolls-Royce RB211-535F turbofans
Accommodation: three (flight deck), maximum of 214 passengers (standard 190)
Dimensions: span 137 ft 9½ in (42 m); height 45 ft 6½ in (13.88 m); length 151 ft 7¾ in (46.22 m)
Weights: operating, empty 130,070 lb (59000 kg); maximum take-off 244,170 lb (110755 kg)
Performance: (estimated with PS-90AT engines) cruising speed at 40,000 ft (12200 m) 528 mph (850 km/h); maximum range, with 196 passengers and reserves 2,392 miles (3850 km)

Vickers Viscount

The world's first true turboprop-powered airliner, the **Vickers Viscount** was developed as a short-haul airliner for European routes. The new aircraft was essentially based on the Vickers Viking (itself a direct descendant of the wartime Wellington bomber), but with tricycle landing gear, four of the newly-developed turboprop engines on a stressed-skin, single-spar wing, and a pressurised circular-section fuselage. The choice of the primitive but ultra-reliable Dart was crucial to the Viscount's eventual success, the axial compressor-equipped Armstrong Siddeley Mamba having been the first choice of the British Air Ministry.

First flying on 16 July 1948, the 32-seat **V.630 Viscount** was stretched to accommodate 47 passengers before entering production in **V.700** series form with 1,400-hp (1044-kW) Rolls-Royce Dart 505/RDa.3 engines, having been renamed from Viceroy when India gained its independence.

Ordered for BEA in 1950, international sales success soon followed, customers including Air France, Capital Airlines, Aer Lingus and Trans Canada. More powerful 1,600-hp (1193-kW) Dart 510/RDa.7 engines resulted in the **V.745**, and underwing slipper tanks were introduced to produce the **V.700D**.

A 9-ft 6-in (2.82-m) cabin stretch and increased structural strength produced the **Series 800**, with progressive increases in engine power and all-up weight producing the **V.802**, **V.806** and **V.810**. Viscount production totalled 444, some going to corporate customers and others to air forces,

British World Airways (formerly British Air Ferries) flies two all-cargo Viscount Freightmasters, which date from 1958 and are still going strong.

including India and Turkey. Secondhand civil aircraft found their way into Ministry of Defence hands for the Empire Test Pilot's School and Royal Radar Establishment. The last military Viscounts in Britain and Turkey were withdrawn from use during 1993 and 1994.

Today only about 15 Viscounts remain active, although many of the aircraft retired during the recession of the late 1980s remain in storage in Britain, Canada, the Philippines, the USA (where until recently there were several flying) and Zaïre. The largest fleet of active Viscounts is operated by British World Airways (formerly British Air Ferries), a specialist charter operator which flies eight. These aircraft can be found operating passenger services (with 74 seats), but are now heavily involved in Royal Mail Parcelforce operations (wearing a striking overall red colour scheme). Two much modified V.806s operate as **Freightmasters**, with side cargo doors. Other Viscounts can be found flying with Bouraq Airlines in the Philippines (one), Guila Air, Trans Service Airlift Air Charter Service (one each), and Fil Air (with two) in Zaïre.

The UK has remained a haven of Viscount operations, latterly with British World (BAF), which has leased out aircraft to many other operators.

SPECIFICATION:
Vickers Viscount 800
Powerplant: four 1,740-ehp (1300-kW) Rolls-Royce Dart Mk 510 turboprops
Accommodation: two (flight deck), maximum of 74 passengers
Dimensions: span 93 ft 8 in (28.55 m); height 26 ft 9 in (8.15 m); length 85 ft 8 in (26.11 m)
Weights: operating, empty 41,000 lb (18600 kg); maximum take-off 64,500 lb (29260 kg)
Performance: maximum cruising speed 325 mph (523 km/h); service ceiling 25,000 ft (7620 m); maximum range, with maximum fuel and 28 passengers 1,180 miles (1900 km)

The **Yak-40 'Codling'** represents the USSR's most successful (and perhaps most radical) attempt to develop a DC-3 replacement. Powered by three turbofan engines, with clamshell thrust reversers, the Yak-40's performance gives it a still-enviable mix of high sector speeds and excellent short/rough-field capability. The aircraft can take off and climb with two engines, and can maintain height in the cruise on one engine. With its rear-mounted engines and slightly swept fin, the Yak-40 resembles a miniature Tu-154, although it has an unswept, tapered wing with hydraulically operated three-section plain flaps and conventional, manually actuated ailerons. The simple but rugged undercarriage has single nose and mainwheels.

The main cabin is usually configured to seat 27 passengers, in nine three-abreast rows, with two seats on the starboard side of the aisle. Alternatives include a layout with eight four-abreast rows, or a mixed-class layout with six or eight seats (including a four-place inward-facing settee) in the forward cabin and 12 seats (in standard three-abreast rows) in the rear cabin. An 11-seat executive configuration is another option.

First flown in prototype form on 21 October 1966, the Yak-40 entered production in 1967, and began passenger-carrying operations with Aeroflot

Yakovlev's small tri-jet is now fading from regular airline service, although many VIP-configured versions remain. Cubana still relies on 10 32-seat aircraft.

The Yak-40 was the best short-range jet airliner available to Eastern European airlines, combining a degree of comfort with surprising performance.

during September 1968. The Yak-40 rapidly became the most popular short-range aircraft on Soviet domestic routes, and huge numbers were procured for Aeroflot and its regional directorates; most of these remain in service with the various private companies that have succeeded the monolithic state airline. The Yak-40 also enjoyed considerable export success and was exported widely to both civilian and military customers, including some outside the traditional Russian sphere of influence such as France, Germany and Italy.

A 40-seat high-density variant announced in 1971 was stillborn, as was the stretched **Yak-40M** and the **Yak-40B** and **Yak-40V**, both of which were versions with uprated AI-25T engines. An intended freighter variant reached the prototype stage. The **Yak-40TL** was announced in 1991 as a possible conversion, with two 7,000-lb (31.14-kN) Textron Lycoming LF 507-1N turbofans replacing the three 3,300-lb (14.7-kN) Ivchenko AI-25s to give dramatically reduced fuel burn and operating costs. Its almost 50 per cent greater thrust would give a 10 per cent improvement in cruising speed and even bigger improvements in take-off and landing performance, especially under hot-and-high conditions. Conversions, which also involve rebuilding the rear fuselage, fin and tailcone are now available.

SPECIFICATION:
Yakovlev Yak-40
Powerplant: three 3,300-lb (14.7 kN) Ivchenko AI-25 turbofans
Accommodation: two (flight deck), maximum of 32 passengers (24 standard)
Dimensions: span 82 ft 0¼ in (25.0 m); length 66 ft 9½ in (20.36 m); height 21 ft 4 in (6.5 m)
Weights: empty 20,725 lb (9400 kg); maximum take-off 35,275 lb (16000 kg)
Performance: maximum cruising speed 342 mph (550 km/h); maximum range with 27 passengers at 292 mph (470 km/h) 1,118 miles (1800 km) with reserves

Yakovlev Yak-42/-242

Two-/three-engined short- to medium-range airliner

Yakovlev developed the **Yak-42 'Clobber'** as a short-haul medium-capacity airliner to replace the Il-18, An-24 and older Tu-134s in Aeroflot service. Design work commenced in the early 1970s, and the aircraft emerged as a scaled-up Yak-40. It retained its predecessor's austere strip capability, needing the minimum of ground support equipment for operations in the Soviet Union's more remote regions. The Yakovlev Bureau suffered some obvious difficulties in the type's early stages as three prototypes were built, all with differing wings, to determine the optimum angle of sweep (which was settled on 23°). The first of these flew on 7 March 1975 and the aircraft entered initial production at Smolensk. Much refinement remained to be done, as Aeroflot only placed its Yak-42s into service on the Moscow-Krasnodor route in 1980/81.

Production Yak-42s could carry 120, using the uniquely Soviet system of passengers carrying on their own luggage and stowing it in the cabin. They also featured four-wheeled main undercarriage bogies instead of the prototype's two-wheeled units. The type suffered many difficulties once in service and was withdrawn from use after accidents in 1982. By October 1984 aircraft with modified wings had been returned to Aeroflot service. The first major development was the **Yak-42D**, which offered an increased fuel load to extend range with 120 passengers to 1,365 miles (2200 km). Production of the Yak-42 has been slow with just over 100 delivered to Aeroflot and its successors.

The unusual Yak-42F carries two underwing pods housing unidentified electro-optical sensors that are reputedly for potential civil use.

Yak-42D exports have been made to Cubana (four) and the China General Aviation Corp. (five). In addition, aircraft are now available for lease directly from the manufacturer, trading as Saratov Avia. During 1993 seven were built. Specialist versions include the **Yak-42E-LL**, a testbed for ZMKB Progress D-236 propfan engines, which first flew in 1991', and the **Yak-42F** with two large underwing sensor pods for survey and earth science duties, several of which were delivered to Aeroflot.

Future developments included the stretched three-engined **Yak-42M** announced in 1987, which has been replaced by the twin-engined **Yak-242**. In mid-1994, the prototype was under final assembly at Saratov. This version features two underwing 26,525-lb (118-kN) Aviadvigatel PS-90A12 turbofans. The 180-seat (typically 162-seat) Yak-242 will also have a Bendix/King EFIS cockpit, fly-by-wire controls and winglets. Certification is planned for mid-1996, and Aeroflot maintains a requirement for 200. The proposed **Yak-46** will share the same fuselage and have two rear-mounted D-27 propfans; a turbofan-powered version is planned also.

Avioimpex is a carrier based in Macedonia (one of Yugoslavia's former republics) and operates this Yak-42D, leased from Saratov Avia.

SPECIFICATION:
Yakovlev Yak-42D
Powerplant: three14,330-lb (63.74-kN) ZMKB Progress D-36 turbofans
Accommodation: two (flight deck), maximum of 120 passengers
Dimensions: span 114 ft 5¼ in (32.87 m); height 32 ft 3 in (9.83 m); length 119 ft 4¼ in (36.38 m)
Weights: empty, equipped 76,058 lb (34500 kg); maximum take-off 125,660 lb (57000 kg)
Performance: maximum cruising speed 503 mph (810 km/h); maximum cruising height 31,500 ft (9600 m); maximum range, with 120 passengers and reserves 1,243 miles (2000 km)

Major Airlines of the World

Each entry is presented in the form of company name followed by IATA and ICAO codes in **bold**, then main base of operations in *italic*.

Adria Airways (JP/ADR)

Ljubljana Airport

DHC-7-102: **2**
DC-9-30: **3**
MD-81: **1**
MD-82: **4**
A320-200: **3**

Slovenia's Adria Airways (formerly Inex Adria Aviapromet) is weathering a downturn in holiday traffic by continuing to leaseout its aircraft to other European airlines.

Aer Lingus (EI/EIN)

Dublin Airport

S340B: **4**
Fk 50: **6**
737-548: **10**
737-448: **6**
A330-300: **3**

In June 1994 Aer Lingus became one of the first Airbus A330 operators when it took delivery of three new aircraft, to replace its long-serving Boeing 747-100s on North Atlantic routes.

Aeroflot Russian Intl (SU/AFL)

Moscow-Shermetyevo Airport

Most of Aeroflot's aircraft have been distributed among its now autonomous regional divisions. Its international divsion operates a large but variable number of A310-300s, B767s, Il-76M/Ts, Il-62Ms, Il-86s, Il-96-300s, Tu-134s and Tu-154s.

Western types such as the A310 and Boeing 767 are a valuable part of the Aeroflot fleet.

Aerolineas Argentinas (AR/ARG)

Buenos Aires-Ministro Pistarini Airport

F28 Mk 1000: **3**
737-200: **10**
MD-88: **6**
727-200: **8**
747-200: **7**

Established by Perón in 1950, Aerolineas Argentinas became the national flag carrier, absorbing the aircraft and routes of three existing airlines.

Aeromexico (AM/AMX)

Mexico City Airport

DC-9-30: **18**
MD-87: **2**
MD-82: **10**
MD-83: **2**
MD-88: **12**
757-200: **6**
767-200: **2**
767-300: **2**
DC-10-15: **2**
DC-10-30: **4**

Aeromexico (or, to give it its full name, Aerovias de México SA) operates a mix of early DC-9s and late-model MD-80s, including the short-fuselage MD-87 and three versions of the stretched MD-80, as seen here.

Air Afrique (RK/RKA)

Abidjan Airport

737-200: **1**
707-300C: **2**
A310-300: **5**
A300B4: **3**
DC-10-30: **2**

While based in the Ivory Coast, Air Afrique also flies as the national airline for Benin, Burkina Faso, the Central African Republic, Chad, Congo, Mali, Mauritania, Niger, Senegal and Togo.

Air Algerie (AH/DAH)

Algiers Airport

F27 Mk 400M: **7**
737-200: **16**
727-200: **11**
L-100-30: **2**
A310-203: **4**
767-300: **3**

In addition to its commercial air transport fleet, Air Algerie operates a variety of other types, from crop-sprayers and light helicopters to executive jets, around its North African home.

Air Canada (AC/ACA)

Montréal/Toronto Airports

RJ 100ER: **4**
DC-9-30: **35**
A320-200: **34**
767-200: **21**
767-300: **6**
L-1011: **4**
747-100: **3**
747-200: **3**
747-400: **3**

Airbus features large in Air Canada's future, as the airline has sizeable numbers of A319s, A320s and A340s on order. More 767s are due also.

Air China (CA/CCA)

Beijing-Capital/Hohhot Airports

Y-7: **6**
146-100: **4**
737-200: **3**
737-300: **15**
An-12: **2**
L-100-30: **2**
707-300C: **2**
767-200: **6**
767-300: **4**

747SP: **4**
747-200: **4**
747-400: **8**

Air China is the chief international airline of the People's Republic of China.

Air France (AF/AFR)

Paris-Charles de Gaulle/Orly Airports

F27 Mk 500M: **14**
737-200: **19**
737-500: **21**
737-300: **6**
A320-111: **7**
A320-211: **20**
727-200: **5**
A310-200: **7**
A310-300: **4**
A300B4: **14**

767-300: **6**
Concorde 101: **6**
A340-200: **6**
A340-300: **4**
747-100: **9**
747-200: **24**
747-300: **2**
747-400: **13**

An Air France Boeing 737-228.

Major Airlines of the World

Air India (AI/AIC)

Bombay Airport

A310-300: **8**
A300B4: **3**
747-200: **9**
747-300: **2**
747-400: **4**

Air India's fleet of Airbuses and Boeings concentrates largely on long-haul flights worldwide, while rival Indian Airlines undertakes many more domestic services.

Air Inter (IT/ITF)

Paris-Orly Airport

Mercure 100: **8**
A320-100: **6**
A320-200: **27**
A321-100: **2**
A300B2: **14**
A300B4: **5**
A330-300: **4**

Air Inter is unique in operating the 156-seat Dassault Mercure, an unsuccessful French Boeing 737 rival that entered service in 1972. They will finally be withdrawn in late 1994/early 1995.

Air Malta (KM/AMC)

Malta-Luqa Airport

ATP: **1**
RJ70: **2**
737-200: **6**
737-300: **3**
A320-200: **2**

While Air Malta's fleet has been centred around the Boeing 737 (as seen here) for many years, in 1994 it began to accept the first of four RJ70s on order from Avro (British Aerospace).

Air New Zealand (NZ/ANZ)

Auckland/Wellington/Christchurch Airports

737-200: **12**
767-200ER: **7**
767-300ER: **7**
747-200: **5**
747-400: **3**

Air New Zealand has begun fitting its 737-200s with Nordam hush-kits and is a prospective customer for the 737-X. In the interim, it may lease 737-300s.

Air UK (UK/UKL)

Norwich/Stansted Airports

SD-360: **2**
F27 Mk 100: **1**
F27 Mk 200: **10**
F27 Mk 500: **5**
F27 Mk 600: **1**
Fk 50: **8**
146-100: **1**
146-200: **2**
146-300: **7**
Fk 100: **9**

Air UK, Britain's third largest scheduled airline, is the world's largest F27 operator. Between 1993 and 1994, these were joined by substantial numbers of new Fk 50s and Fk 100s.

Air Ukraine/Intl (6U/UKR)

Kiev-Borispol/Zhilyani Airports

L 410UVP: **5**
Yak-40: **18**
An-24: **49**
An-30: **11**
An-26: **14**
An-32: **5**
An-72: **1**
Tu-134: **28**
Yak-42: **22**

Il-18: **2**
737-400: **2**
Tu-154B: **36**
Tu-154M: **3**
Il-62M: **7**

Air Ukraine's International division flies a pair of 737-4YOs.

Air Zimbabwe (UM/AZW)

Harare International Airport

146-200: **1**
737-200: **3**
707-300: **2**
767-200ER: **2**

Air Zimbabwe's three JT8D-17A-powered Boeing 737-2NOs are all comparatively young aircraft, as they rolled off the Seattle line in 1986/87.

Alaska Airlines (AS/ASA)

Seattle-Tacoma International Airport

737-200: **9**
737-400: **20**
MD-82: **10**
MD-83: **31**
727-100C: **1**
727-200: **4**

From its base in Washington state, Alaska Airlines flies a substantial MD-80 fleet. There are 40 more MD90-30s on order or option for delivery from 1996.

Alitalia (AZ/AZA)

Roma-Fiumicina Airport

DC-9-30: **29**
MD-82: **46**
A321-100: **5**
A300B2: **2**
A300B4: **12**
MD-11/F: **8**
747-200: **14**

Italy's Alitalia has rejuvenated its fleet in recent times through the addition of new MD-11s and A321s. More MD-82s, A321s and 747-400s are also on order.

All Nippon Airways (NH/ANA)

Tokyo-Haneda Airport

YS-11A: **7**
737-200: **9**
A320-200: **17**
767-200: **25**
767-300/ER: **38**
L-1011-1: **5**
747-100SR: **16**
747-200: **6**
747-400/D: **17**

All Nippon's long-haul fleet is soon to be joined by the Boeing 777, Airbus A340 and more 747-400s. The company is also actively seeking even larger future designs.

Major Airlines of the World

American Airlines (AA/AAL)
Dallas-Forth Worth/Tulsa Airports

Fk 100: **75**
MD-82: **227**
MD-83: **33**
727-200: **115**
757-200: **74**
767-200ER: **22**
A300-600R: **35**
767-300ER: **22**
DC-10-10: **39**

DC-10-30: **8**
MD-11: **19**

Quite apart from its own huge fleet, American Airlines also operates feeder services under the banner of American Eagle.

America West Airlines (HP/AWE)
Phoenix Airport

737-100: **1**
737-200: **22**
737-300: **33**
A320-200: **18**
757-200: **11**

America West was a 1980s success story, operating international services with 747s. It filed for Chapter 11 bankruptcy protection in 1991, but is now once more in profit.

Ansett Australia (AN/AAA)
Melbourne International Airport

Fk 50: **8**
F28 Mk 1000: **5**
F28 Mk 3000: **2**
F28 Mk 4000: **7**
146-200/QT: **9**
737-300: **19**
A320-200: **12**
727-200: **6**
767-200/ER: **6**

Ansett Airlines was founded in 1937 and has gone through various manifestations before adopting its current incarnation of Ansett Australia.

Austrian Airlines (OS/AUA)
Vienna-Schwechat Airport

DHC-8-103: **3**
Fk 50: **8**
MD-87: **5**
MD-81: **7**
MD-82: **6**
MD-83: **2**
A310-300/ET: **4**

Long a committed McDonnell Douglas customer, Austrian began operating Airbuses in 1988. These A310s will soon be joined by A320, A321s and A340s.

Avianca (AV/AVA)
Bogota-Eldorado/Barranquilla Airports

Fk 50-300: **8**
MD-83: **11** .
757-200: **2**
767-200ER: **2**
747-200: **1**

Colombia's Avianca was founded in 1919. Its aircraft are largely leased, with the Fk 50s still on the Dutch register, MD-80s, 757s and 747 on the Irish, and 767s on the US.

Major Airlines of the World

Balkan Airlines (LZ/LAZ)

Sofia Airport

Mi-8: **2**
Yak-40: **4**
An-24: **14**
Tu-134A/B: **9**
737-500: **3**
An-12: **4**
Il-18: **6**
A320-200: **4**
Tu-154B: **16**

Tu-154M: **8**
767-200ER: **2**

***Balkan Bulgarian
Airlines was one of
the slower Eastern
Bloc airlines to
begin operating
Western aircraft.***

Bangladesh Biman (BG/BBC)

Dhaka Airport

ATP: **2**
F28 Mk 4000: **2**
DC-10-30: **5**

***Bangladesh's
small national
carrier operates an
international
network with its
five 272-seat
DC-10-30s. Three
are former
Singapore Airlines
aircraft.***

British Airways (BA/BAW)

London-Heathrow/-Gatwick Airports

737-200: **14**
737-400: **39**
A320-211: **10**
757-200: **39**
767-300ER: **22**
Concorde 102: **7**
DC-10-30: **7**
747-100: **15**
747-200: **17**

747-400: **30**

***Apart from some
A320s and DC-10s
inherited from
British
Caledonian,
'BA' operates
almost an all-
Boeing fleet.***

British Midland (BD/BMA)

East Midlands Airport

DHC-7-110: **1**
DC-9-14/15: **5**
Fk 100: **3**
DC-9-30: **8**
737-500: **7**
737-300: **5**
737-400: **6**

***British Midland is
adding to its 737
fleet through the
introduction of
four 107-seat
Fokker 100s in
1994 and, in 1995,
five 75-seat
Fokker 70s.***

BWIA International BW/BWA)

Port of Spain Airport

MD-83: **9**
L-1011-500: **4**

***BWIA
International
(British West
Indian Airlines, or
'Beewee') has
been the flag
carrier of Trinidad
and Tobago since
1940.***

Major Airlines of the World

Canadian Airlines (CP/CDN)

Calgary/Vancouver/Toronto Airports

737-200: **49**
A320-200: **8**
767-300ER: **11**
DC-10-30/ER: **8**
747-400: **3**

Canadian (or Canadien to French-speaking nationals) was established in 1987 with the merger of Canadian Pacific and Pacific Western Airlines.

Cargolux (CVC/CLX)

Luxembourg Airport

747-200C(SCD): **3**
747-200F(SCD): **2**
747-400F(SCD): **2**

Cargolux has a long-established reputation as a (profitable) specialist all-cargo airline. It was the launch customer for the 747-400F and has a third aircraft on order.

Cathay Pacific Airways (CX/CPA)

Hong Kong-Kai Tek Airport

L-1011-1: **17**
L-1011-100: **2**
A340-211: **2**
747-200: **11**
747-300: **6**
747-400: **18**
747-400F: **1**

A battle involving 747s, 777s, A330s and A340s is growing between Boeing and Airbus to replace Cathay's TriStars and provide future long-range capacity.

China Airlines (CI/CAL)

Taipei-Sung Shan/-Chiang Kai Shek Airports

737-200: **3**
A300B4: **6**
A300-600R: **5**
MD-11: **4**
747SP: **5**
747-200/F: **6**
747-400: **4**

Until the recent deregulation of the national airline market, China Airlines was Taiwan's sole international flag carrier.

Condor Flugdienst (DE/CFG)

Frankfurt Airport

737-300: **4**
757-200: **18**
767-300ER: **9**
DC-10-30: **3**
747-400: **1**

Condor undertakes charter flying, chiefly for the German travel industry. Its single 747-400 is leased from Lufthansa (which owns Condor) for use on scheduled services to China.

Major Airlines of the World

Continental Airlines (CO/COA)

Houston Airport

DC-9-30: **34**
737-100: **12**
737-200: **20**
737-500: **6**
737-300: **58**
MD-81: **5**
MD-82: **57**
MD-83: **2**
727-200: **82**

757-200: **2**
A300B4: **21**
DC-10-10: **6**
DC-10-30: **13**
747-100: **2**
747-200: **3**

***Continental has
737s, 757s and 777s
on order.***

Croatia Airlines (OU/CTN)

Zagreb Airport

ATR42-300QC: **2**
737-200: **5**

***Croatia Airways
now operates a
pair of ATR42s and
five ex-Lufthansa
737-230s alongside
a variety of Cessna
twins and Cessna
and Piper
lightplanes.***

Crossair (LX/CRX)

Basel/Zurich Airports

SF340A/QC: **10**
S340B: **15**
Fk 50: **5**
S2000: **2**
RJ85: **4**
146-300: **2**

***Crossair is the
Saab 2000 launch
customer, with an
order for 20. They
will be dubbed
'Concordinos', as
the 146/RJs are
'Jumbolinos'. Saab
340s are simply
'Skyliners'.***

CSA (OK/CSA)

Prague-Ruzyne Airport

ATR72-200: **4**
Tu-134A: **5**
737-500: **5**
Tu-154M: **4**
A310-300: **2**
Il-62M: **3**

***Founded in 1923,
CSA is now the
flag carrier for the
Czech and Slovak
Republics. It is in
the process of
retiring the last of
its Soviet-built
aircraft.***

Cubana (CU/CUB)

Havana Airport

An-2: **1**
Mi-8: **5**
Yak-40: **10**
F27 Mk 600: **8**
An-24: **12**
An 26: **26**
Yak-42: **4**
Tu-154B: **4**
Tu-154M: **4**
Il-62M: **13**

Il-76M: **2**

***Cubana is
suffering a
crippling spares
and fuel shortage.
Former Spanish
F27s are replacing
older Antonovs
and Yaks.***

Major Airlines of the World

Delta Airlines (DL/DAL)

Atlanta Airport

737-200: **58**
737-300: **14**
MD-88: **110**
727-200: **141**
757-200: **84**
A310-200: **7**
A310-300: **20**
767-200: **15**
767-300/ER: **44**

L-1011-1: **32**
L-1011-250: **7**
L-1011-500: **17**
MD-11: **15**

Delta has further substantial numbers of Boeing and McDD types on order.

DHL Airlines (ER/DHL)

Cincinnati Airport

SA227AT: **10**
727-100F: **11**
727-200F: **6**
DC-8-73AF: **5**

In addition to operating its own aircraft in the United States and Europe, DHL has established a UK-based offshoot, DHL Air, which has recently acquired more 727s.

Ecuatoriana (EU/EEA)

Quito Airport

707-300B: **2**
DC-10-30: **1**

Founded in 1957, Ecuatoriana became Ecuador's national airline. Best known for its gold-painted 707s, the airline suspended all operations in 1993, pending a restart in 1994.

Egyptair (MS/MSR)

Cairo International Airport

737-200: **2**
737-500: **5**
A320-200: **7**
767-200ER: **3**
A300B4: **5**
A300-600R: **9**
767-300ER: **2**
747-300(SCD): **2**

Egyptair was founded in 1932, taking up its present name in 1974. It currently has six A321s, three A340s and three Boeing 777s on order.

El Al Israel Airlines (LY/ELY)

Tel Aviv-Ben Gurion International Airport

737-200: **2**
757-200: **7**
767-200/ER: **4**
747-100(SCD): **1**
747-200: **8**
747-400: **2**

The 757 is the second most numerous type in El Al's all-Boeing fleet. In 1994 the airline introduced its first Boeing 747-400s. It has options on two more aircraft.

Emery Worldwide (GJ/EWW)

Dayton/Indianapolis/San Jose Airports

DC-9-15F: **5**
727-100F: **32**
727-200F: **5**
DC-8-54F: **2**
DC-8-60F: **19**
DC-8-73F: **8**

Emery Airfreight was acquired by Consolidated Freightways to form Emery Worldwide in 1989. Aircraft are also operated for the US Postal Service.

Emirates (A6/UAE)

Dubai Airport

727-200: **2**
A310-300: **9**
A300-600R: **6**

Based in Dubai, Emirates provides air services for the United Arab Emirates. Currently relying chiefly on Airbuses, it has seven Boeing 777s on order, from 1996.

Ethiopian Airlines

Addis Ababa Airport

DHC-6-300: **5**
ATR42-300: **2**
DHC-5: **1**
737-200: **1**
L-100-30: **2**
757-200: **5**
707-300C: **1**
767-200ER: **3**

Operating a diverse fleet on a variety of passenger and freight services, Ethiopian Airlines is among the most advanced and profitable of African airlines.

Federal Express

Memphis/Indianapolis Airports

C.208A/B: **266**
F27 Mk 500: **24**
F27 Mk 600: **8**
727-100F: **75**
727-200F: **88**
A310-200F: **13**
A300-600F: **6**
DC-10-10CF: **11**
DC-10-30CF: **19**

MD-11AF: **13**
747-200F: **6**

In July 1994 Federal Express unveiled a new (overall white) colour scheme, and its official retitling as 'FedEx'.

Finnair (AY/FIN)

Helsinki-Vantaa Airport

DC-9-40: **5**
DC-9-50: **12**
MD-87: **3**
MD-82: **9**
MD-83: **5**
A300B4: **2**
DC-10-30: **5**
MD-11: **4**

Finnair began life as a seaplane operator. It has become a faithful McDonnell Douglas customer, with only two leased A300s interrupting the picture.

Major Airlines of the World

Garuda Indonesian (GA/GIA)

Jakarta-Soekarno Hatta Airport

DC-9-30: **5**
737-300: **8**
737-400: **7**
A300B4: **9**
A300-600R: **10**
DC-10-30: **6**
MD-11: **6**
747-200: **7**
747-400: **2**

Future additions to the Garuda fleet include three MD-11s in 1995, nine Boeing 737-400s between 1996 and 1997, and seven Boeing 747-400s by 1998.

Gulf Air (GF/GFA)

Bahrain Airport

737-200: **5**
A320-200: **12**
757-200F: **1**
767-300ER: **20**
L-1011-200: **8**
A340-300: **3**

Gulf Air is the national airline of Bahrain, Oman, Qatar and the UAE. Its expanding fleet will soon be joined by a further six A320s, six A340s and up to 12 Boeing 777s.

Iberia (IB/IBE)

Madrid-Barajas Airport

DC-9-30: **18**
MD-87: **24**
A320-200: **22**
A321-100: **4**
727-200: **30**
757-200: **8**
A300B4: **8**
DC-10-30: **8**
747-200: **7**

Already an A320 operator, Iberia has over 30 A321s on order. It will also begin replacing its long-serving DC-10s with A340-200s in 1995, while adding 15 more 757s.

Icelandair (FI/ICE)

Reykjavik/Keflavik Airports

Fk 50: **4**
737-400: **4**
757-200: **3**

Icelandair's Fokker 50s undertake domestic flights, while international routes are the responsibility of 737s and 757s that replaced 727s and DC-8s.

Iran Air (IR/IRA)

Tehran Airport

Fk 100: **6**
737-200: **3**
707-100: **2**
727-200: **5**
707-300C: **4**
A300B2: **5**
A300-600R: **2**
747SP: **4**
747-100: **1**
747-200: **4**

Having been starved of spares for its US equipment in recent years, Iran Air has recently looked to European manufacturers for its new aircraft needs, acquiring Fokker 100s and A300-600Rs.

Major Airlines of the World

Japan Air Lines (JL/JAL)

Tokyo-Haneda/-Narita Airports

767-200: **3**
767-300: **16**
DC-10-40: **15**
MD-11: **6**
747-100/SR: **8**
747-200/SR/F: **31**
747-300/SR: **16**
747-400D: **39**

Japan Air Lines is the world's largest 747 operator, with a fleet of over 90 in service. JAL has options on another 35 747-400s, plus 777s and more MD-11s.

Kenya Airways (KQ/KQA)

Nairobi Airport

Fk 50: **3**
737-200: **2**
A310-300: **3**

Kenya Airway's trio of A310-300s is named 'Nyayo Star', 'Narambee Star' and 'Uhuru Star', and was delivered in 1986 (two) and 1989 (one), replacing ageing Boeing707s.

KLM (KL/KLM)

Amsterdam-Schipol Airport

Fk 100: **6**
737-300: **15**
737-400: **12**
A310-200: **10**
DC-10-30: **4**
MD-11: **6**
747-200SUD: **10**
747-300: **3**
747-400/(SCD): **16**

KLM (Royal Dutch Airlines) is one of the world's most senior airlines, and the oldest to have retained the same name since its inception, in 1919.

Korean Air (KE/KAL)

Seoul-Kimpo Airport

F28 Mk 4000: **1**
Fk 100: **9**
MD-82: **10**
MD-83: **2**
727-200: **5**
A300B4/F4: **10**
A300-600R: **24**
DC-10-30: **3**
MD-11: **5**

747SP: **2**
747-200/F: **14**
747-300: **4**
747-400: **16**

Korean Air is yet another expanding Asian airline, with orders for A330s, 777s and 747-400s.

Kuwait Airways (KU/KAC)

Kuwait City Airport

GIV: **3**
A320-200: **3**
727-200 (VIP): **1**
707-300C: **3**
767-200ER: **1**
A310-300: **4**
A300-600R: **5**
747-200(SCD): **4**
747-400(SCD): **3**

Kuwait Airways has more than replaced the aircraft lost in the Iraqi invasion of 1990. Some of the pre-war fleet survives, like this 747-269 in Kuwait's new colour scheme.

Major Airlines of the World

LAN-Chile (LA/LAN)

Santiago-A. Merino Benitez Airport

146-200: **2**
737-200: **4**
707-300C: **1**
DC-8-71AF: **2**
767-200ER: **2**
767-300ER: **2**

A sizeable portion of the LAN Chile fleet – indeed, every aircraft bar the BAe 146s and Boeing 707 – are leased from Irish lessors Guinness Peat Aviation.

Lithuanian Airlines (TE/LIL)

Vilnius Airport

An-24: **4**
An-26: **3**
Tu-134A: **8**
737-200: **1**
Yak-42/D: **12**

Since it was founded in 1991, Lithuanian Airlines has experimented with several colour schemes. Some other aircraft now wear a more adventurous red and grey scheme.

LOT-Polish Airlines (LO/LOT)

Warsaw-Okecie Airport

ATR72-200: **8**
An-26: **2**
737-500: **5**
737-400: **4**
767-200ER: **2**
767-300ER: **2**

LOT retired the last of its Soviet-built jets (the Tu-134) in March 1994, leaving only a pair of An-26 freighters as survivors from the airline's old Eastern Bloc days.

LTU International (LT/LTU)

Dusseldorf Airport

L-1011-1: **4**
L-1011-200: **2**
L-1011-500: **3**
MD-11: **4**

Apart from its Dusseldorf operations, Germany's LTU charter airline owns LTU Sud, which flies nine 757-200s and four 757-300ERs from Munich.

Lufthansa (DL/DLH)

Frankfurt/Berlin/Cologne/Hamburg/Munich

737-200: **30**
737-500: **31**
737-300/QC: **43**
737-400: **7**
A320-200: **33**
A321-100: **9**
A310-300: **12**
A300-600R: **11**
A340-211: **6**
A340-300: **6**
747-200/(SCD): **12**
747-400/(SCD): **17**

Lufthansa also operates regional services from Cologne as Lufhansa Cityline, with 28 Fokker 50s and 15 Canadair Regional Jets.

Major Airlines of the World

Luxair (LG/LGL)

Luxembourg Airport

Fk 50: **4**
737-500: **2**
737-400: **2**

Operating from the tiny Grand Duchy of Luxembourg (between France and Germany), Luxair's fleet is augmented by Luxair Commuter EMB-120 Brasilias.

Malaysia Airlines (MH/MAS)

Kuala Lumpar/Saba/Sarawak Airports

DHC-6-300: **6**
Fk 50: **11**
737-500: **9**
737-300F: **2**
737-400: **52**
A300B4: **4**
DC-10-30: **6**
747-200: **2**
737-300(SCD): **1**

747-400/(SCD): **11**

Malaysia has become a committed Boeing 737 operator, replacing earlier examples with CFM56-powered aircraft.

Malev Airlines (MA/MAH)

Budapest-Ferihegy Airport

Yak-40: **2**
Tu-134A: **6**
737-200: **3**
737-300: **3**
Tu-154B: **12**
767-200ER: **2**

While Hungary's Malev was one of the first Eastern European airlines to introduce Western aircraft, it still has many Soviet-built types in service.

Mexicana (MX/MXA)

Mexico City Airport

Fk 100: **10**
A320-200: **12**
727-200: **26**
DC-10-15: **5**

Mexicana, Mexico's second main airline, introduced a series of striking hand-painted tail designs, but has found them too costly to complete and maintain.

Middle East Airlines (ME/MEA)

Beirut Airport

720-023B: **2**
A310-200: **2**
707-300B/C: **8**
A310-300: **1**
747-200(SCD): **3**

Lebanon's MEA is returning to stable operations after over a decade spent struggling to survive the fighting in its homeland. It is the last airline operator of the Boeing 720.

Major Airlines of the World

Northwest Airlines (NW/NWA)

Minneapolis-St Paul Airport

DC-9-14/15: **22**
DC-9-30: **77**
DC-9-40: **12**
DC-9-50: **28**
MD-82: **8**
A320-200: **50**
727-200: **56**
757-200: **33**
DC-10-40: **21**

DC-10-30: **8**
747-100: **12**
747-200/F: **28**
747-400: **10**

Despite the advent of newer types, Northwest is still the world's largest DC-9 operator.

Olympic Airways (OA/OAL)

Athens-Hellenikon Airport

737-200: **11**
737-400: **7**
727-200: **9**
A300B4: **8**
A300-600R: **3**
747-200: **4**

Greece's Olympic Airways was founded by Aristotle Onassis, but is now 100 per cent state-owned. It has A300-600Rs, Boeing 737s, 767s and 747s on order.

Pakistan Intl Airlines (PK/PIA)

Karachi Airport

DHC-6-300: **2**
F27 Mk 200: **13**
F27 Mk 400: **1**
737-300: **6**
707-300C: **2**
A310-300: **6**
A300B4: **9**
747-200/(SCD): **8**

Pakistan International was founded in 1954 and currently serves 44 destinations in 39 countries, in addition to dedicated freight services by the 707s and 747s.

Philippine Air Lines (PR/PAL)

Manila Airport

Fk 50: **10**
737-300: **12**
A300B4: **8**
DC-10-30: **2**
747-200/(SCD): **11**
747-400: **2**

In recent times Philippine Air Lines has placed many of its older types, such as BAC One-Elevens and Shorts 360, into storage, while introducing Fokker 50s, 737-300s and 747-400s.

QANTAS Airways (QF/QFA)

Sydney-Mascot/Melbourne Airports

737-300: **16**
737-400: **17**
767-200ER: **7**
A300B4: **4**
767-300ER: **15**
747-338: **6**
747-400: **18**

QANTAS began life in 1920 as the Queensland And Northern Territories Air Service. Retaining that name, today it styles itself as 'The Australian Airline'.

Major Airlines of the World

Royal Air Maroc (AT/RAM)

Casablanca Airport

ATR42-300: **3**
737-200: **6**
737-500: **5**
737-400: **6**
727-200: **6**
757-200: **2**
707-200C: **2**
747SP: **1**
747-200/(SCD): **2**

Quite apart from its modern, largely Boeing-built fleet, RAM still maintains two Caravelles and a Lockheed L.749 Constellation at its Casablanca home base.

Royal Brunei Airlines (BI/RBS)

Bandar Seri Begawan Airport

Fk 50: **2**
757-200: **3**
767-300ER: **8**

In addition to flying its own schedules, Royal Brunei operates the Sultan of Brunei's personal A340-200. He also has his own Boeing 747-400.

Royal Jordanian Airlines (RJ/RJA)

Amman Airport

A320-200: **2**
727-200: **2**
707-300C: **3**
A310-30: **3**
L-1011-500: **5**

Until 1986, Royal Jordanian was known as Alia Airlines (in honour of King Hussein's daughter). All its aircraft are named after various Middle Eastern princesses or major cities.

Royal Nepal Airlines (RA/RNA)

Kathmandu Airport

DHC-6-300: **9**
HS 748: **2**
757-200/F: **2**
A310-300: **1**

Royal Nepal operates the unique 757-200F (SCD) and has begun offering sightseeing flights around the Kingdom's Himalaya range.

SABENA (SN/SAB)

Brussels National Airport

EMB-120ER: **10**
DHC-8-300: **5**
F28 Mk 3000: **1**
F28 Mk 4000: **2**
146-200: **6**
737-200/C: **13**
737-500: **6**
737-300: **6**
737-400: **3**
A310-200: **3**

DC-10-30CF: **2**
747-200(SCD): **1**
747-300(SCD): **2**

SABENA is slowly introducing this new scheme. Its smaller types are operated by regional subsidiary DAT.

Major Airlines of the World

Saudia (SV/SVA)

Jeddah Airport

737-200: **19**
DC-8-63AF: **1**
A300-600: **11**
L-1011-200: **17**
747SP: **1**
747-100: **9**
747-200F: **1**
747-300: **10**

Saudia is about to embark on a massive re-equipment spree involving over 60 new Boeings and MD-11s. Saudia also operates a huge VIP fleet, from small turboprops to 747s.

SAS (SK/SAS)

Copenhagen/Olso/Stockholm Airports

F28 Mk 1000: **3**
F28 Mk 4000: **16**
DC-9-20: **9**
DC-9-40: **26**
MD-87: **16**
MD-81: **31**
MD-82: **16**
MD-83: **2**
767-200/ER: **3**

767-300ER: **14**

Scandanavian Airlines System is the national airline of Norway, Sweden and Denmark, with aircaft registered in all three countries.

Singapore Airlines (SQ/SIA)

Singapore-Changi Airport

737-300F: **1**
A310-200: **6**
A310-300: **17**
747-200/F: **8**
747-300/(SCD): **14**
747-400: **24**

Singapore prides itself on having one of the youngest fleets in the world. 777s are due to replace the A310s, with the airline also now ordering A340s .

South African Airways (SA/SAA)

Johannesburg-Jan Smuts

737-200: **14**
A320-200: **7**
767-200ER: **1**
A300B2: **4**
A300B4: **4**
747SP: **5**
747-200: **6**
747-300: **2**
747-400: **4**

SAA, or SAL (Suid-Afrikaanse Lugdiens) in Afrikaans, was formed in 1934. It has a commuter division – SA Express – that operates DHC-8s.

Southwest Airlines (WN/SWA)

Dallas-Love Field/Houston Airports

737-200: **50**
737-500: **25**
737-300: **82**

Apart from a brief flirtation with leased 727s, Southwest has long been a 737 airline. Easily the largest 737 operator, it has substantial (150+) numbers (including 63 737-Xs) on order.

Swissair (SR/SWR)

Zurich-Kloten Airport

Fk 100: **10**
MD-81: **24**
MD-82: **1**
A310-200: **5**
A310-300: **5**
MD-11: **13**
747-300/(SCD): **5**

As Swissair awaits the arrival of the first of its five A319s, 16 A320s and eight A321s (beginning in 1995), it has unveiled a new overall white colour scheme.

Syrianair (RB/SYR)

Damascus Airport

Yak-40: **6**
An-24: **24**
An-26: **5**
Tu-134B: **6**
Se 210-10B3: **2**
727-200: **6**
Tu-154M: **3**
Il-76M: **4**
747SP: **2**

Syrianair – Syrian Arab Airlines received a boost to its varied and slightly ageing fleet in 1994 with the lifting of US sanctions and the arrival of several ex-Kuwaiti 727s.

TAP – Air Portugal (TP/TAP)

Lisbon Airport

737-200: **8**
737-300: **9**
A320-200: **6**
A310-300: **5**
L-1011-500: **7**

TAP (Transportes Aéreos Portugueses) was founded in 1945. Its TriStars have now been supplemented by A310-300s, and A340-300s are on order for 1994/95.

TAROM (RO/ROT)

Bucharest-Otopeni/-Baneasa Airports

An-24: **17**
BAC 1-11/500: **7**
ROMBAC 1-11: **6**
737-300: **5**
Il-18: **4**
Tu-154B: **8**
707-300C: **1**
A310-300: **3**
Il-62/M: **3**

Romania's TAROM (Transporturile Aeriene Romane) is one of several Eastern European airlines to adopt the A310 for long-range services.

Thai Airways Intl (TG/THA)

Bangkok International Airport

ATR42-300: **2**
ATR72-200: **2**
146-300: **5**
737-200: **3**
737-400: **7**
A310-200: **2**
A300B4: **12**
A300-600: **6**
A300-600R: **10**
DC-10-30ER: **3**

MD-11: **4**
747-200: **6**
747-300: **2**
747-400: **9**

Thai has further wide-bodies on order in the shape of A300-600Rs and Boeing 777s.

Major Airlines of the World

THY Turkish Airlines (TK/THY)

Istanbul Airport

RJ100: **8**
DC-9-30: **9**
737-500: **2**
737-400: **26**
727-200: **10**
A310-200: **8**
A310-300: **7**
A340-300: **3**

With the introduction of its current colour scheme, THY restyled itself as Turkish Airlines. It moved into a new era in 1994, with the delivery of its first A340-300s.

Tunis Air (TU/TAR)

Tunis-Carthage Airport

737-200: **4**
737-500: **3**
A320-200: **7**
727-200: **7**
A300B4: **1**

With its roots in a historic part of North Africa, it is no surprise that some of Tunis Air's aircraft carry the name of ancient heroes such as 'Hannibal'.

TWA (TW/TWA)

Kansas City/St Louis/New York-J.F.K.

DC-9-15: **7**
DC-9-30: **36**
DC-9-40: **3**
DC-9-50: **12**
MD-82: **29**
MD-83: **11**
727-100: **5**
727-200: **51**
767-200ER: **10**

767-300ER: **3**
L-1011: **21**
747-100: **10**
747-200: **2**

TWA is one of the US majors that has recently emerged from bankruptcy protection.

United Airlines (UA/UAL)

Chicago-O'Hare/San Francisco Airports

737-200: **69**
737-500: **57**
737-300: **101**
A320-200: **21**
727-200: **75**
757-200: **88**
767-200/ER: **19**
767-300ER: **23**
DC-10-10: **42**

DC-10-30: **8**
747SP: **10**
747-100: **18**
747-200: **9**
747-400: **24**

With the collapse of Aeroflot, United is the world's largest airline.

UPS (5X/UPS)

Louisville Airport

SA227AT: **11**
727-100C/F: **50**
727-200F: **8**
757-200F: **46**
DC-8-71AF: **23**
DC-8-73AF: **26**
747-100F/(SCD): **12**

US-based United Parcel Service has undertaken the re-engining and refitting of its 727 fleet as 'Quiet Freighters', in addition to launching specialist aircraft like the 757-200F and 767-330F.

Major Airlines of the World

US Air (US/USA)

Pittsburgh/Washington Airports

F28 Mk 100: **17**	727-200: **8**
F28 Mk 4000: **24**	757-200: **22**
Fk 100: **36**	767-200ER: **13**
DC-9-30: **72**	
737-200: **81**	***USAir is one of the***
737-300: **101**	***'Big Five' US***
737-400: **54**	***carriers. In 1993***
MD-81: **19**	***British Airways***
MD-82: **12**	***acquired a major***
	stockholding.

VARIG (RG/VRG)

Rio de Janeiro Airport

737-200: **17**	747-400: **3**
737-300: **28**	
727-100F: **5**	***Brazil's VARIG***
767-200ER: **6**	***(Viaçao Aérea Rio-***
767-300ER: **4**	***Grandense) was***
DC-10-30/CF: **10**	***founded in 1927***
MD-11: **6**	***and serves 44***
747-200(SCD): **3**	***internal Brazilian***
747-300/(SCD): **5**	***destinations and***
	44 international.

VIASA (VA/VIA)

Caracas-Maquetia (Simon Bolivar) Airport

727-200: **5**	***VIASA***
A300B4: **2**	***(Venezolana***
DC-10-30: **5**	***Internacional de***
	Aviacion) is
	Venezuela's
	national airline
	and uses DC-10-30s
	for its long-range
	routes.

Virgin Atlantic (VS/VIR)

London-Gatwick/-Heathrow Airports

A340-311: **4**	***Richard Branson's***
747-100: **1**	***pioneering Virgin***
747-200: **7**	***Atlantic Airways***
747-400: **2**	***became the first***
	UK airline to
	introduce the A340
	in 1994. 747-400s
	joined the fleet
	that year also.

Zambia Airways (QZ/ZAC)

Lusaka Airport

ATR42-300: **2**	***Zambia Airways***
737-200: **2**	***has been in***
DC-8-71: **1**	***operation since***
DC-10-30: **1**	***1967. This Boeing***
	757-23APF was
	leased to the
	African carrier by
	Ansett Worldwide
	Aviation Services
	for a period
	beginning in 1990.

INDEX